REVELATION OF THE MESSIAH

THE MESSIAH, AS MANIFESTED THROUGHOUT THE WHOLE OF SCRIPTURE

DELORIS BIOCIC

Published by Deloris Biocic Dumpsterboycooper@gmail.com

ISBN 979-8-989-526-0-0
.

ACKNOWLEDGEMENTS

Thanks to my lovely daughter, Raven, for all your help and support.

For James, Thomas, Lyndsey, Brooklynn, and Beau,

To all my friends and family who think I have joined a weird cult or have become 'Jewish.'

Let us call upon YAHUAH, who is perfect and is the provider of perfection through our perfect high priest, YAHUSHA HAMASHIACH, that he might grant that our mind discover the truth about the matters that will be investigated and their composition, and thus let us proceed to what follows. - Origen, Commentary on the Book of John, book 28 (14)

The Hebrew names for the Most HIGH ELOHIYM, as they will appear in quotes from the eth Cepher, are listed below with their common interpretation:

ELOAH, ELOHAI, ELOHIYM: God

EL SHADDAI: God Almighty YAHUAH,

YAH: Lord God

YAHUAH ELOHAI: The Lord my God

YAHUAH ELOHAYKEM: The Lord your God (group of people)

YAHUAH ELOHAYHEM: The Lord your God

YAHUAH ELOHAYKA: The Lord your God (singular person)

YAHUAH TSEVA'OTH: The Lord of hosts

YAHUSHA: YAH's salvation

YAHUSHA HAMASHIACH: YAH's salvation in the Messiah

RUACH HA'QODESH: Holy Spirit

REFERENCES

eth Cepher
3rd Edition, Rev 1
Cepher Publishing Group, C
Everett, Washington 98208

Aramaic English New
Testament
Andrew Gabriel Roth
Large Print Parallel Study
Edition
AENT 4th Edition 2011 2011
Netzari Press LLC

A New English Translation of
the Septuagint
Albert Pietersma and
Benjamin G. Wright, editors
Oxford University Press, NY
Tsiyon Edition

Targum Isaiah in English 2012
Eliyahu Ben David and Tsiyon
Radio
Zarathustra College Station,
Texas

The Targum of Jonathan
BenUzziel on the Pentateuch
with The Fragments of the
Jerusalem Targum from the
Modern English Translation
Edited by Luis Smith

Anti-Nicene Father's
Hendrickson Publishers, Inc.
Peabody, Massachusetts
Second printing 1995

The Works of Flavius Josephus
Translated by William Whiston
Baker Book House Grand
Rapids Michigan 1978

The Works of Philo Translated
by C.D. Younger Hendrickson
Publishers, Inc. Thirteenth
printing 2018

The Gospel of the Kailedy 1998
Culdian Trust Cormandel,
New Zealand

The Kolbrin
1994 the Hope Trust
2676 Rings Road, Cormandel
New Zealand

TABLE OF CONTENTS

INTRODUCTION

These are the words of Agur, the son of Yaqeh, who prophesied and received power. He said to Ithliel, Surely, I am weak minded, and have not the understanding of men. I know not wisdom, nor have I learned the knowledge of the holy men. Tell me, who has ascended up into heaven and come down? Who has gathered the wind in his fists? Who has bound the waters in a handkerchief? Who has established all the borders of the earth? What is his name, and what is his son's name, if you can tell? Every word of YAHUAH is pure; he is a shield to those who put their trust in him. Do not add to his words, lest he reprove you, and you be found a liar. Proverbs 30:1 – 6

We will explore the nature of our Messiah, the Son of our ELOHIYM. The definition of Messiah is promised deliverer. We will see that not only did YAHUAH deliver his people throughout scripture, but he also promised to be the ultimate deliverer of his people in the last days, with the promise of raising us from death to eternal life, living in his presence. We will explore the various manifestations in the Old Testament scriptures of YAHUAH as our Savior. Besides our bibles the Messiah was also written of in the Dead Sea Scrolls. Scroll 4q 246 is an Aramaic apocalypse very fragmented, but the subject of the Messiah is clear. It says the spirit of ELOHIYM dwells on him and that he will be designated the Son Of ELOHIYM. Besides the son, in the following pages, I would like to demonstrate that YAHUSHA the Messiah is indeed on every page of the scriptures under other titles and manifestations, just as he told the Pharisees that he was before Abraham, as well as to his fellow travelers on the road to Emmaus, where he laid out the scriptures, starting with Moses, which pointed to him.

Even the Samaritan woman at the well of Jacob on Mount Gerizim in John chapter 4 knew to be looking for a Messiah who would "tell us all things." How did the Samaritans know to be looking for a Messiah? They only read the first five books of the Bible.

Maybe they knew the Messiah would come from their reading of Genesis 49:8,10, which reads: "Yehuda, you are he whom your brethren shall praise; your hand shall be in the neck of your enemies; your father's children shall bow down before you. The scepter shall not part from Yehuda, nor a Torah giver from between his feet until Shiloh come; and unto him shall the gathering of the people be."

Or maybe the Samaritans knew there would be a future Messiah from their reading of Numbers 24:7-9 and 17-19, which reads from the Septuagint: "A person will come forth from his (Israel's) offspring and he shall rule over many nations, and reign of him shall be exalted beyond Gog. And his reign shall be

2

increased; a god guided him out of Egypt; like a unicorn's glory, he was to him. He shall devour his enemies' nations and de- marrow their stoutness and shall shoot down an enemy with his missiles. He lay down and rested like a lion and like a welp. Who will raise him up? Blessed are those who bless you, and cursed are those who curse you." Verses 17 through 19 again from the Septuagint reads: "I will point to him, and not now; I deem him happy; but he is not at hand. A star shall dawn out of Jacob, and a person shall rise up out of Israel, and he shall crush the chiefs of Moab, and he shall plunder all Seth's sons. And Edom will be an inheritance, and Esau, his enemy, will be an inheritance, and Israel acted with strength. And one shall rise out of Jacob, and he shall destroy one being saved from a city." And maybe the Samaritans could see the Messiah or the coming Messiah in Deuteronomy 33:7, which reads from the Septuagint: "And this of Yehuda: listen, oh Lord, to the voice of Yehuda, and you could enter into his people; his hands will decide for him, and you will be a helper from his enemies."

Before we continue, I want to establish that I am not a teacher. I am a student and a lover of YAHUAH. This is information I have learned during my studies over the years, and I thought I would share some of my discoveries with the people I love. Do not believe anything I have written here at face value. I encourage you to pick up the scriptures, verify what is written here, and discern the truth for yourself. If you think I am incorrect in anything I have written, open your scriptures and study it for yourself. I would ask that before proceeding, you pray and ask the Holy

Spirit to lead you into knowledge and understanding and to have an open mind to the truth. The truth will set you free.

Before I proceed, I need to address a matter of housekeeping. I am sure you are curious about the name YAHUSHA that I use instead of the name Jesus. This name Jesus came into existence around 600 A.D. I choose to use the name given to the Messiah by his mother, which is identical to that of Joshua, son of Nun, as stated in Numbers 13:16: "and Moshe called Husha the son of Nun, Yahusha." The name of the Messiah was replaced with Elizeus in the 1611 King James Version of the scripture so as not to confuse the Messiah with Yahusha, son of Nun (Joshua). Elizeus is a name that weds the pagan deity Zeus with the Elohim of Israel, so I will not use it unless it is used in a direct quote.

As to the name of the creator of all, the Most High, YAHUAH, this name has been replaced in the scripture some 7,000 times with Lord or God. Jeremiah foretold the replacement of the NAME when he wrote in chapter 23:25-27 of the book of Jeremiah; "I have heard what the prophets said that prophecy lies in my name, saying, I have dreamed, I have dreamed. How long shall this be in the heart of the prophets that prophesy lies? Yea, they are prophets of the deceit of their own heart; which think to cause my people to forget my name by their dreams which they tell every man to his neighbor, as their fathers have forgotten my name for Ba'al".

Besides being a Phoenician deity, the word ba'al also means lord. Also, notice how this verse admonishes against substituting another name for the

Most High. You can't say to someone who worships Buddha that we are honoring the same Elohim because the Most High creator of all doesn't like being called by another name any more than he likes the worship practices established for and given to other gods attributed to him like tree worship which is traced to the worship of Ishtar in ancient Samaria found in tablets and cylinders from 2,500 BC.

According to Roy Blizzard, Jr., in his book Understanding the Difficult Words of Jesus, "By the time of the second temple, Jews had developed an aversion to using the name of God for fear of violating the third commandment. They substituted evasive synonyms for 'God' such as 'the name,' 'the place,' 'the power,' and 'Heaven' as in Matthew 21:25, which states: "The baptism of John, where was it from, heaven, or from men?"". In the phrase Kingdom of Heaven, this substitution is seen in Luke 15:18, when the prodigal son says, "I have sinned against heaven." There, heaven is a clear substitute for the name of God. With this in mind, examining the scriptures takes on a different meaning.

As to the pronunciation of the name of the Most High, many big brains have written and discussed how they believe the tetragrammaton (YHWH) should be pronounced. There are arguments for adding the 'v' sound or the 'w' sound. I am not dogmatic concerning the pronunciation of any of the names.

I prefer to use the pronunciation of the tetragrammaton of an ear witness. Josephus (A.D. 37-100 A.D.), in his book The Wars of the Jews, book 5, chapter 5, section 7, hints as to how the name of the

Most High ELOHIYM's name is pronounced in his description of the high priests' garments. He describes the High Priest's headdress or miter as having a golden crown on which the sacred name is engraved. Josephus further states that that name consists of four vowels. YHWH should sound like ee, aa, oo, aa, much like taking a breath. YAHUAH, the father's name is in the son's name, and you can see that YAHUSHA is similar. I will speak on it again, but I do not want to get too technical since there is plenty of information for anyone to read, study, and come to their own conclusions. It is essential because many verses tell us to praise the name of our creator. YAHUSHA stated that he did proclaim the father's name. You need to know it.

Origen of Alexandria (A.D. 185–253 A.D.) expounded on this idea of substituting names in his book, Against Celsus, book five, chapters 45 and 46, where he admits there is a mystical power in the use of names. I like his example of there being power in calling on the God of Abraham, the God of Isaac and the God of Jacob, since even demons are vanquished and become submissive to him who pronounces these names, "whereas, if we say, the god of the chosen father of the echo, the god of laughter, and the god of him who strikes with the heel, the mention of these names is attended with no result."

In his commentary on the book of John, Origen admits the proper names have been mistranslated from Hebrew to Greek. In chapter 24, he is explicitly talking about proper place names but admits all Hebrew names contain a meaning of their own, which contributes to the understanding of the text. Exodus

20:7 commands that the name of YAHUAH should not be taken in vain or brought to nothing. And it is to be proclaimed. Exodus 9:16 states: "Indeed, for this cause have I raised you up, for to show in you my power; and that my name may be declared throughout all the earth."

Exodus 33:19 is an exciting passage concerning proclaiming the name, which is a good segue into the topic of this writing, which is the revelation of the Messiah. In verse 19 of Exodus 33, it is not clear whom YAHUAH is speaking when he tells Moses, "I will make all my goodness pass before you, and I will proclaim the name of YAHUAH before you." Exodus 34:5-6 describes how YAHUAH appeared with Moses on Mount Sinai: "And YAHUAH descended in the cloud and stood with him (Moses) there and proclaimed the name of YAHUAH. And YAHUAH passed by before him, and proclaimed, YAHUAH, YAHUAH EL." Who is this that YAHUAH passed before? Who is standing next to Moses? And who is passing by proclaiming the NAME?

Who was in the cloud leading the Israelites through the wilderness? Exodus 13:21 tells us that YAHUAH went before them (Israel) by day in a pillar of cloud. Exodus 14:19 calls this entity in the cloud the Angel of ELOHIYM. This exact phrase is repeated in Exodus 23:20-23: YAHUAH tells Moses he will send his Angel before them. YAHUAH admits to appearing to Abraham, Isaac, and Jacob in Exodus 6:3, telling Moses they knew him as El Shaddai, "but by my name YAHUAH was I not known to them." In the following pages, we will explore how YAHUAH manifested himself in his creation and by what names and titles.

What is the father's name, and what is his son's name?

Since there is power in the names, it is essential to know them. You cannot begin a relationship with someone if you do not know their name. What if someone you loved had a book about them explaining their likes and dislikes to you? You would read it often. It would be dog-eared and highlighted in places, and you would do your best to adhere to those likes and avoid doing the things they disliked. I would imagine the cover of the book would contain that person's name and that it would be repeated throughout the text.

What if that same person you love had taken the trouble to buy flowers and strewn a path of petals leading to a room in your house? Wouldn't you follow it to see what you would find? Reading the scriptures is just that. It is the discovery of your creator. Reading it line by line, here a little, there a little, piecing together to come to the truth of who your creator is, that your creator loved you enough to save you from the penalty of death by making the ultimate sacrifice to pay that debt. It started in the Garden of Eden with our expulsion after Adam had adhered to his wife's advice. The WORD OF YAHUAH promised Adam that HE would come in the flesh and save him so that he and his descendants could return to the Garden.

The Most High gave us an instruction book laying out how he is to be worshiped. Yes, there is no Temple made of bricks and mortar standing in Israel; however, we are now those stones that make up the temple of the Most High, and he still desires sacrifice daily as laid out in Leviticus chapters 1 through 7.

Only now, animal blood is not required since YAHUSHA, the Messiah, shed his blood once and for all for us. We are to acknowledge everything belongs to him and offer thanks for what we have. We should praise him for the work he does in our lives. We should offer repentance and a contrite heart for our trespasses. Our Elohim the Most High wants these sacrifices from us, sacrifices of the heart. The Torah is now written on our hearts by the Ruach HaKodesh, the Holy Spirit, once we accept it.

Incredibly, our creator wants to have a personal relationship with us. He wants to live in the presence of his creation. He has left us a book of instruction, the Torah, detailing who he is, what he expects from us, and when he wants us to meet with him. Of course, I am speaking of the Bible, our book of instruction, which will bring us closer to the answers to our questions concerning our creator and his creation.

Most everyone has a Bible on a shelf or a table in their homes. We may read a scripture or two, a passage or a chapter, but have you ever opened it up to the first page in Genesis and read it through to the last chapter of the book of Revelation? I know I certainly had not. For years, the only time I picked up my Bible was to go to church on Sundays and Wednesdays, where I opened it to the prescribed chapter and verse, and at the end of the sermon, I closed it, took it home, and put it back on the shelf or on the table where it stayed.

As a Christian, most of my reading occurred in the New Testament, but mostly in Paul's letters. The front of the book only told stories I had learned as a child, such as the expulsion from the Garden, Noah's flood, and Daniel in the Lion's Den: Children's tales I had learned in Sunday school. It was not until several years ago that I was compelled to sit down and open the book on the first page and read it through.

I started with an old version of the Jerusalem Bible I had bought for $9.00 in 1978, which I had been schlepping around for years and never actually read. While reading several other versions, including a couple of editions of the Cepher, I started seeing the son of my ELOHIYM on every page of the Old Testament. I must say that now, the Old Testament is truly my favorite. I do love the New Testament very much, especially Andrew Gabriel Roth's translation from Aramaic, which is particularly informative, especially with all his footnotes and commentary.

I was raised believing that YAHUSHA died for all my past sins and any future sins that I might think to commit and that all I needed to do was just say I am sorry and go on my merry way. However, in my readings, I realized that YAHUSHA sacrificed his life and spilled his blood to pay our debt, which we incur by sin, which is the death of our soul or an eternity of darkness outside his presence. We are under a death sentence because of our stubbornness not to follow the law that he had set forth on Mount Sinai, which was the same law that was in place when Adam and Eve were in the Garden.

I realized that YAHUSHA paid our ticket, our debt, much like if I received a speeding ticket and someone stepped in and paid that ticket for me. It does not mean that I am free to continue to speed. If I get caught speeding again, I will get another ticket, which I will be obliged to pay. Also, if caught speeding down I-35, my daughter cannot tell the officer that her mother or father had perfectly driven down I-35 last week and expect to be let off the hook for her transgression of the speeding law.

We are obligated to follow the law much like the laws we have in our communities, countries, and states. And I realized that the Covenant was only a renewed Covenant, not an old Covenant that had been nailed to the cross. The only thing nailed to the cross was my ticket of debt. I am now obligated not to incur any further debt. YAHUSHA told the woman accused of fornication in the Book of John chapter 8:11 to go and sin no more. He forgave her debt and instructed her to go and incur no further debt.

There is an allegation against Christians made by the practitioners of Judaism concerning Christianity's acceptance of a surrogate sent in YAH's place to complete the Covenant made between himself and Abraham. The allegation is that since YAHUAH himself cut the Covenant and made the promises, he could not send someone in his place to pay the debt of death. This allegation would be true if you believe that YAHUSHA was in no way part of the Covenant cutting. However, you must conclude, and the evidence shows that YAHUSHA was engaged in these Covenants and promises. I intend to lay out the evidence that proves the manifestations YAHUAH used to interact with his creation.

YAHUSHA tells us in the Book of John 14:6 that he is "the Way, the Truth, and the Life: no man comes unto the Father but by me." In verse 7, he says, "If ye had known me, you should have known my Father also: and from henceforth ye know him and have seen him." Psalms 119 instructs us that the Truth is the Torah. YAHUSHA is telling us he is the Torah, the living, breathing word of YAHUAH!

YAHUSHA is also bringing to the mind of his listeners the third book of Ezra, Chapter 4:35-40, Micah 7:20, and The Wisdom of Solomon 5:7-6:25. That is the one purpose of this book: Learning the Way, the Truth and the Life to know YAHUAH, who sent his only begotten son to redeem us from the penalty of the death sentence we're under, by the shedding of his blood, the perfect sacrifice. During this journey, I pray you will see that it has been YAHUSHA all along who has been interacting with his creation, and if we have eyes to see, he is written on all the pages of our Bible.

Our Messiah knocks on the door of our hearts; all we must do is open and accept the proposal. Our creator will not break down our door and drag us out, kicking and screaming. However, there is no atheist in a foxhole. So, if your house is on fire and you cry out to him, he will kick down the door and bring you out just like HE did for his bride, Israel. While they were in bondage in Egypt, they cried out to YAHUAH, and he brought them out. His bride had come of age, and they realized they needed Yeshu'ah (Yah's salvation). They called, and he went to their rescue. YAHUAH brought them to the wedding feast; the marriage conditions were agreed upon.

The conditions are still in place: He is Holy, so we must be holy. YAHUAH is not going to force us to follow him as foretold in the book of Husha (Hosea) chapter 1, where the Word of YAHUAH tells Husha that He "will have mercy upon the house of Yahuda and will save them by YAHUAH ELOHAYHEM and will not save them by bow, nor by sword, nor by battle, by horse, nor by horseman." Could this passage mean that he will not use force but will give us eyes to see and ears to hear, leading us by his spirit into his word, the truth? This knowledge, once accepted and acted upon, will put us on the path of righteousness.

To be holy, we need to have YAHUAH's instruction: his Torah. Paul tells us so in Galatians 3:24, where he says the Torah is our tutor. The word used there for a tutor is pedagogue. A pedagogue was a teacher who always accompanied his young pupil, instructing him in all things and would guard his safety even at the expense of his own life. I realize this work will rub some people the wrong way. However, Paul can in no way contradict the other disciples or YAHUSHA himself. Paul was a lawyer, and he spoke and wrote as one. I could never go away from reading the scriptures with the knowledge and understanding that Paul had. He was raised in the temple at the feet of Gamaliel. I was raised in a Baptist Church, reading a verse or two on Sunday and Wednesday and listening to someone else's interpretation of said verses. I depended on my pastor to know what he was talking about. We all come from somewhere along the path of righteousness, even if it is in the deep weeds along the side of the road. When trying to understand Paul's writings, it is essential to know what he read to understand what he wrote.

Since Paul tells us that the Torah is our pedagogue, our elementary education, it is incumbent that we learn the basic information about our creator and what we must do to please him. If we do not have this basic information, anyone speaking false doctrine could easily lead us astray. If you do not know YAHUAH's doctrine, you can have no discernment concerning false doctrine. How was Eve deceived? Could Adam have been more precise in his instruction concerning the tree? The serpent told Eve that she would not die. She doubted YAHUAH. Eve wondered what YAHUAH really said. She did not seek confirmation of the information presented to her. Could she not have called out to YAHUAH or Adam to confirm the truth? Instead, she doubted the truth of YAHUAH's word and believed false information. We have the truth sitting on a shelf, or thanks to apps like Blueletterbible.org, we have all the answers in the palm of our hand and can quickly confirm the word.

The first-century followers of YAHUSHA started their day hearing the word, and because the New Testament did not exist then, they were hearing Torah. Acts 15 tells of the Apostles' debate about what commandments new followers should be taught to follow. It was decided to instruct them to abstain from pollution of idols, from fornication, and from eating blood and strangled animals, and in verse 21, it says, "for Moses of old time has in every city them that preach him, being read in the synagogue." Yes, new believers attended synagogue, where they learned the laws of Moses, heard the exhortations and warnings of the prophets, and sang along to the Psalms. According to Christian Charles Josias von Bunsen (A.D. 1791-1860), the early churches, after the believers were expelled from the synagogues for their belief in YAHUSHA as their Messiah, held meetings consisting of sharing bread and wine: a small meal in which members brought as a sacrifice or offering. Other members offered praise, a contrite heart, a sin, a guilt offering, or a thank offering. They also continued to share the good news of Messiah and his works of salvation and continued to learn the books of Moses.

The Kolbrin says, "The purpose of the sacred scriptures is also to show man what life should be, how they should be governed, how they should conduct themselves, what they should keep and what they should discard" (Kolbrin chapter 8 of Elidor). The key word there is 'also' because by learning Torah, they also knew who their Messiah was. Before we begin, let us clear up some of the difficult words of Apostle Paul.

UNDERSTANDING PAUL AND THE WORKS OF TORAH

Wherefore, beloved, seeing that you look for such things, be diligent that ye may be found of him in peace, without spot, and blameless. And account that the long-suffering of YAHUAH is salvation; even as our beloved brother Paul also according to the wisdom given unto him has written unto you; as also in all his cepheriym, speaking in them of these things; and which are some things hard to be understood, which they that are unlearned and unstable pervert, as they do also the other scriptures, and to their own destruction. Ye, therefore, beloved, seeing you know these things before, beware lest ye also, being led away with the error of the Torahless, fall from your own steadfastness. 2 Peter 3:14-17

In Romans 3:20 and 28, Paul says, "Therefore by The Works of Torah, no flesh is justified in his sight: for by the Torah is the knowledge of sin. Therefore, we conclude that a man is justified by belief without the works of Torah." Most Christians would argue that Paul is teaching that the law of Moses (Torah) has been abolished. When you study Paul's words about the Torah, they seem contradictory because, in some places, he advocates that the Torah leads to death, and in others, he requires his listeners to follow the law. This phrase, Works of Torah, predates Paul by hundreds of years.

The term 'works of Torah' was discovered in the Dead Sea Scrolls in the Community Rules, (scrolls 4QMMT; 4Q394-399). In my study of the Dead Sea Scrolls, I learned that it was not just a collection of pseudo epigraphical or extra-biblical works but the whole Temple Library, which included every book of the Bible save the New Testament. The Scrolls were found between 1947 and 1956 in the Judean desert known as Qumran or Damascus, which is where Paul was going when he had his Damascus Road conversion (See Scrolls CD,4Q265-73, 5Q12,6Q15 titled the Damascus document). The Dead Sea Scrolls contain no bills or personal letters, and are all sacred writings written in Aramaic and Biblical Hebrew. The story of how these scrolls may have wound up in the caves surrounding the Dead Sea can be found in the four books of The Maccabees, which used to be in the Canon. However, those books have been removed from most bibles. I would encourage everyone to read The Maccabees since it is there that you learn what the abomination is, which makes the Temple desolate, among other histories leading to the coming of the Messiah. Antiochus IV, a Greek Hellenistic King who ruled the Seleucid empire from 175 BC until his death in 164 BC, tried to enforce a lunar calendar. The Priestly calendar was a solar/lunar calendar, but the Priests refused to abide by this lunar calendar.

In 175 BC, a Hellenized high priest was appointed who agreed to practice the lunar calendar so that the true priests were kicked out of the Temple. They could not take any of the sacred implements of the Temple; however, they did take their sacred writings. It is thought that the Essenes inhabited the Dead Sea area where the scrolls were found. However, I do not believe that is correct. Several writers wrote about the Essenes, who we have been told were the occupants of this Qumran community. Hippolytus (A.D. 170-236 A.D.), in book 9, chapter 13, writes of the Essenes: "There is not one city of them but settle in every city." Most of the information about the Essenes comes from Josephus' writings in his Antiquities, where he states that they are a sect that underwent four divisions. However, he does not put these Essenes in any particular place. In his life story, Josephus reports to have studied with the Essenes for three years, just as Paul studied with the Nazoreans.

This other group, the Nazoreans', are conflated with the Essenes because they were occupants of the Dead Sea or Judean desert area (Qumran) and guardians of the Scrolls. Epiphanius of Selamus (AD 310-320) writes in the Panarion 1,2: "All Christians alike were called Nazoreans". We all know that

YAHUSHA, the Messiah, was called the Nazarene. We will get into that later, but for now, let us just discuss what Epiphanius had to say about the Nazoreans. First, he says they were Jewish, attached to the law, and had circumcision. (6.2) "Everyone called the Christians Nazoreans." Then he cites Acts 24, where Paul is accused of being the ringleader of this sect. In verse 5, the high Priest Khanan-Yah says of Paul, "For we have found this man to be an assassin, and one who does treasonous work among all Yehudeans in the whole land; for he is a ringleader of the sect of the Netzarim." And Paul replied respecting the Netzarim in verse 14, "But this indeed I acknowledge, that in that same doctrine of which they (Netzarim) speak, I do serve the Elohim of my father's, believing all the things written in Torah and the prophets. And I have a hope in Elohim, which they also themselves expect, that there is to be a resurrection of the dead, both righteous and the wicked. And for this reason, I also labor to have always a pure conscience before Elohim, and before man".

We learn the Nazorean doctrine in Epiphanius 7.1- 9,3: "But they are Jews in every way and nothing else. They use not only the New Testament but the Old Testament as well, as the Jews do. For they do not repudiate the legislation, the prophets, and the books which are called the writings by the Jews and by themselves. They have no different views but confess everything in full accord with the doctrine of the law and, like the Jews, except that they are believers in Christ. For they acknowledge both the resurrection of the dead and that all things have been created by God, and they declare that God is one and that his son is

Jesus Christ. They are perfectly versed in the Hebrew language, for the entire law, the prophets and the so-called writings-I mean the poetic books. They are different from the Jews and different from Christians only in the following ways. They disagree with Jews because of their belief in Christ, but they are not in accord with Christians because they are still fettered by the laws. - Circumcision, the Sabbath, and the rest. This sect of Nazoreans is to be found in Beroea near Coelesyria in the Decapolis near Pella. for that was its place of origin, since all the disciples had settled in Pella after their remove from Jerusalem. Yet, to the Jews, they are very much enemies. Not only do Jewish people bear hatred against them; they even stand up at dawn, at midday, and toward evening, three times a day when they recite their prayers in the synagogues and curse and anathematize them, saying three times a day, 'God curse the Nazoreans'".

Epiphanius finishes by saying, "But now that we have detected this sect - like a stinging insect that is small, and yet causes pain with its poison - and have squashed it with the words of truth." So, you see, we have one group who is much hated by both sides of the WAY: the Jews and the "Christians," and Paul was in the middle because he does not deny being a part of them. Paul and the Nazoreans were like the followers from Revelation 12:17: "And the dragon was wroth with the woman and went to make war with the remnant of her seed, which guard the Commandments of YAHUAH, and have the testimony of YAHUSHA ha'Mashiach."

According to the Dead Sea Scrolls, the initiation process for entry into the community took three years of study. Acts 9:18-19 tells how Paul received his sight, was baptized, and was with the disciples, those who were in Damascus "certain days." Paul tells us what happened in Galatians chapter 1, starting in verse 17, after his Damascus Road conversion. He states, "Neither went I up to Jerusalem to them which were Apostles before me; but I went to Arav and returned again unto Damascus. Then, after three years, I went up to Jerusalem to see Kepha (Peter) and abode with him for 15 days".

Arav is Mount Sinai, and Damascus is Qumran. In Acts 17:10, the brethren sent Paul and Silas to Beroea, where they found ready and willing hearers of the word who searched the scriptures daily, testing the teachings of Paul and Silas. Suppose Paul is a member of the Nazoreans, the exiled Levitical Priesthood from the second Temple with their followers. In that case, the works of Torah Paul is speaking about in The Book of Romans and other places could be the written Mishna in the form of the Community Rules and the Damascus documents because the Mishna that we know of today was not transmitted into writing at the time of Paul's ministry.

The Mishna is the oral tradition of the Rabbis. It is believed that Moses received spoken laws and those written by the hand of YAHUAH onto tablets. These oral laws the rabbis designated as Torah, sheh b'al peh, as distinguished from the written law, Torah sheh-bichtav. The Rabbis considered these oral laws as binding as the written ones. These sayings were considered handed down from Moses to Joshua to the elders and the elders to the prophets, and the prophets transmitted it to the men of the great assembly. Saying by saying and generation by generation, the oral law has coexisted with the written law ever since. Additional laws not found in the written law appear in the oral law as laws given to Moses at Sinai. The rest of the oral law is implied in the written law. It can be deduced from it by principles of interpretation developed by Rabbis during the time of YAHUSHA, the Messiah. This view is verified by an anecdote from Rabbi Shammai (50 B.C.- 30 A.D.): "It is related that a certain man stood before Shemmai and said, Rabbi, how many Torahs do you have?' The rabbi replied, 'Two - one written and one oral.' (Avot d'Rabbi Natan) (Shabbat 31a).

The oral law was never transmitted into written form for public use until Rabbi Yehudah ha-Nasi, circa 200 CE. He broke with tradition and published his work, a compilation of laws. The Tosephta appeared early in the 5th Century AD, roughly 200 years after Rabbi Yehudah's Mishna. The Mishna and the Tosephta contained readings, rulings, and maxims divided into six orders: seeds, festivals, women, damages, sacred things, and purity. These books were subdivided into 63 books or tractates. These laws were created to keep the people from violating the laws of Moses which if violated brought death. However, living under these laws became more tyrannical.

The truth is that the Torah can mean one of two things to someone practicing Judaism or Christianity. It can mean the opinions and discussions of rabbis that have been put to writing, or it can mean the laws of Moses as put forth in the first five books of the scriptures. The term' works of Torah' means something different to the listener.

Two people who hold opposing definitions for one word can converse and seem to agree but are not because their definitions are different. For example, who is Jesus? Is he the son of Elohim, the divine being who created all things, or was he a man with some good moral teachings who lived an exemplary life? You can have a perfectly compelling conversation about Jesus Christ while still talking about two different entities.

It is important to understand what Paul, John, and the Messiah YAHUSHA mean when they use the word law. It also helps to know what your scriptures say. John 1:17 in most scriptures reads, "For the Torah was given through Moses but grace and truth came by YAHUSHA." However, the word 'but' is absent if you look at the underlying Hebrew. It has been added. The verse should read, "For the Torah was given through Mosheh, grace and truth came by YAHUSHA HAMASHIACH." Grace, the YAHUSHA gave forgiveness of our trespasses as opposed to instant death and Truth as clarification of the Torah.

The teachings of Paul, John, and YAHUSHA, the Messiah, cannot contradict one another. In Matthew 9:14, Mark 2:18, and Luke 5:17, we see YAHUSHA teaching and being challenged by Pharisees, Sadducees, and doctors of the law. YAHUSHA directed them to the written law in many places (Matthew 21:41, 22:31).

I never really gave much thought to why these Pharisees and Sadducees were hanging out and listening to YAHUSHA. We first read about them in Matthew 3:7, and it's John the Baptist who is talking to them because many of the Pharisees and the righteous were coming to be immersed by him, and he calls them a generation of vipers and asks them, "who has warned you to flee from the wrath to come." Well, that is a good question, how did they know to come?

I discovered that many were coming to John because he was the true Zadok high priest. The Messiah knew to come to the true high priest for his own baptism. We are told some of these Pharisees and righteous left the temple and followed John the Baptist. In the book of Acts 13:1, we find a list of people assembled at Antioch, certain prophets, and teachers. Among the names is Manaen, who we are told was brought up with Herod the Tetrarch and Sha'ul (Paul).

There was a Saint Manaen who was a teacher at the church of Antioch, and he was King Herod Antipas's foster brother and lifelong friend. This connection with the royal family may have made him one of the eyewitnesses and ministers of the word mentioned in Luke 1:2. This Manachem (Manaen) is mostly stricken from the Talmud (a commentary on the Mishna and is a significant text of Rabbinic Judaism second only to the Bible).

However, he is listed once in the tractate Sanhedrin 98b. Later in the Babylonian Talmud, there is a dispute among the Sages over Manaen and what caused him to be stricken from the Mishna. The last Judge (Av Beit Din) of the Sanhedrin in about 20 BC was said to be Manaen the Essene. He and many others walked out from the Sanhedrin, thus making it illegitimate when a majority left to follow the king's service. The Babylonian Talmud cites a dispute among the sages over what Manhaen went forth to do. The third Century Rabbi Abaya argues that he went forth out into evil courses or culture, while Rava (Abba Ben Joseph bar Hama (A.D. 280-352 A.D.) argues he went forth out to the Kings (God's) service. The Talmud then quotes a baraita supporting Rava's opinion: "Thus it is also taught: Manahem went forth out to the King's Service, and there went forth out with him 80 pairs of disciples dressed in silk".

This Menahem is believed to be the same as spoken of by Josephus in Antiquities 15:10:5, where he records that Menahem prophesied that Herod would be king, announcing to him that he would reign successfully despite Herod not being in the line of the royal dynasty.

When Herod became king, he asked Manahem how long his reign would be. Initially, he did not reply, and Herod urged him until he prophesied that Herod would reign for at least 30 years but did not specify the exact number. Herod was pleased with Menahem's answer, dismissed him with a clasp of the hand, and thenceforth bestowed special honors upon the Essenes, who I believe to be the Nazoreans.

As recorded in the books of the Maccabees, there were many upheavals and divisions among the Pharisees leading up to the coming of Messiah, including assassinations. John the Baptist's father Zachariah was murdered, and his wife Elizabeth, with

John, fled to the desert. Remember that John was six months older than YAHUSHA and would have been of the age when Herod ordered that all male children under two years be murdered. Zechariah refused to hand over his son to be murdered, which is why he was killed. YAHUSHA, the infant, and his family fled to Egypt.

The Apostle Peter knew there was danger in Jerusalem. A false Sanhedrin could be raised with blood on its hands, no question about it, and YAHUSHA the Messiah ignited that flame as he said in Luke 12:49, "I am coming to send fire on the earth; and what will I if it be already kindled?" And a fire of revolution he kindled when, in John chapter 8, he separates salvation from DNA. YAHUSHA speaks the famous verse from John 8:32, "You shall know the truth, and the truth shall make you free."

From Psalms 119:142, we know that Truth equals the Commandments of YAHUAH. Then, in John 8:39, the Jews tell YAHUSHA that Abraham is our father, to which YAHUSHA replies, "If you were Abraham's children, you would do the works of Abraham." The works of Abraham are the written law of YAHUAH.

Now we can see a difference between the works of the law, which were the walls built around YAHUAH'S written laws given to Moses on Mount Sinai, and the oral traditions or works of Torah, which were written early, as found in the Dead Sea Scrolls Damascus Document. These oral laws were given to protect the laws of Moses from being broken. There was a wall of rules built around the law that ensured that you did not break a commandment because breaking a commandment brought death.

There are many examples in the Gospels of YAHUSHA confronting the Jews. They accuse YAHUSHA'S Apostles of not washing their hands without the prescribed prayer before they ate, gathering grains into their hands, or carrying a bed on the Shabbat. Nowhere in Scripture are there laws admonishing one for carrying a bed, walking a certain distance, or praying while you wash your hands.

There is a command in Deuteronomy 4:2, which says, "You shall not add to the word that I command you, nor take from it, that you may keep the Commandments of YAHUAH your ELOHIYM that I command you." Ultimately, YAHUSHA tells these Jews that they are not of YAHUAH, the Father, but are from their father, the devil. In John 8:44, YAHUSHA states, "The devil was a murderer from the beginning and abode not in the truth." Again, the truth is the Commandments of YAHUAH.

Hearing many sermons about this particular passage of John calling these adversaries of YAHUSHA Jews, it never occurred to me that YAHUSHA and his disciples were also Jews. It is in the Book of John where we see the word Jew. The title of Jew is not used in an adversarial way. John uses it to differentiate between themselves, the branches or the Netzer, and the people refusing to accept the Messiah in the person of YAHUSHA, the son of the virgin Mary, of the lineage of King David. The word Jew in the Book of John refers to a person following the oral traditions, given to keep a person from breaking the laws given to Moses. It is not meant to be an ethnic slur because they were all biological sons of Abraham.

In Matthew 23. While addressing the multitude, YAHUSHA says, "The scribes and the Pharisees sit in Moses's seat: all therefore whatsoever he bids you guard, that diligently guard and do; but do not ye after their reforms and traditions; for they say and do not. For they bind heavy burdens and grievous to be born and lay them on men's shoulders; but they themselves will not move them with one of their fingers". Notice the pronoun 'he' refers to the proper noun Moses, not the Pharisees. It is Moses, i.e., the Commandments, that we are to be guarding and doing and not the mitzvot, these oral traditions that the Pharisees have commanded to keep the people from violating the laws of Moses. Those laws brought death if they were broken. We now have grace that allows us to make mistakes, learn from those mistakes, and take that knowledge to implement changes in our lives so that we may continue on our path toward righteousness.

As the good news spread of the Messiah, people were coming to belief who did not have the traditions of the law. The Canaanite woman from Matthew chapter 15 came to YAHUSHA in search of help for her daughter, who was vexed by a devil. Starting in verse 23, YAHUSHA "answered her, not a word, and his Talmidiym came and besought him, saying, send her away; for she cries after us, but he answered and said I am not sent but unto the lost sheep of the house of Yashar'el. Then came she and worshiped him, saying ADONAI help me. But he answered and said, it is not meet to take the children's bread and to cast it to dogs". He called her a dog. She was not of the house of Yashar'el. Now read the parable of the one lost sheep in Luke 15. And remember the commission YAHUSHA gave to his Talmidiym in Matthew 10:6 "but go rather to the lost sheep of the house of Yashar'el."

How do we become members of the House of Israel? How do we, being of the wild olive tree, become grafted into the cultivated tree? We learn from the writings of Clement of Rome (AD 35 - 99) that this Canaanite woman gets grafted in. To understand how, we must go to the Book of Acts chapter 15, where the debate was raging about what to tell the new converts to the way. It was determined to tell them not to worship idols, not to eat blood, not to eat strangled animals, and to refrain from fornication: the basics, the people were to attend synagogue every Shabbat to hear Moses. Moses is Torah, the first five books of the scriptures, and through hearing, they would live in them, not because they felt they had to but because they had a heart for it.

There was always provision for all peoples to live in the camp of YAHUAH. Remember, a mixed multitude was brought out of Egypt. See Exodus 12:48,49, Leviticus 24:22, Numbers 9:14, and 15:14-16,26. Leviticus 19:34 says, 'The stranger that dwells with you shall be unto you as one born among you, and you shall love him as yourself'.

In Galatians, chapter 2, Paul talks about Titus. He says that Titus was not compelled to be circumcised. Titus learned the Commandments, and he wanted to be circumcised. Titus was circumcised because of his heart condition. He heard the Torah, learned by listening to the Commandments, and then acted upon that knowledge he had obtained on what he needed to do as a follower to be grafted into the cultivated Olive Tree, Yashar'el.

To sum up, the works of the Torah, because I feel I have gone far afield here, are those rules that the rabbis developed to guard against violating the Torah. These rules became more important and ritual than the Torah itself, which also in and of itself brought death. In case any of you readers see this and are feeling righteous in that you do not follow the rabbinic laws, I would caution you by saying the Roman Catholic Church (RCC), is no different. The RCC believes that the Bible alone is not considered the word of YAHUAH. To the RCC, the way to salvation is 'tradition' plus 'magisterium,' which is the teaching authority of the institution. To any of you who would say I am not Catholic or a practicing Jew, I would ask what day you consider to be the Sabbath or which feast days you are celebrating.

If you believe Sunday is the Sabbath, then you are under the authority of the Roman Catholic church. Here is a brief history of how that came about: Egyptian Mithraism was introduced into Rome in the second century AD as a festival on Sunday dedicated to the worshiping of the Sun. In 313 AD, emperor Constantine made Christianity legal and made Sunday a civil day of rest. By 321 AD, emperor Constantine appointed himself Bishop of Rome. On March 7th, 321 AD, he issued the Declaration stating, "On the venerable day of the sun let the magistrates and the people residing in cities rest, and let all workshops be closed" (Codex Justinian's 3.12.3). It was in 325 AD that Pope Sylvester I officially named Sunday the Lord's Day. In 338 AD, Eusebius, the court Bishop of Constantine, wrote, "All things whatsoever that it was the duty to do on the Sabbath (the seventh day of the week) we (Constantine, Eusebius, and other Bishops) have transferred to the Lord's Day (the first day of the week) as more appropriately belonging to it. It was not until 364 A.D, during the Council of Laodicea, that it was declared that Christians should not Judaize and be idle on Saturday but shall work on that day. I would also ask if your denominational leaders are among the signatories of the Manhattan Declaration of 2009 or the Evangelical and Catholics Together project, which began in 1994. But I digress.

I will discuss more the difficult words of Paul throughout this work and especially next, where the case is made for YAHUSHA being the Messiah, the Son of ELOHIYM in the book of Hebrews, which I do not believe Paul wrote. Still, I do think he had a hand in writing, maybe dictating to a scribe. In 2 Corinthians 11:24 and 25, Paul states that he five times received 39 stripes from the Jews. He was beaten with rods three times and survived a stoning once. He also survived a shipwreck. I have in my past life come across a man who survived a prison riot that involved rock throwing. He obtained a crushed orbital socket, which plagued him for the rest of his life, and he had the luxury of a surgeon who could piece his socket back together with pins and plates. Paul had no such luxury.

I have heard the theory that a devil mentally tormented Paul. This theory is in response to Paul's complaining in 2 Corinthians 12:7 of a thorn in the flesh and being buffeted by a messenger of Satan. The word there for buffeted is Strong's Concordance number G2852 kolaphizo, which means to wrap with the fist. People who live with chronic pain can relate to this statement of Paul. I will say that if you believe a demon-possessed Paul, you must throw his letters out. However, I know from experience and seeing the trials and tribulations he endured for his savior that it was a physical malady he was suffering from and could explain why he could not sit and write a letter to the Hebrews.

All the disciples were commissioned to teach the lost sheep the good news that the promised Messiah had come. YAHUSHA referred to YAHUAH as his father in Heaven seven times in the book of Matthew. Citing Old Testament prophecies concerning the coming Son of ELOHIYM and pointing out how YAHUSHA, the son of the Virgin Mary, fulfilled those prophecies was the disciples' only tactic. The writer of Hebrews makes a convincing case; therefore, I will breakdown the first couple of chapters of the Book of Hebrews to demonstrate how the front of the Bible is all about the promise of salvation, which would come from YAHUAH in the manifestation of a Son and show how salvation also came in other forms as well which YAHUSHA the Messiah admitted to being., demonstrating that he was written into every page of Scripture.

MESSIAH YAHUSHA IS THE SON OF ELOHIYM

"YAHUSHA HA'MASHIACH is the power of YAH. HE is the reason, HE is his Wisdom and Glory; he enters into a virgin; being the Holy Spirit; HE is endued with flesh; YAHUAH is mingled with man. This is our ELOHIYM, this is our Messiah, who, as the mediator of the two, puts on man that he may lead them to the Father. What man is, YAHUSHA was willing to be, that man also may be what YAHUSHA is". Cyprian, The Treatises number 6, paragraph 11.

How did anyone in the first century know YAHUSHA, the son of Mary, was the son of ELOHIYM? Yes, YAHUSHA himself said he was the son of ELOHIYM in Matthew 27:43 and John 10:36. But why believe him? How did they know ELOHIYM had a son? They did not have the New Testament, the gospels, or the letters of Paul. All they had was Moses, the prophets, and the songs. They had Isaiah 9:6, which reads from the Targum, "The Prophet said to the house of David, for unto us a child is born, unto us a son is given, and he has taken the law upon himself to keep it. His name is called from eternity, wonderful, the mighty ELOHIYM, who liveth to eternity, the messiah, whose peace shall be great upon us in his days." Just two chapters before this verse in 7:14, it says, "Therefore the Lord himself shall give you a sign; behold, a virgin shall conceive, and bear a son, and she shall call his name Immanuel." This name means 'with us is God,' from Strong's Concordance number H6005.

By the time of the first century, Israel knew from the prophecy of Daniel 9:24-27 to be looking for the Son, the Messiah. Daniel 9:24-27 reads, "Seventy weeks are determined for the people and the holy city, to finish the transgression, and to make an end of sins, and to make atonement for iniquity, and to bring everlasting righteousness, and to seal up the vision and the prophets, and to anoint the Holy of Holies. Know and understand that from the going forth of the word to return and to build Yerushalayim until MASHIACH the Prince is seven weeks; and three score and two weeks; returning to build the wide street of gold in times of distress. And after three score and two weeks, MASHIACH is cut off, but nothing of the holy city is ruined, and the people of the prince to come, the end of which is in a flood, and even until the end of the battle, devastation is determined. And the strength of the Covenant multiplies for one week: and in the middle of the week, the sacrifice, and the oblation cease, and upon the end, abominations destroy, until the consummation is determined and poured over the desolation".

There is a popular television series portraying the story of the Messiah YAHUSHA from the point of view of the disciples, who are portrayed as not knowing their scriptures, which I believe is false. However, in contradiction to that portrayal, in one episode, YAHUSHA asks children if they knew the Shema and if they could recite it, proving they were learning Moses at an early age. If all we had were Old Testament scriptures, could we substantiate YAHUSHAS' claim of being the Son of ELOHIYM? Could we have identified YAHUSHA as the Messiah just as they did? Everyone knew ELOHIYM had a son, and many believed YAHUSHA was the Messiah they sought. They also knew it was time for the Messiah, ELOHIYM's Son, to appear.

Nathaniel knew ELOHIYM had a son. The Book of John, chapter 1:49, says: "Nathaniel answered and said unto him, Rabbi, you are the son of ELOHIYM; you are the king of Yashar'el," Satan also knew. The Book of Luke 4:9 says: "And he (Satan) brought him to Jerusalem, and set him on a pinnacle of the temple, and said unto him, if you be the Son of ELOHIYM, cast yourself down from hence." Even devils knew ELOHIYM had a son. In the Book of Matthew chapter 8, starting in verse 28, it says: "and when he (YAHUSHA) was come to the other side into the country of the Girgashiym, there met him two possessed with devils, coming out of the tombs, exceeding fierce, so that no man might pass by that way. And behold, they cried out, saying, what have we to do with you, YAHUSHA, Son of ELOHIYM?"

The Pharisees knew YAHUAH had a son. In the Book of Matthew, chapter 26:63 it says, "But YAHUSHA held his peace. And the high priest answered and said unto him, I adjure you by the living EL, that you tell us whether you be HA'MASHIACH, the Son of ELOHIYM". Even the Roman Centurion knew.

Mark chapter 15:39 says: "And when the centurion, which stood over against him, saw that he (YAHUSHA) so cried out, and gave up his ruach (spirit), he said, 'Truly this man was the Son of ELOHIYM." Given that they only had the words of Moses, the prophets, and the songs, how did they know?

First-century people only read or heard works such as those found in the caves of Qumran, which included the book of Enoch. Their scriptures, as ours, are the infallible word of YAHUAH. In The Book of Enoch, chapter 104, starting in verse 8, it says, "But when they shall write all my words correctly in their own languages, they shall neither change or diminish them; but shall write them all correctly; all which from the first I have uttered concerning them. Another mystery also I point out. To the righteous and the wise shall be given cepheriym (books) of joy, of integrity, and of great wisdom. To them shall cepheriym be given, in which they shall believe; and in which they shall rejoice. And all the righteous shall be rewarded, who from these shall acquire the knowledge of every upright path. In those days, says YAHUAH, they shall call to the children of the earth and make them listen to their wisdom. Show them that you are their leaders; and that remuneration shall take place over the whole earth; for I and my **son** will forever hold communion with them in the paths of uprightness, while they are still alive. Peace shall be yours. Rejoice, children of integrity, in the Truth".

Earlier in Enoch chapter 46, he is shown the Ancient of Days who is described with a head like white wool, which is like the description given in

Daniel 7:9 and Revelation 1:14 and again in Enoch 71 where Enoch reiterates the woolen head of the Ancient of Days he adds "and his robe was indescribable." But in Enoch 46, he beholds the Ancient of Days "and with him another, whose countenance resembled that of man. His countenance was full of grace, like one of the Holy angels." Here, we see Messiah YAHUSHA is a separate being from YAHUAH, a spiritual being individual from YAHUAH.

Detractors rightfully would direct you to Deuteronomy 4:35, which says: "Unto you it was showed, that you might know that YAHUAH he is ELOHIYM: there is none else beside him." Or they would direct you to the book of Isaiah 44:24. It says there: "Thus says YAHUAH, your Redeemer, and he that formed you, from the womb, I am YAHUAH that makes all things; that stretches forth the heavens alone, that spreads abroad the earth by myself." Then there is Isaiah 42:8, which says: "I am YAHUAH: that is my Name: and my glory will I not give to another, neither my praise to graven images."

Some will scoff at my use of Enoch and say it is not scripture. I will point you to 2 Peter 2:4, which says, "For if YAH spared not the angels that sinned, but cast them down to She'ol, and delivered them into chains of darkness, to be watched unto the judgment of anguish." The story of these angels who were cast into darkness can be found in Enoch chapter 13.

Similarly, Jude quotes Enoch chapter 2:1, saying, "Behold, YAHUAH comes with ten thousands of his qodeshiym, to execute judgment upon them, and to convince all that are wicked among them of all their wicked deeds which they have wickedly committed, and of all their hard speeches which wicked sinners has spoken against him."

Tertullian (160-240 A.D.) advocated for the sacredness of the Book of Enoch in his apology, as well as Origen (A.D. 185-253 A.D.). However, I will leave this topic with the words of the Messiah himself in Matthew 22; from verse 30, he says to the Pharisees who were testing him, "You do err, not knowing the scriptures, nor the power of YAHUAH. For in the resurrection, they neither marry, nor are giving in marriage, but are as the angels of EL in heaven." The fact that Angels do not have wives in heaven can be found nowhere in the canonized scriptures. You will only see this in the Book of Enoch, chapter 15. YAHUAH tells Enoch to address the Watchers who had fallen, cohabited, and mated with the earthly women, as described in Genesis 6. Enoch was given this message from YAH to tell the angels, starting in verse 6, "But you from the beginning were made spiritual, possessing a life which is eternal, and not subject to death forever. Wherefore I made not women for you because being spiritual, your dwelling is in heaven".

We must also use the front of our Bibles to reconcile the belief that ELOHIYM had a son to answer the previous verses from Deuteronomy and Isaiah. In the book of Isaiah, chapter 28:7-13 it says: "but they also have erred through wine, and through strong drink are out of the way; the priest and the prophet have erred through strong drink; they are swallowed up of wine, they are out of the way through strong drink; they err in vision, they stumble in judgment. For all tables are full of vomit and filthiness, so that there is no place clean. Whom shall teach knowledge? And whom shall he make to understand doctrine? Them that are weaned from the milk and drawn from the breasts; For precept must be upon precept, precept upon precept: line upon line, line upon line; here a little, and there a little".

Proverbs chapter 25:2 says: "It is the glory of ELOHIYM to conceal a thing, but the honor of kings to search out a matter." So, we are on a treasure hunt for the truth, and YAHUSHA said the truth would set you free. YAHUSHA also said in the book of John chapter 5:39, "Search the scriptures; for in them you think you have eternal life: and they are they which testify of me." It is interesting that earlier in verse 37 he said, "and the Father himself, which has sent me, has borne witness of me. You have neither heard his voice at any time nor seen his shape. And you have not his word abiding in you: for whom he has sent, him you believe not". If no one has ever seen the shape or heard the voice of YAHUAH, the Father, whose voice were they hearing, and who did they see?

A midrash pulls several passages together to make a point or even doctrine. Scripture should prove scripture and interpret itself. Hence, line upon line, here a little, there a little. Our Evangelical preachers do the same. However, the rabbi would use a part of a scripture passage in a discussion, assuming their audience's knowledge of scriptures would allow them to deduce the fuller meaning of the passage. If you do not know these scriptures and their context, how can you recognize when the New

Testament writers are quoting from the Old Testament?

The writer of Hebrews does precisely this in chapters 1 & 2, where he quotes a dozen or so passages from the Old Testament and pulls these passages, along with parallel passages, together to prove the claim made at the time that YAHUAH had a Son who created the world, and that this son was sitting on the right hand of the Most High in heaven. Most importantly, this Son was YAHUSHA, the son of the virgin Mary. At this point, I would encourage you to open your Bible to the book of Hebrews, chapter 1, and read that the writer of Hebrews makes a claim and uses Old Testament verses to prove that YAHUAH created the world through his son. The writer expected his readers to know these verses. And not just the verses but the context in which they were written, the whole chapter, and even the whole book. Let us go through these verses that are quoted in the Book of Hebrews to prove to the listeners, the Hebrews, that YAHUAH had a son, and that son was YAHUSHA, the son of Mary.

The writer of Hebrews in chapter 1 starts, "YAHUAH, who at sundry times and in diverse manners spoke in time past unto the fathers by the prophets, has in these last days spoken unto us by his son, whom he has appointed heir of all things, by whom also he made the worlds; who being in the brightness of his glory and the express image of his person, and upholding all things by the word of his power, when he had by himself purged our sins, set down on the right hand of the Majesty on high; being made so much better than the angels, as he has by inheritance obtained a more excellent Name than they. For unto which of the Angels, has he said at any time"

Then the writer quotes from Psalms chapter 2:7, which says: "I will declare the decree: YAHUAH has said unto me, you are my Son; this day have I begotten you." Before this verse 7 quote, Psalms 2:2 says: "the kings of the earth set themselves, and the rulers take counsel together, against YAHUAH, and against his MASHIACH." So, we know that in verse 7, YAHUAH is talking about his MASHIACH, his anointed and his son.

On the surface of this verse in Psalms 2, most people would say he is talking about David. But the sod meaning, that being the mystical or secret meaning of the phrase, takes on a deeper meaning when reading further down in verse 8 of the Psalm where YAHUAH says: "Ask of me, and I shall give you the heathen for your inheritance, and the uttermost parts of the earth for your possession. You shall break them with a rod of iron; you shall dash them in pieces like a Potter's vessel". We know that David nor his son Solomon ruled to the uttermost parts of the earth and never broke the other nations to pieces like a potter's vessel. This verse cannot be about David.

The writer of Hebrews then quotes 2 Samuel chapter 7:14: "I will be to him a Father, and he shall be to me a son." In this verse, YAHUAH is speaking to David through the prophet Nathan about building the Temple. Verse 17 says that his (David's) kingdom will be established forever. The Psalms were written long before the northern kingdom was dispersed and before the dispersion of Judah to Babylon. The kingdom of Israel was not established forever. This same kind of interaction is also recorded in 1 Chronicles chapter 17; the specific quote is in verse 13. This son is clearly not David or Solomon who are lying dead in a tomb.

The writer of Hebrews expected his listeners to know chapter 7 of 2 Samuel, in which the Word of YAHUAH appeared to Nathan and instructed David concerning the building of a temple. What I say next may seem controversial to most; however, it must be noted that an earthly temple was never intended by YAHUAH to be built. Cyprian (200–258 A.D.) addressed this in his treatise number 12 concerning the house of Elohim. He quotes the book of Second Kings, which in his day would have been 2 Samuel chapter 7, verses 4, 5,12-16, which reads, "And the Word of the Lord came to Nathan, saying, go and tell my servant David, thus saith the Lord, 'Thou shalt not build me an house to dwell in; but it shall be, when thy days shall be fulfilled, and thou shalt sleep with thy fathers, I will raise up thy seed after thee, which shall come from thy bowels, and I will make ready his kingdom. He shall build me an house in my name, and I will raise up his throne forever; and I will be to him for a father, and he shall be to me for a son; and his house shall obtain confidence, and his kingdom forever more in my sight."

It was after David's death that his seed would be raised to build a temple. Solomon was alive at the time of this prophecy, so YAHUAH could not have been talking about him and his Temple. Also, notice that it is when this son should arrive that YAH will "make ready his kingdom." We are now allowed to forge a path in our hearts that will enable YAHUAH to reside by his spirit in us, thus making us temples.

Continuing in Hebrews 1:6, the writer says: "And again, when he brings his yachiyd (son) into the world, he says, 'And let all the angels of YAH worship Him.'" This quote is taken from Deuteronomy 32:43, and reading from the Septuagint, you get "Be glad, O skies, with him, and let all the divine sons do obeisance to him. Be glad, O nations, with his people, and let all the angels of YAHUAH prevail for him". The writer is calling these Divine Sons angels.

Just a side note on the Septuagint: according to Philo, it was translated from Chaldaic to Greek on the island of Phanos in front of Alexandria. It is estimated to have been written about 282 BC. While reading the anti-Nicene fathers and trying to match up their quotes from scripture, it becomes clear they were reading from the Septuagint, which was translated from a much older Hebrew text than any of our modern-day scriptures. An example of this can be found in Origen's homily on Psalm 15 (16), a prophecy of the Messiah to come, which reads:

> *"A monument- inscription to David.*
> *Protect me, O EL, because I have hoped in you. I have said to YAHUAH, you are my ADONAI because you do not have a need for my good things. He has made wonders for the holy ones who are in the land; all his things willed are in them. Their weaknesses have been multiplied; they hasten after these things. I by no means gather with their assemblies because of blood, nor will I*

mention their names with my lips. YAHUAH is the portion of my inheritance and of my cup. You are the one restoring my inheritance to me. My boundary lines have fallen in my strongest, for indeed my inheritance is strongest for me. I shall bless YAHUAH, who causes me to apprehend, yet also until night, my kidneys have disciplined me.

I have foreseen YAHUAH face to face through everything because he is at my right hand so that I may not be shaken. Therefore, my heart rejoiced, and my glory exalted. But still, my flesh will set up a tent in hope because you will not abandon my soul in hades. Nor will you allow your devout one to see corruption. You have made me know roads of life. You will fill me with rejoicing with your persona, the very thing that is a delight in his right hand".

Now compare this with any of your scripture, even the Septuagint, which is much closer to what Origen quoted. Also, Origen, as well as others that I will cover later, says that this Psalm and other passages are being spoken by the Messiah. If you are concerned about the line, 'nor will I mention their names (those who have been humbled) with my lips.' It just means he will not merely give lip service to them but will be mentioned in his heart and in his depth.

Let us return to the Book of Hebrews, chapter 1. In verse 7, the writer says, "And of the angels He says," then the writer quotes Psalms 104:4, which says, "Who makes his angels ruachoth (spirits), his ministers a flaming fire". This Psalm describes how

YAHUAH created all things and describes his rule over creation. Please read Psalms 104. Continuing in Hebrews 1:8, the writer quotes from Psalms chapter 45:6-7: "But unto the son, he says, 'Your throne, O ELOHIYM, is forever and ever: a scepter of righteousness is the scepter of your kingdom. You have loved righteousness and hated iniquity: therefore ELOHIYM, even your ELOHIYM, has anointed you with the oil of gladness above your fellows". Who is anointing who?

Psalm 45:7 says: "Therefore ELOHIYM even your ELOHIYM has anointed you". This Psalm is sung about the King. It says in verse 1, "My heart bubbles forth good news, and I will tell my deeds to the king; my tongue is the pen of a ready writer." But which king? The writer of Hebrews claims this verse is about the son of ELOHIYM. Reading the same Psalm verses from the Septuagint, which has this as the 44th Psalm starting in verse 6: "Your throne, O ELOHIYM, is forever and ever. A rod of equity is the rod of your rule; you loved righteousness and hated lawlessness. Therefore, ELOHIYM, your ELOHIYM, anointed you with oil of rejoicing and beyond your partners. Myrrh and myrrh oil and cassia waft from your clothes, from ivory bastions, with which they made you glad. Daughters of kings are in your honor; the queen stood at your right in gold woven clothing, decked out in many colors". Again, who is anointing who? The writer of Hebrews concludes it is the Father who is anointing the Son here in Psalms chapter 45 because in Hebrews 1:8-9 it says, "but unto the son he says" and then quotes Psalm45:6-7. Therefore, it is safe to conclude the King who is being spoken of here in Psalm 45 is the King of the universe, not an earthly king.

Starting in verse 10 of Hebrews chapter 1, the writer quotes Psalms 102, which talks about the coming Messiah. It says in Psalms 102:12-21: "But you, O YAHUAH, shall endure forever; and your mention unto all generations. You shall arise and have mercy upon Zion, for the time to favor her, yea, the set time is come. For your servants take pleasure in her stones and favor the dust thereof. The heathens shall fear the name of YAHUAH, and all the kings of the earth your glory. When YAHUAH shall build up Zion, he shall appear in his glory. He will regard the prayer of the destitute and not despise their prayer. This shall be written for the generation to come, and the people which shall be created shall praise YAH. For he has looked down from the height of his sanctuary; from heaven did YAHUAH behold the earth: to hear the groaning of the prisoner; to loose those that are appointed to death; to declare the name of YAHUAH in Tsiyon, and his praise in Jerusalem; when the people are gathered together, and the kingdoms, to serve YAHUAH". When YAHUAH delivered Israel from Egypt, he did not save them from death. Therefore, this passage must be speaking of the coming Messiah, specifically YAHUSHA, when he came and laid down his life, shedding his blood to deliver us from that sentence of death and granting us eternal life. YAHUSHA fulfilled this prophecy of Psalms 102 when he says in the Gospel of John 17:26, "And I have declared unto them your name, and will declare it: that the love wherewith you have loved me may be in them, and I in them." The further fulfillment of Psalms 102:21 is shown in Acts chapter 2:5: "And there were dwelling at Jerusalem Jews, devout men out of every nation under heaven."

In Hebrews 1:10, the writer is quoting Psalms 102:25-27 which says: "You, YAHUAH, in the beginning, have laid the foundation of the earth; and the heavens are the works of your hands; they shall perish; but you remain, and they all shall wax old as does a garment: and as a vesture shall you fold them up, and they shall be changed: but you are the same, and your years shall not fail." Here, the writer concludes that YAHUAH created the earth with His hands. Later, we will explore scriptures concerning the hand of YAHUAH, which will prove that YAHUSHA, the Messiah, is YAHUAH made flesh through the Virgin Mary.

Returning to the book of Hebrews chapter 1, starting in verse 13, the writer asks: "But to which of the Angels said he at any time, 'sit at my right hand, until I make your enemies your footstool?" This quote is from Psalms 110:1, which says: "YAHUAH said unto my Adonai, sit at my right hand until I make your enemies your footstool." There is a parallel verse in Ecclesiasticus chapter 51:10 which says: "I called upon YAHUAH, the father of my ADONAI, that he would not leave me in the days of my trouble, and in the time of the proud when there was no help." Remember, the reader of Hebrews is expected to recall Psalms 110 and Ecclesiasticus 51. Combining these two chapters, Psalms 110, and Ecclesiasticus 51, it is clear David and Solomon recognized YAHUAH had a son. David calls him Adonai, and Solomon calls him the son of ELOHIYM.

As we continue, in Hebrews chapter 2, we see the writer attempting to establish that YAHUAH made himself flesh. Interestingly, the writer of Hebrews in 2:3 refers us back to the book of Deuteronomy, chapter 32. The writer in Hebrews 2:3 says, "How will we escape if we hate the things which are our life, things which began to be spoken by our Master (Yeshua) and were confirmed to us by them who heard from him." This quote is taken from Andrew Gabriel Roth's translation of the New Testament from the Aramaic. Deuteronomy 32 is the song of Moses in which he goes over the history of the world and the history of Israel, which was not very pretty, considering they continually left YAHUAH and followed other gods.

Starting in Deuteronomy, chapter 32:44-47 says: "And Moses came and recited all the words of this song before the people, he and Yahusha the son of Nun. And when Moses had finished reciting all these words to all Israel, he said to them, set your hearts to all the words which I testify among you this day, which you shall command your children to do, all the words of this law. For it is not a vain thing for you because it is your life, and through this thing, you shall prolong your days in the land which you are crossing the Jordan to possess".

By pointing the listeners back to the song of Moses, the writer of Hebrews is reminding his listeners that adherence to the commands given on Mount Sinai, the laws of Moses, and the Torah meant life. A parallel verse in Psalm 119:93 states, "I will never forget thy commandments because they are my very life." The writer of Hebrews is teaching A

Renewed Covenant, not a new covenant. Israel broke the Covenant or marriage contract. The divorced Israel and put away Judah can now be reconciled to her husband because YAHUSHA, the Messiah, gave his life on the cross, shedding his blood, laying down his life, and resurrecting from the dead. The husband died, thus making a way for us to enter into this renewed Covenant thus removing the debt of death. The writer stresses that this message he delivers means the salvation of our soul. It means eternal life. It means a return to the garden as promised to Adam in the First book of Adam and Eve, where they would live in the presence of YAHUAH, regaining their bright nature. I will speak briefly about the bright nature that I first read about in the first book of Adam and Eve.

I realize that the book of Adam and Eve is apocryphal. However, extra-biblical texts provide us with a backdrop or an explanation of the scriptures we find in the Bible. When Adam and Eve fell, they lost their bright nature, and they were promised by the word of YAHUAH to get it back. Scripture confirms this in 1 John 3:2 which states, "Beloved, now are we the sons of YAHUAH, and it does not yet appear that we shall be: but we know that, when he shall appear, we shall be like him; for we shall see him as he is." John also writes in the Book of Revelation 21:23: "And the city had no need of the sun, neither of the moon, to shine in it; for the glory of YAHUAH did lighten it, and the lamb is the light thereof." Paul writes in 1 Corinthians chapter 15:4,42: "There is one glory of the sun, and another glory of the moon, and another glory of the stars: for one star differs from another star in glory, so also is the resurrection of the dead. It is sown in corruption; it is raised in incorruption". In the Book of Matthew, chapter 13:43, YAHUSHA the Messiah says himself: "Then shall the righteous shine forth as the sun in the Kingdom of their Father. Who has ears to hear, let him hear". Is there scriptural support for these promises of Paul, John, and the Messiah?

The return of our bright nature may be found in Psalms 17:15, which states, "As for me, I will behold your face in righteousness; I shall be satisfied, when I awake, with your likeness." Or Daniel chapter 12:2-3: "And many of them that sleep in the dust of the earth shall awake, some to everlasting life, and some to shame and everlasting contempt. And they that be wise shall shine as the brightness of the expanse; and they that turn many to righteousness as the stars forever and ever". Isaiah chapter 60, starting in verse 1, says, "Arise oh Jerusalem; for your light is come, and the glory of YAHUAH is risen upon you. For, behold, the darkness shall cover the earth, and gross darkness the people; but YAHUAH shall arise upon you, and His glory shall be seen upon you. And the other nations shall come to your light, and Kings to the brightness of your rising". In the book The Wisdom of Solomon, starting in 2:23 and ending in 3:7, it says: "For ELOHIYM created man to be immortal and made him to be an image of his own eternity. Nevertheless, through envy of the devil came death into the world; and they that do hold of his side do find it. But the souls of the righteous are in the hand of ELOHIYM, and there shall no torment touch them. In the sight of the unwise, they seem to die, and their departure is taken for misery, and their going from us to be utter destruction, but they are in peace. For though they be punished in the sight of men yet is their hope full of immortality. And having been a little chastened, they should be greatly rewarded; for ELOHIYM proved them and found them worthy for himself. As gold in the furnace has he tried them and received them as a burnt offering. And in the time of their visitation, they shall shine and run to and fro like sparks among the stubble."

Second Baruch chapter 51:7-11 states: "But those who have been saved by their works and to whom the Torah has been now a hope and understanding an expectation and wisdom a confidence shall wonders appear in their time. For they shall behold the world which is now invisible to them, and they shall behold the time which is now hidden from them: And time shall no longer age them. For in the heights of that world shall they dwell, and they shall be made like unto the angels and be made equal to the stars, and they shall be changed into every form they desire, from beauty into loveliness, and from light into the splendor of glory. For there shall be spread before them the extents of paradise, and there be shown to them the beauty and the majesty of the loving creatures which are beneath the throne and all the armies of the Angels who are now held fast by My Word, unless they should appear, and are held fast by a command that they may stand in their places till their advent comes".

4 Ezra 7:55-56 states: "And that the faces of them which have used abstinence shall shine above

the stars, whereas our faces shall be blacker than darkness. For a while, we lived and committed iniquity; we considered not that we should begin to suffer for it after death". Job 14:14 states, "If a man dies, shall he live again? all the days of my appointed time will I wait, till my change come". I could continue and quote from The Apocalypse of Moses, The Apocalypse of Abraham, the Book of Nicodemus, or the Book of Enoch; still, we get the general idea. Just as Moses's face shone after being in the presence of YAHUAH, as described in Exodus chapter 34:35, we will live in ELOHYIM's brightness forever. However, I will finish this topic with a quote from the First Book of Adam and Eve, chapter 55, which pulls it all together.

After being expelled from the garden, Adam and Eve tried to reenter it, but YAHUAH tells them it "cannot be today; but only when the Covenant I have made with you is fulfilled. Then Adam, when he heard the Word of Elohim and the fluttering of the Angels whom he did not see, but only heard the sound of them with his ears, he and Eve cried, and said to the angels; oh spirits, who wait on ELOHIYM, look at me, and that my being unable to see you! For when I was in my former bright nature, then I could see you, and sang praise as you do; and my heart was far above you. But now that I have transgressed, that bright nature is gone from me, and I am come to this miserable state. And now I have come to this that I cannot see you, and you do not serve me like you used to do. For I have become animal flesh". You see the Covenant was that YAHUAH would come in the flesh and save Adam from his sentence of death and return him to the garden and return him his bright nature, which is obtained by living in the presence of YAHUAH.

This promise is extended to Adam's descendants as promised in the Psalm of Solomon chapter 3:11-12 reading from the Septuagint, which says: "The destruction of the sinner is forever, and he will not be remembered when HE visits the righteous. This is the portion of sinners forever, but those who fear the Lord shall rise to everlasting life, and their life is in the light of the Lord and shall never end".

What is righteousness? Psalms 119:172 States, "My tongue shall speak of your word: for all your Commandments are righteousness." 1 John 5:17 states, "all unrighteousness is sin." Just before that, in chapter 3 and verse 5 of the first book of John, we are told, "For sin is the transgression of the Torah." Sin is unrighteousness, and John is clear that sin is the transgression of The Commandments of YAHUAH, which we find in the first five books of our Bible. The writer of Hebrews is pointing us back to this: that the work of our Messiah, the Son of ELOHIYM, came to deliver to us everlasting life. Understanding this demonstrates just how important it is to know the front and back of the Bible because by knowing the beginning, we can understand the end.

The goal, the hope of YAHUSHA the Messiah, is our reconciliation with our creator as described in the book of Jeremiah 31:31, which says: "Behold, the days come, says YAHUAH, that I will cut a renewed Covenant with the house of Yashar'el, and with the house of Yahuda: Not according to the Covenant that I cut with their fathers in the day that I took them by the hand to bring them out of the land of Mitsrayim (Egypt); which my Covenant they broke although I was a husband to them, says YAHUAH; but this shall be the Covenant that I will cut with the House of Yashar'el; after those days, says YAHUAH, I will put my Torah in their inward parts, and write it in their hearts; and I will be their ELOHIYM, and they shall be my people."

YAHUAH is not rewriting the Torah. He will write it on our hearts instead of on tablets of stone. To enter into this renewed Covenant, by law, the husband had to die for the bride to marry again legally because the marriage vows had been broken and a divorce decreed (Jeremiah 3:7-11). We also must die to ourselves and to the world once we agree to enter into this renewed covenant and become the people of the Creator, the Most High ELOHIYM, just as Paul said in Galatians 6:14, "Never should I glory, save in the cross of our ADONAI YAHUSHA HAMASHIACH by whom the world is crucified unto me, and I unto the world."

We must incorporate all of scripture into our lives. In the Book of Revelation, chapter 15, in verse 1, it says: "And I saw another sign in heaven, great and wonderful; seven Messengers having seven plagues, the last in order, because with them the wrath of Elohim is completed. And I saw as it were a sea of glass mixed with fire; and they, who had been innocent over the beast of prey and over its image and over the number of its name, were standing on the sea of glass; and they had the harps of Elohim. And they sing the song of Moses the servant of Elohim, and the song of the Lamb, saying: 'Great and marvelous are your deeds, master YHWH Elohim Almighty; just and true are your ways, O King of the worlds,'" This is quoted from the English translation of the Aramaic by Andrew Gabriel Roth.

We need to know both songs just as Revelation 12:17 says, "And the dragon was enraged against the woman; and he went to make war upon the remnant of her seed who keep the Commandments of Elohim and have the testimony of Yeshua." It is sad to know that the practitioners of Judaism do not have the testimony of YAHUSHA, the Messiah, and that most Christians do not keep the Commandments of YAHUAH. They believe those were nailed to the cross instead of the bill of debt they owe.

If I am stopped speeding down Mesquite Avenue, I cannot use as an excuse that my husband did the speed limit yesterday while coming home. I will have to pay my fine and speed no more. YAHUSHA, the Messiah, has paid for our ticket, and we are to go and sin no more. Christians today do not seem to understand that YAHUSHA the Messiah came to show what was possible through obedience to the Commandments. By not understanding the front of the book, Tertullian's words are correct when he writes in Against Marcion book 1, chapter 27, "A better god has been discovered, who never takes offense, is never angry, never inflicts punishment, who has prepared no fire in hell, no gnashing of teeth in outer darkness! He is purely and simply good. He indeed forbids all delinquency, but only in word. He is in you if you are willing to pay him homage, for the sake of appearances, that you may seem to honor YAH, for your fear he does not want. And so satisfied are the Marcionites with such pretenses, that they have no fear of their god at all".

Establishing the goal of Messiah, the writer of Hebrews continues in chapter 2:6 by quoting Psalms 8:4-6, "To the Messengers he has not subjected the world to come, of which we speak. But as the scripture testifies and says: what is man that you are mindful of him? And the son of man, that you attend to him? You have made him somewhat lower than the messengers: Glory and Honor have you put on his head, and you have invested him with authority over the work of your hand. And all things have you subjected under his feet. And in this submitting of all things to him, you left out nothing which he did not submit to him. But now, we do not yet see all things subjected to him. We see that he is YAHUSHA the Messiah, who humbled himself to become a little lower than the messengers through his suffering and death, but now he is crowned with honor and glory because he tasted death for the sake of everyone apart from Elohim". Most translations of the Bibles will end that last sentence with "that he by the grace of YAHUAH should taste death for every man." I quote this verse in Psalms from the Aramaic, which also agrees with the Septuagint, which Origen also quoted. YAHUSHA tasted death for everyone except his Father, who did not have to taste it.

This quote in Hebrews 2 implies a separation here and is supported by YAHUSHA's many statements concerning the will of the Father in which he said, "Not my will but Your Will." I will not get into Monophysites, which was an early heresy claiming the Messiah was holy divine and only had the appearance of a human form. YAHUAH promised to come in the flesh and sacrifice himself to save Adam and his descendants from the curse of death. He is promising us a return to the garden and eternal life in the presence of YAHUAH. Acts 20:28 confirms this, which reads: "Take great care of yourselves, and of all the flock over which The Ruach haKodesh has established you as overseers for, that you feed the assembly of Mashiach, which he has acquired by his blood."

The Book of John chapter 5:26 reads: "For as to the Father, there is life in his Qnoma, and likewise he also gives to the son, that there might be life in his Qnoma." Qnoma means underlying substance. YAHUSHA the Messiah, in his flesh, contained the substance of his Father, the Most High ELOHIYM. The price of redemption was in Mashiach's blood. Hebrews 2:9 represents both ELOHIYM in him, as well as YASHUAH's "humanity"; obviously, it was his humanity that was laid down that he might take it up again, as stated in John 10:17 where Messiah says: "because of this, my Father loves me that I may lay down my life that I might take it up again ." This was the will of the Father made manifest in the Son by his life, death, and resurrection.

We receive a hint of this soul or spirit entanglement in the Book of Genesis 44:30. Judah pleads with his brother Joseph to allow them to return to Canaan with the younger brother Benjamin. He explains that it would be impossible for the brothers to return without Benjamin because, as he says, "his (Jacob's) life is bound up in the lad's life." In the prior verse, Judah stated that if they failed to return with Benjamin, it would cause Jacob's death. You could say the same of Abraham and

Isaac. When Abraham was willing to sacrifice his beloved Son of Promise, he was not Abraham's only son; remember, Abraham had Ishmael, his firstborn.

I realize at this point someone is going to bring up Matthew 27:46, which tells of YAHUSHA the Messiah just before dying crying, "My God, My God, why hast thou forsaken me." Some people believe that the Father, the Most High ELOHIYM, abandoned YAHUSHA, his son, at that point. There is also a belief that the Messiah went to hell and fought and was beaten up by Satan and his army for three days, with YAHUSHA ultimately prevailing in the end. This teaching is outrageous. I would challenge anyone to find scripture that shows anything but obedience by demons or Satan to YAHUSHA, the Messiah, while he was walking the earth. What would make anybody believe that that changed when he went to She'ol to preach and deliver Adam and his descendants as promised? Psalms 107:16 states: "For he has broken the gates of brass and cut the bars of iron in sunder." You can read the book of Nicodemus and learn the story of what happened in She'ol when YAHUSHA appeared in his brightness and did just that.

YAHUSHA, while on the cross, points readers back to Psalms 22, which prophesied his suffering. The Aramaic has "My EL! My EL! (Lamana Shabakthani) Why have you spared me?" In other words, Father, I am ready. Why can't we finish this? Of course, at the time, even the people standing there watching the crucifixion were confused about what YAHUSHA was saying. I prefer to believe that his work was finished, and there was no other reason to prolong the agony he was enduring because he gave up his spirit and died right after that. Remember, though, the Roman soldier standing by who heard and saw what was happening, remarked that YAHUSHA was indeed the son of Elohim.

Returning to Hebrews 2:6, some would say that Adam had all things subjected under his feet. Adam was made a little lower than the angels. However, the writer of Hebrews makes it clear that it is the Messiah he is talking about. Through his suffering, he brings many sons to his glory to perfect the practice of their life by suffering the cross. Verse 10 of Hebrews chapter 2 reads: "For it became him, for whom are all things, and by whom are all things, and bringing many sons into glory, to make the captain of their yeshu'ah perfect through sufferings." The Aramaic reads "the prince of their life." Merriam-Webster Dictionary defines a Prince as a member of a royal family, especially a son of the sovereign. Was Adam a son of ELOHIYM? Adam was a holy created being, brought forth from the dust of the earth, and received the Breath of Life from YAHUAH.

Interestingly, this verse calls YAHUSHA the captain of our salvation. The word Tseva'oth is the plural for Saba (host), which is Strong's H6635, which means a mass of persons primarily organized for war, by implication, a campaign literally or figuratively. YAHUAH TSEVA'OTH is often translated into English in scripture as Lord of Hosts. I do not want to get sidetracked by this phrase because it will require its chapter. But if you follow what I am putting down here, the writer of Hebrews here, in verse 10 of chapter 2, is equating YAHUSHA the Messiah, the captain of our salvation, with YAHUAH TSEVA'OTH (Lord of Hosts) from the front of the book.

Continuing in Hebrews 2:11, the writer confirms that YAHUSHA HAMASHIACH was flesh and blood, becoming a brother to his disciples. The text reads: "For both he that sanctifies (Messiah), and they who are sanctified (the believers of Messiah) are all of One (flesh): for which cause he is not ashamed to call them brethren." In verses 12 and 13, He quotes Psalms 22:23-25 and Psalms 16:1, and then he quotes Isaiah chapter 8:18. Hebrews 2:12-13 reads, "I will declare your name unto my brethren, in the midst of the called out assembly will I sing praise unto you. And again, I will put my trust in him. And again, behold I and the children which YAHUAH has given me". Remember, Psalm 22 is a Prophecy of the Messiah and his crucifixion. Psalm 16 is a prophecy of the resurrection of the Messiah. When one reads this Psalm, now maybe with eyes to see and ears to hear, you will see or question who exactly is talking here. The Hebrews writer calls you back to it by quoting the first line, assuming the readers or his listeners know this Psalm.

The listeners would also be familiar with the prophecy of the coming Messiah in Isaiah chapter 8 in verse 4. It reads: "For before the child shall have knowledge to cry, my father, and my mother, The riches of Damascus and the spoil of Shomeron shall be taken away before the king of Ashshur." Most all agree this is a prophecy of the gifts the three kings came and presented to the Messiah after his birth in Bethlehem: gold, frankincense, and myrrh. The writer of Hebrews is quoting Isaiah 8:18, which reads, "Behold, I and the children whom YAHUAH has given me are for signs and for wonders in Yashar'el from YAHUAH TSEVA'OTH which dwells in Mount Zion." Not only does Isaiah chapter 8 foretell of the Messiah coming in the flesh but also of his ministry and his preaching to the disciples and ultimately that the word of YAHUAH is the messiah when the writer of Hebrews says in verse 14 and 15: "Because the children participated in flesh and blood, he also, in like manner, took part in the same; that by his death, he might bring to nothing him who held the kingdom of death, namely Satan; and might release them who, through fear of death were all their lives subject to bondage." Who else has the power to bring Satan to nothing? Even Michael, the great archangel, when disputing with Satan over Moses's body, only rebuked him in the name of YAHUAH.

To finish Hebrews chapter 2, verses 17 and 18 reads: "Wherefore in all things, it behooved him to be made like unto his brethren, that he might be a merciful and faithful high priest in things pertaining to YAHUAH, to make reconciliation for the sins of the people. For in that he himself has suffered being tempted, he is able to help them that are tempted". The writer reminds us that YAHUSHA the Messiah, a man of flesh could forgive our sins. Because of this, the scribes and Pharisees accused YAHUSHA of blasphemy. In Luke 5:17, they said that only ELOHIYM alone can forgive sins. How did YAHUSHA reconcile our sins? Isaiah 53, a powerful prophecy of the Messiah, tells us that the Messiah would die for our sins. Tertullian quotes Isaiah 53:12 in Against Marcion

Book 4 Chapter 10: "He shall remit to many their sins and shall himself take away their sins." The image of a suffering, servant messiah is a continuation of the theme set forth in Isaiah 1:18, which says: "Come now, let us reason together, says YAHUAH: though your sins be scarlet, they shall be white as snow."

There is an argument about Isaiah 53, claiming the subject is not the Messiah but Israel itself. However, this is a recent claim. Historically, even the rabbis agreed that this chapter in Isaiah is about the messiah. It was not until the Middle Ages that opinion changed about Isaiah 53. Most of the rabbis and scholars for the first thousand years of Christianity agreed that not only did Isaiah 53 predict the suffering Messiah, but a parallel chapter in Zechariah Chapter 12 did as well.

Zechariah 12 is a chapter concerning the pending judgment of Jerusalem, and specifically in verse 10, it states: "And I will pour upon the house of David, and the inhabitants of Jerusalem, the spirit of grace and supplication and they shall look upon me whom they have pierced, and they shall mourn for him, as one mourns for his beloved son, and shall be in bitterness for him, as one that is in bitterness for his firstborn." Verse 1 of this chapter starts: "the burden of the Word of YAHUAH for Jerusalem, says YAHUAH, which stretches forth the heavens, and lays the foundations of the earth, and forms the spirit of man within him." In verse 10 it is YAHUAH himself who says, "shall look upon me whom they have pierced".

In his book Against Celsus, Origen writes about chapter 53 of Isaiah and the problem that Celsus and his followers had in accepting that YAHUAH himself could come and take on the flesh of a man let alone be pierced. What Origen argues is that if you say that YAHUAH cannot do something, you are then not understanding the power of the Creator when you think that he could leave his abode in heaven empty to come to earth, not being able to occupy two spaces at the same time. The Wisdom of Solomon 1:7 says: "For the Ruach YAHUAH fills the world: and that which contains all things has knowledge of the voice, therefore he that speaks unrighteous things cannot be hid."

The Apostle Paul taught the Athenians in Acts 27:28, we all "in Him live, and move, and have our being." Origen says it best: "Although the God of the universe should through his own power descend with Jesus into the life of man, and although the Word which was in the beginning with God, which is also God himself, should come to us, he does not give his place or vacate his own seat, so that one place should be empty of him, and another which did not formally contain him be filled. But the power and Divinity of God comes through him whom God chooses and resides in him in whom he finds a place, not changing its situation, nor leaving its own place empty and filling another". In the Gospel of John 10:30, YAHUSHA says "I and the father are one." Zechariah Chapter 11, starting in verse 1 states: "And there shall come forth a shoot out of the stem of Jesse, and a branch shall grow out of his roots; and he shall be at peace, and the spirit of YAHUAH shall rest upon him, the spirit of wisdom and understanding, the spirit of counsel and might, the spirit of knowledge and the reverence of YAHUAH." And it is this verse that YAHUSHA is referring his listeners to when he says in John 15:1, "I am the true vine, and my Father is the laborer. Every branch in me that does not bear fruit, he prunes so that it may bring forth more fruit". Notice here that YAHUAH is the laborer. He is the one that is pruning the branches of the Vine, which would be us. Now you can understand how the Pharisees could bring the charge of blasphemy upon YAHUSHA, the Messiah, when he forgives sins.

Reading Isaiah 53 leads us back to Psalms 22, another suffering Messiah prophecy. The bystanders at the cross who heard the Messiah quote the first line of Psalm 22, "Eliy, Eliy, why have you forsaken me?", would have known this Psalm and not just that Psalm but also Isaiah 53, the parallel scripture. Well, not everybody, only those with ears to hear and eyes to see. Read them for yourself and see if you disagree that that is who these verses are talking about. The Hebrews writer reminds listeners of these scriptures and tells them that this foretold Messiah is YAHUSHA. He came, and the vow of salvation was accomplished.

One more parallel scripture is Psalm 16, which I quoted earlier in full. On the surface of the text, you would think that the psalmist, David, is talking about himself. But when you get to verse 10, it says, "For thou hast left not my soul in She'ol; neither has thou suffered the Holy One to see corruption." This verse is talking about a death and a resurrection. Repeatedly, early church writers referred to this passage and reminded their listeners that David's grave was still with them. David's body was corrupted and still in his grave. As shown in the earlier quote from Psalm 16, verse 9 which reads, "Still my flesh will set up a tent of hope." YAHUSHA becomes the Tabernacle of our rest. The last verse of Psalm 16 from the Cepher states, "Thou wilt show me the path of life, and I shall be filled with the joy of thy countenance, with the pleasure of victory of thy right hand."

Today, we have the New Testament scriptures, so in hindsight, we can see that Psalm 15 (16) and all the parallel verses clearly talk about The Messiah. We know that because the Israelites at the time, the people living in and around Jerusalem recognized YAHUSHA as the Messiah whom they were waiting for because they knew all the scriptures which pointed to him, as YAHUSHA the Messiah said in Mark 14:21, "The son of man will go as it is written of him." Where was it written of him? When he said these words, there was no New Testament. Also, the writer of Hebrews says in chapter 4 that the gospel was taught to the Israelites 40 years in the wilderness. That gospel is the five books of Moses.

The writer of Hebrews makes a convincing case that YAHUSHA, the son of the virgin Mary, was the Messiah; the Messiah they were anticipating, the Messiah who, as the scriptures said, was to be the Son of ELOHIYM made flesh. YAHUSHA the Messiah checked all the boxes of the prophecies concerning the coming Messiah. The lineage of the Messiah, as foretold in 2 Samuel 7:12-16 and 1 Chronicles 17:11, that he must be a descendant of David, is indeed true. The birthplace of Messiah in Micah 5 predicted the Messiah would be born in Bethlehem; that is where he was born. The timing of the Messiah's first coming was foretold in Daniel 9: that the Messiah would come before the destruction of the second Temple, which he did. He would be sentenced to a violent death, which he was.

The Messiah's birth, coming reign and that he would have a nature like ELOHIYM himself as foretold in Isaiah 7, Daniel 7, Isaiah 9, and Zechariah 12, were all fulfilled. Zachariah 9:9 foretold the humility of the Messiah, who would enter Jerusalem riding on a donkey. Isaiah 35 prophesied the healing power of the Messiah. YAHUSHA himself referred to Isaiah 35 in Matthew 11 when he told John's disciples to "go and tell John what you hear and see: the blind receive their sight and the lame walk, lepers are cleansed, and the deaf hear, and the dead are raised up, and the poor have good news preached to them. And blessed is the one who is not offended by me". And through the Messiah, the Gentiles would be redeemed through him as predicted in Isaiah chapter 53 and Psalms 22, which we have covered. In Isaiah 53, there is a prophecy that his own people would reject him and that the other nations would be saved by that rejection. The Messiah's death was foretold in Psalm 22, Isaiah 53, and Zechariah 12 that he would be pierced. Zechariah 12 also prophesied the resurrection, as well as Psalm 16.

As a side note concerning Psalms 22:16, it says, "For dogs have compassed me; the assembly of the wicked have enclosed me: they pierced my hands and my feet." There has been a controversy for many years between the Jewish and the Christian interpretation of Psalms 22. With the discovery of the Dead Sea scrolls, verse 16 makes more sense when we realize there was a translation error and that the original text agrees with the bore a hole in my hands and feet rendition. In the Septuagint, it is Psalm 21:16-18. It reads, "Because many dogs encircle me, a gathering of evildoers surrounded me. They gouged my hands and feet; I counted all my bones, but they took note and observed me; they divided my clothes among themselves, and for my clothing they cast lots". George M. Lamsa's translation from the Aramaic of the Peshitta also agrees with this translation.

Before moving on to the next claim to YAHUSHA'S divinity and other forms of interaction with mankind, I would like to address the other 'son' issue, and that being the Messiah was to be the son of King David of the tribe of Judah. YAHUSHA makes this claim in Matthew 22:41, Mark 12:35, and Luke 20:39-43 who record the conversation between the Pharisees who emphasize oral law (Matthew 23:1- 2) and the scribes who emphasize written law (Mark and Luke). YAHUSHA asks the Pharisees, "What do you think about the Mashiyach? Whose son is he?" The Pharisees' answer, 'David,' is given in Matthew. Each disciple addresses the different answers to YAHUSHA'S questions. From the Aramaic, Matthew 22:41-45 states, "While the Pharisees were together, YAHUSHA the Messiah questioned them, 'What do you think about the Mashiyach? Whose son is he? 'David's,' they told him. He asked them, how is it then that David, inspired by the spirit, calls him Master YHWH, for he said Master YHWH said to my master, sit at my right hand until I put your enemies under your feet. If then, David calls him YHWH, how is he his son?"

YAHUSHA the Messiah quotes Psalm 110:1-7: "YAHUAH said unto my ADONAI, sit at my right hand, until I make your enemies your footstool. YAHUAH shall send the rod of your strength out of Tsiyon: rule thou in the midst of your enemies. Your people shall be willing in the day of your power, in the beauties of holiness from the womb of the morning; you have the dew of your youth. YAHUAH has sworn and will not repent; you are a priest forever after the order of Melchizedek. YAHUAH at your right hand shall strike through kings in the day of his wrath. He shall judge among the heathen; he shall fill the places with the dead bodies; he shall wound the heads over many countries. He shall drink of the brook in the way; therefore, shall he lift up the head." The Apostle Peter in Acts 2:14-36 addresses the people of Judah on the day of Shavuot when the Holy Spirit had descended upon the gathered crowd. Peter quotes Psalm 110:1. He reminds the people that David is still in his grave and had not ascended to heaven.

Peter further testifies that YAHUSHA has been raised from the dead and sits upon the throne of heaven. Peter's listeners knew Psalm 110 as we should also. In Acts 36:36, Peter says, "Therefore let all the house of Yashar'el know assuredly, that YAHUAH has made that same YAHUSHA, whom you have crucified, both YAHUAH and MASHIACH." Also, note from the above verse in Psalm 110 that YAHUAH is at the right hand. The subject of the verse is the ADONAI of YAHUAH, who is at the right hand that will be bringing judgment. In 4 Ezra 2:45- 47, Ezra sees on

Mount Zion a multitude of people exalting YAHUAH, who in their midst was a young man setting crowns on everyone's head. Ezra inquired of the angel as to who this young man was, and the angel answered and said, "It is the Son of ELOHIYM, whom they have confessed in the world."

As the disciples Matthew, Mark, and Luke described, Peter witnessed this conversation with the Pharisees and Scribes. Peter knew the answer YAHUSHA had anticipated from the Pharisees when he asked the question in M a t t h e w 22; however, the Pharisees answered 'David,' which is also correct because YAHUSHA is a descendant of King David. The disciple Mark records in 12:35: "While teaching in the temple, YAHUSHA answered and said, how do the Scribes say that the Mashiyach is the son of David?" After YAHUSHA receives the answer from the Pharisees, he turns to the Scribes and asks them for their answer to the question. He was, again, referring to Psalm 110. Mark has left out the initial question to the Pharisees. Luke 20:39 has the answer the Scribes gave, "Teacher, you have spoken well. And they no longer dare to ask him anything. Then He said to them, 'How can they say that the Mashiyach is the son of David? David himself says in the Book of Psalms: Master YHWH said to my master, sit at my right hand until I make your enemies your footstool. David then calls him my master, so how is he, his son?" Clearly, YAHUSHA is intimating that HE is the ADONAI from Psalm 110.

By my count, the New Testament writers quote from the Psalms 125 times, as much as any other book in the Old Testament. The rabbis believe this is a misappropriation or abuse of Psalms since they do not consider it a book of Prophecy but instead a book of prayer by David and others for the people to pray to their Elohiym. I believe Psalms is a book of Prophecy and that the spirit of YAHUAH spoke through David as stated in 2 Samuel 23:1, which says, "Now these be the last words of David. David the son of Yishai, and the man who was raised up on high, the anointed of the ELOHAI of Ya'aqov, and the sweet psalmist of Yashar'el said, the RUACH YAHUAH spoke by me, and his word was in my tongue."

The Psalms can be divided into five distinct books. The first two chapters of Psalms serve as an introduction to these books. The rabbis believe the first Psalm, or the first two Psalms, is about King David. However, if you look closely, you see it is about the rebellion against the Messiah and YAHUAH himself. Chapter 2:1 says: "Why do the heathen rage, and the people imagine a vain thing? The kings of the earth set themselves, and the rulers take counsel together, against YAHUAH, and against his MASHIACH." YAHUAH enthrones his King, and in verse 2:7, this enthroned King responds to this rebellion with: "YAHUAH has said to me, you are my son; this day have I begotten you."

Begotten does not necessarily have to mean born, in a physical sense. The word 'begotten' can also mean to bring forth, or to set up. Therefore, an only begotten son could mean an entity manifested or brought forth. This idea that YAHUAH could manifest himself in the flesh, i.e., born of water and blood has been hotly debated.

For centuries, this led to many heresies concerning the Messiah's divinity. Nestorians held the belief that the Messiah was 2 separate individuals. Apollinarianism believed YAHUSHA's human intellect was replaced with one divine. Docetism held that YAHUSHA only seemed to have a body. Arianism believed YAHUSHA to be a created being, due to YAHUAH's inability to manifest himself in a form that could allow him to interact with his creation. There is also confusion concerning the two Hebrew words for 'son' used in Psalms 2:7 and 12. The word used in verse 7 for 'son' is 'ben,' Strong's Concordance number H1121, which means son. Then, verse 2:12 says: "Kiss the Son, lest he be angry, and you perish from the way, when his wrath is kindled but a little. Blessed are all they that put their trust in him." The Hebrew word for son in this verse is Bar, H1248, which means heir (apparent) to the throne or son. Rabbis would tell you that bar does not mean son in Hebrew; however, in Proverbs 31:2, bar is used three times: "What, my son? And what, the son of my womb? and what, the son of my vows?" Bar of my womb indicates a child born. Bar must mean son in Psalms 2:12 to complete the reconciliation, which happens in the conclusion of Psalms, the last four chapters. Because both words for son are used, Psalms 22:7,12 indicate the son is also the heir apparent.

The disciples knew the Psalms were prophetic, and the Messiah confirmed that belief when he said in Luke 24:44: "And he, YAHUSHA, said unto them, these are the words which I spoke unto you, while I was yet with you, that all things must be fulfilled, which were written in the Torah of Mosheh, and in the prophets, and in the Psalms concerning me." YAHUAH's **word,** through the RUACH HAKODESH, spoke through David, who was not only a king but also a prophet. The Psalms were the top 150 chart hits of the day. Think of an old song you knew growing up, and just by hearing one line you hear on the radio, you know the rest of the song and the meaning. The Psalms are no different.

MESSIAH YAHUSHA IS THE WORD OF YAHUAH

"In the beginning was the Word, and the Word was with ELOHIYM, and the Word was ELOHIYM. The same was in the beginning with ELOHIYM. All things were made by him; and without him was not anything made that was made. John 1:1-3

Psalms 33:6 says: "By the Word of YAHUAH were the heavens made; and all the host of them by the breath of his mouth." The word used here for breath is Ruach, which is Strong's Concordance number H7307, which means wind, by resemblance breath, or spirit. This word is used 232 times in scripture. The first time Ruach is used is in Genesis 1:2, which says, "And the earth was without form and void; darkness was upon the face of the deep. And the Ruach ELOHIYM moved upon the face of the waters". The Word came from the breath of YAHUAH, which spoke everything into existence. The creator is Indeed, on every page of the scriptures, he is the strongarm or the hand, the Fountain of water, the Word, a messenger, or angel, or even the captain of The Host, or, as we just explored, the only begotten Son of YYAHUAH. Let us return to the original question: how did John know that YAHUSHA, the son of the virgin Mary, was indeed the Messiah and particularly the word of ELOHIYM? Remember, all they knew was the Old Testament books: Moses, the prophets, and the psalms. Let us go to the beginning. Genesis chapter 1:27 reads, "Elohim created man in his own image, in the image of Elohim created he him; male and female created he them." The same verse from the Jerusalem Targum reads, "And the Word of the Lord created man in his likeness, in the likeness of the presence of YAHWEH he created him, the male and his yokefellow he created them."

The Targum, which means translation, is a translation of the Hebrew Bible into the Aramaic language. The word Targum initially indicated a translation of the Old Testament in any language but later came to refer specifically to an Aramaic translation. The earliest Targums date from the time after the Babylonian exile when Aramaic had superseded Hebrew as the spoken language of the Jews in Palestine. It is impossible to get more than a rough estimate as to the period in which Aramaic displaced Hebrew as a spoken language. It is certain, however, that Aramaic was firmly established in Palestine by the first century AD. Although Hebrew remained the learned and sacred language, the Targums were designed to transmit the Hebrew scriptures to synagogue attendees of whom the Hebrew of the Old Testament was unintelligible. Not just anyone could translate the Hebrew scriptures for the unlearned people. It had to be a very learned scribe. I will use the Targum for this subject because they extensively refer to the **Word of the Lord**.

To finish a discussion on Genesis 1:27, I would like to read what Philo had to say about this verse. Philo, usually known as Philo the Jew or Philo of Alexandria (a city in Egypt), which contained a large Jewish diaspora population in the Greco-Roman times, lived from about 20 B.C. to about 50 A.D. Philo's comment on Genesis 1:27 reads, "Why, then, does he use the expression, 'in the image of God I made man, as if he were speaking of that of some other god, and not of having made him in the likeness of himself? This expression is used with great beauty and wisdom. For it is impossible that anything mortal should be made in the likeness of the Most High God, the Father of the universe; but it could only be made in the likeness of the second god, who is the word of the other; for it is fitting that the rational type in the soul of man should receive the impression of the Word of God, since the God below the Word is superior to all and every rational nature; and it is not lawful for any created thing to be made like The God who is above reason, and who is endowed with the most excellent and special form appropriated to himself alone". Interestingly, when Philo quotes Genesis 1:27, He states, ' **I** made man'. Philo's quote was taken from On Providence fragment 1. The Targumist says further in Genesis 2:8, "And a garden from the Eden of the just was planted by the Word of the Lord God before the creation of the world, and he made there to dwell the man when He had created him."

I do not want to get off into a discussion on trinitarianism, Unitarianism, or any kind of ism because I do not believe them to be valid or relevant to the topic. However, some would look at this text of Philo's' and think he is making a case for trinitarianism. However, I do not believe he was. That 'ism' is a much later idea that developed around the third century.

Paul may explain the image of ELOHIYM that Christ carried in himself in 2 Corinthians 4:4, where he says, "To them whose minds the god of this world has blinded, in order that they might not believe, or else the light of the flame (Good News) of the glory of the Mashiyach (who is the likeness of Elohim) should dawn upon them." In this passage, The Good News, the flame of the glory of Mashiyach who the likeness of ELOHIYM is, uses the word *Damota d'Alaha* for 'likeness of ELOHIYM,' which is an interesting word choice according to Andrew Gabriel Roth, whose work I quoted from, where he says that damota denotes likeness but is not equivalent.

In Hebrews 1:3, we are told that YAHUSHA is the radiance of YAHUAH's glory, His light, like a spark that bursts forth from a fire. Just as if you were to light a candle with another candle, you would not diminish the light of the previous candle, and that light which has been transferred to the new candle is not weaker than the first.

Once you can understand that the Father and the Son are the same in essence and substance but not the same in aspect, you can see a prophecy of the Messiah coming in the form of man in the story of Gideon in the Book of Judges, chapter 7. Gideon orders his soldiers to put torches into pots. The pots were made of clay, just as man is also made of clay. In the battle during the middle watch, the soldiers blew their trumpets. They broke the pots containing the torches in their hands, which I believe is a foreshadowing of the risen Messiah who has broken out of his clay pot and will come amidst blaring shofars on the final day to put down his enemies. Just as it says in the Book of Revelation chapter 19, when YAHUSHA the Messiah comes at the last trump it says, starting in verse 11, "And I saw heaven open and behold a white horse; and he that sat upon him was called Faithful and True, and in righteousness he judges and makes war. His eyes were as a flame of fire, and on his head were many crowns, and he had a name written that no man knew but he himself. And he was clothed with a vesture dipped in blood: and his name is called The WORD of YAHUAH".

In Genesis chapter 3:10, Adam is speaking, saying, "I heard your voice in the garden, and I was afraid because I was naked, and I hid myself." Who is this Voice? In John 5:37, YAHUSHA, the Messiah, tells us, "The Father who sent me testifies concerning me. You have neither heard His voice nor have you seen His appearance. And his Word does not dwell in you because you do not believe in him whom he sent. Search the scriptures, because in them you think you have that life that is eternal, and they testify concerning me". According to YAHUSHA, we have not seen The Voice nor witnessed the image of YAHUAH. Notice also that he says no one. Does that also include the angels? What is it or who was it that everyone seen and heard? My guess is that this is the reason there was so much confusion, and still is today, concerning who YAHUSHA was. Since before his birth, death, and resurrection, he had been seen and had come as The Voice, as the messenger, in the agency and speaking the words of his Father.

In Genesis chapter 11, we come to the Tower of Babel incident. Verse 6 from the Cepher reads, "and YAHUAH said, behold the people is one, and they all have one language; and this they begin to do; and now nothing will be restrained from them, which they have imagined to do. Go to, let us go down, and there confound their language that they may not understand one another's speech". In the Targum, these same verses are interesting. It reads, "And the Lord said, Behold the people is one, and the language of all of them one: and this they have thought to do: and now they will not be restrained from doing whatever they imagine. And the Lord said to the 70 Angels who stand before him, come, we will descend and will there commingle their language, that a man shall not understand the speech of his neighbor. And the Word of the Lord was revealed against the city, and with him, seventy angels, having reference to 70 nations, each having its language, and then the writing of its hand; and he dispersed them from thence upon the face of all the earth into 70 languages".

This idea of the 70 angels may sound outrageous to most, but there is support for these passages in the Targum and scriptures. From the Septuagint Deuteronomy, chapter 32:8, says, "When the Most High was apportioning nations, as he scattered

Adam's sons, he fixed boundaries of nations according to the number of divine sons, and his people Jacob became the Lord's portion.". Clement of Alexandria (A.D 153-193-217), in his Stromata book 6 chapter 17, confirms this when he wrote concerning Deuteronomy 32:8, "For regiments of angels are distributed over the nations and cities. And, perchance, some are assigned to individuals as well."

This idea of ruling angels may clear up the words of the Messiah himself in Matthew 25, starting in verse 31, where he says, "When the Son of Adam shall come in his glory, and all the Holy Angels with him, then shall he sit upon the throne of his glory; and before him shall be gathered all nations, and he shall separate them one from another, as a shepherd divides his sheep from the goats." In Genesis chapters 15-17, we are told that 'YAHUAH' appeared to Abram and said to him, "I am EL SHADDAI," and promised to make a covenant with him. The Targum reads, "And the Lord appeared to Abram, and said to him, I am EL SHADDAI, serve before me and be perfect in your flesh, and I will set my covenant between my Word and you and will multiply you very greatly" (Genesis 17:1-2). During the covenant-making in Genesis 15, YAHUAH caused Abram to become unconscious. At the same time, YAH appeared as a smoking furnace and a burning lamp walking through the divided parts of the sacrifice. (Genesis 15:17).

Just before this cutting of the covenant in Genesis 15, we are told of a war against Amraphel, aka Nimrod, and the other three kings that had come against Sodom and Amora and taken Lot captive (Genesis 14). In Genesis 15:1, "The Word (pithgama) of the Lord came to Abram in a vision saying fear not, if these men should gather together in Legions and come against you, my Word (memra) will be your shield; and also, if these fall before you in this world, the reward of your good works shall be kept, and be prepared before me in the world to come great exceedingly." Interestingly, the Targumist used the word pithgama, which means command, work, affair, decree, word, or report. The word memra is used, which would be Abrams' shield.

Memra of YAHUAH is used in the Targum in places where it might appear as though YAHUAH is speaking to himself or of himself, which occurs in Genesis 35:1. It reads from the Targum, "The Lord said to Jacob, arise, go up to Bethel and dwell there, and make there an altar to Eloha, who revealed himself to you in your flight from before Esau, your brother." From the Cepher, this verse reads, "And ELOHIYM said unto Ya'aqov, arise, go up to Beyt-EL, and dwell there; and make there an altar unto ELOHIYM, that appeared unto you when you fled from the face of Esau, your brother." Who is Jacob making an alter to? The underlying Hebrew text has Elohim speaking and telling Jacob to make the altar to EL. Why wouldn't the text just say, make an altar to me?

Again, in Genesis 19:23,24: "The sun was risen upon the earth when Lot entered into Tso'ar. Then YAHUAH rained upon Cedom and upon Amorah brimstone and fire from YAHUAH out of the heavens". Luke 12:49-50 is extraordinary because

YAHUSHA indirectly claims to be YAHUAH himself when he says, "I have come to cast fire on earth. And I desire it had been kindled, if not already". In the Old Testament, YAHUAH is described as a consuming fire. He comes with fire or kindles a fire of judgment. He says I will send fire, or I will set fire. It is a recurring phrase in the Old Testament. Fire means judgment. When you hear people calling for fire to be rained down upon them from Heaven, RUN! They are not calling for something good. They are calling for judgment to be rained down on them. However, I will acknowledge that a spiritual fire does exist, which could be a euphemism for trials and tribulations.

In his Commentary on John Book 13 (138), Origen states, "If however, [there is spiritual] wood, grass, and straw, perhaps when our God is said to be a consuming fire, it refers to the fire that consumes such matter (Hebrews 14:29) it is fitting indeed for the Lord to destroy such things and obliterate inferior materials. When this happens, there is suffering and distress, but not from any physical punishment, in the ruling parts of the soul, for it is there that the building worthy of being destroyed exists."

YAHUSHA's listeners must have been shocked to have heard him say that he had come to cast fire onto the earth in Luke 12:49-50. They must have thought that YAHUSHA was equating himself with YAHUAH, who rained fire on earth, or at least recognized that he was admitting to being the entity acting in the agency of YAHUAH. Again, Genesis chapter 19:23 says, "The sun was risen upon the earth when Lot entered into Tso'ar. Then YAHUAH rained upon Cedom and upon Amorah brimstone and fire from YAHUAH out of the heavens; and he overthrew those cities, and all the circle of the Yardan, and all the inhabitants of the cities and that which grew upon the ground". It appears from this verse that there is an entity on earth acting by the power of an entity in heaven.

The Targum is more precise concerning this verse, it states, "And the Word of the Lord had caused showers of favor to descend upon Sodom and Gomorrah, to the intent that they might work repentance, but they did it not; so that they said, 'wickedness is not manifest before the Lord.' Behold then, there are now sent down upon them sulfur and fire from before the Word of the Lord from heaven". It is the Word that is acting here in the agency of the Most High ELOHIYM in heaven. A confirming verse in Psalms 18:12-13 says, speaking about the destruction of Sodom and Gomorrah, "At the brightness that was before him his thick clouds passed, hailstones and coals of fire. YAHUAH also thundered in the heavens, and EL ELYON gave **His voice** hailstones and coals of fire". In this Psalm, one could argue that David talks about Exodus 9:21, where hailstones mixed with fire are sent upon Egypt. Fair enough, it could. David states that EL ELYON gave his voice hailstones and coals of fire, which could be describing both events.

While we are on the topic of fire, let us continue to explore the fire of YAHUAH. Scriptures tell us that YAHUAH is a consuming fire (Deuteronomy 4:24). The Wisdom of Solomon, chapter 17, talks about the days of darkness, one of Egypt's ten plagues. It says, starting in verse 5, "No power of the fire might give them light; neither could the bright flames of the stars endure to lighten that horrible night. Only there appeared unto them a fire kindled of itself, very dreadful; for being much terrified, they thought the things which they saw to be worse than the sight they saw not". Is this a description of the outer darkness? Is this the darkness that comes from being outside the presence of YAH? Think of the wedding guest in the parable of the great wedding banquet in Matthew chapter 22 and verse 13 when the wedding guest who had not come dressed in a proper garment was cast out into outer darkness where there shall be weeping and gnashing of teeth.

Exodus 11:4 says, "And Mosheh said, thus says YAHUAH, about midnight will I go out into the midst of Mitsrayim, and all the firstborn in the land of Mitsrayim shall die." In Deuteronomy 9:3, YAHUAH tells Moses that He will go over the Jordan before them (the Israelites) as a consuming fire to destroy and bring down the people in the land of Canaan. There is the pillar of fire by night, which leads the Israelites out of Egypt. Exodus 13:21 says, "And YAHUAH went before them by day in a pillar of a cloud, to lead them in the way; and by night in a pillar of fire, to give them light; to go by day and night." Further, in chapter 14:19, it says that the angel of ELOHIYM, which went before the camp of Israel, removed, and went behind them; and the pillar of the cloud went from before their face and stood behind them: and it came between the camp of the Egyptians and the camp of Israel". This fire is clearly a manifestation of YAHUAH.

Deuteronomy chapter 1:32-33 says, "Yet in this thing you did not believe YAHUAH ELOHAYKEM, who went in the way before you, to search you out a place to pitch your tents in, in fire by night, to show you by what way you should go, and in a cloud by day." The Targum, however, has the same verse but tells us that the Israelites did not believe "in the **Word** of the Lord your Elohim who led before you in the way to prepare you the place of your encampments."

In Matthew 28:20, YAHUSHA tells his disciples, "Lo I am with you always," and in John chapter 14, he says that he is the way, the Truth, and the life and that he was going to go prepare a place for them in his father's house. These verses are hearkening back to the verses in Exodus. It was the Word that was the fire. Exodus 14:24 States, "And it came to pass, that in the morning watch YAHUAH looked unto the host of the Egyptians through the pillar of fire and of the cloud and troubled the host of the Egyptians." Was the pillar of fire between YAHUAH and the Egyptians, or was YAHUAH the pillar of fire himself?

Moses tells the Israelites in Deuteronomy 4:33-36, "Did ever people hear the voice of ELOHIYM speaking out of the midst of the fire, as you have heard, and lived? Or has ELOHIYM assayed to go and take him a nation from the midst of another nation, by temptations, by signs, and by wonders, and by war, and by a mighty hand, and by a stretched-out arm, and by great terrors, according to all that YAHUAH ELOHAYKEM did for you in Mitsrayim before your eyes? Unto you it was showed that you might know that YAHUAH he is ELOHIYM; there is none else beside him. Out of Heaven he made you to hear his voice, that he might instruct you; and upon earth he showed you his great fire; and you heard his words out of the midst of the fire." Notice here that it is from heaven that The Voice was heard from the midst of the fire, much like a ventriloquist dummy: the throne in heaven was not empty. The Word, The Voice, was heard from the midst of the fire and seen on the mountain.

Concerning Deuteronomy 4:33-36 the Targum tells us the Israelites were hearing the Word of YAHUAH. It reads, "Had it ever been that people should hear the voice of the Word of the Lord, the living GOD, speaking from the midst of the fire, as you heard and remained alive? In Deuteronomy 5 of the Targum, Moses tells Israel, "Word to word did the Lord speak with you at the mountain from the midst of the fire. I stood between the Word of the Lord and you at that time, to declare to you the Word of the Lord, because you were afraid before The Voice of the Word of the Lord, which you heard from the midst of the fire". We are told that the Messiah would be a prophet like Moses who would stand as a shield between us and the consuming fire, which is YAHUAH. It is a clear divinity statement when YAHUSHA tells his disciples he goes before them to prepare a place, he is intimating that HE is that Angel in the column of flame, and we know from the scriptures that the column of fire was YAHUAH.

Let us look at Genesis 15 again. During The Cutting of the Covenant between YAHUAH and Abraham, in verse 17, YAHUAH himself walks through the pieces. Moses sees a smoking furnace like a lamp. The Hebrew word used for the smoking furnace is Lapid, H3940. Lapid is the word used in the Book of Judges chapter 7, which I covered earlier, telling the story of Gideon and his lamps. Lapid is also used in the Book of Daniel chapter 10:6, where he explains the appearance of the man clothed in linen. He had eyes as lamps of fire, which is similar to the description of YAHUAH in the Book of Revelation chapter 1, whose eyes were as a flame of fire. Lapid is also used in Exodus 20:18, where YAHUAH is on the mountaintop for all of Israel to see. It says, "And all the people saw the thunderings, and the lightnings (H3940 Lapid) and the noise of the trumpet, and the mountain smoking, and when the people saw it, they removed, and stood afar off". By walking through the divided parts of these animals the vow was made that if I break this covenant then the same thing will happen to me that happened to these animals. It was YAHUAH alone who completed the curse of the covenant. Therefore, it is YAHUAH who must pay the ultimate price when the vows are broken. You must believe that YAHUSHA, the WORD of YAHUAH, was in that flame walking through the divided animal parts. Otherwise, he cannot be that perfect sacrifice who pays the price for our debt.

In Genesis 15, YAH commands Abram to circumcise himself and his family and promises Sarah a son. But I want to point out that YAHUAH sets the Covenant between His Word and man. Later in Genesis 30, when YAHUAH remembers Sarah, he says, from the Targum, "And the remembrance of Sarah came before the Lord, and the voice of her prayer was heard before him, and he said in His Word that he would give her sons." The exact wording is used in Genesis 9 when YAHUAH made a covenant with Noah in verse 12, "And ELOHIYM said, this is the sign of the covenant which I make between me and you and every living creature that is with you, for perpetual generations; I do set my bow in the cloud, and it shall be for a sign of a covenant between me and the earth." The Targum reads, "And the Lord said, this is the sign of the Covenant which I established between My Word and between you and every living soul that is with you, to the generations of the world. I have set My bow in the cloud, and it shall be for a token of the Covenant between My Word and the earth". Going back to Genesis chapter 7, when Noah enters the Ark before the deluge begins, according to the Targum it is the "Word of the Lord" that seals Noah and his family into the Ark.

Isaiah chapter 1:9-10 says, "Except YAHUAH TSEVA'OTH had left unto us a very small remnant, we should have been as Cedom, and we should have been like unto Amorah. Hear the Word of YAHUAH, ye rulers of Cedom; give ear unto the Torah of our ELOHIYM, ye people of Amorah". I find this verse interesting because the Hebrew often repeats an idea, just reworded differently to get the point across. It is Hebrew poetry, much like the Psalms of David. All the prophets could be said to be psalmists as well. That idea is born out in 1 Chronicles 25:1-6 where the men were to prophesy with musical instruments and song. Even in 2 Kings 3:11-15, a minstrel, a singer, or a poet did the prophesying. In this verse in Isaiah 1:9-10, the reader is told to listen to the Word of YAHUAH (His edicts), to the Torah of ELOHIYM. Both are the same. YAHUSHA, the Messiah, was the living Torah.

You will find that all the prophets and Patriarchs had the Word of YAHUAH appearing or coming to them. And now that we know that it is YAHUAH's edicts, his commands, his memra, his voice, that is appearing to them and understanding this to be YAHUSHA the Messiah, it makes it easier to understand what His mission was here on earth when he took on flesh. The prophets' messages always urged the Israelites to return to the laws (the Covenant) of YAHUAH. That is what repentance looks like. The Israelites were commanded to give up their idols and return to the true worship of their Most High creator.

The Word came to Ezekiel many times. However, the most significant is in chapter 45:17,25 from the Targum, which reads, "But Israel shall be saved by the Word of YAHUAH with an everlasting salvation by the Word of YAHUAH shall all the seed of Israel be justified." Here, YAHUAH is referred to as the savior. The Word came to Husha (Hosea). Notice that his name is the same as Husha son of Nun, whom Moses later changed to Yahusha, whom we call Joshua, the same name as our savior Messiah. Hushas' book starts in chapter 1, verse 1: "The Word of YAHUAH that came unto Husha." The prophet Joel's book also begins with the Word coming to him. The Word also appears to Jeremiah 1:2, to Jonah in 1:1, Micah 1:1, Zephaniah 1:1, Haggai 1:3, and Zechariah 1:1.

If YAHUSHA the Messiah is the Word of YAHUAH made flesh, then you should wonder about the meaning behind Malachi 4:2, in which YAHUAH gives a final warning to Israel, saying the day will come as a burning oven wherein all the wicked shall be burned up but then says, "But unto you, that fear my name shall the brilliance of righteousness arise with healing wings; and you shall go forth, and grow up as calves of the stall. And you shall tread down the wicked; for they shall be ashes under the soles of your feet in the day that I shall do this, says YAHUAH TSEVA'OTH".

Malachi is an enjoyable book; it is in chapter 3 where you find the prophecy of John the Baptist and the Book of Life, which I will cover later. I also believe that if you read the prophets and know their prophecies you will gain a better understanding of the Book of Revelation. In the book of Revelation, John is clearly drawing from the prophets and telling of their prophecy's final fulfillment. I will leave the prophets with a verse from First Baruch 3:35: "This is our ELOHIYM, and there shall none other be accounted of in comparison of him. He has found out all the way of knowledge, and has given it unto Ya'aqov his servant, and to Yashar'el his beloved. Afterward he did show himself upon earth and conversed with men". How could he have conversed with men in his full Shekinah? It is not possible for us to see YAHUAH and live. However, his voice walking amongst them was possible, just as it was with Adam after the expulsion from the garden.

John was not the only disciple who recognized that YAHUSHA the Messiah was the Word of YAHUAH. Peter also knew. In second Peter 3:5, "For this they willingly forget, that the heavens were of old; and the earth rose up from the waters, and by means of water, by the Word of ELOHIYM. And by means of these Waters the world which then was being submerged, again perished in the waters. And the heavens that are now that now are, and the earth, are by his Word stored up, being reserved for the fire at the day of judgment and the tradition of wicked men". The Apostle Paul also knew. However, to understand what Paul wrote, we must understand what Paul read, and because he is so easy to misunderstand, we must take a studious route to his understanding of the Word of YAHUAH and how he taught it in his day.

In Ephesians 1:13, Paul, talking about YAHUSHA the Messiah says, "In whom you also have heard the Word of Truth, which is the good news of your life, and have believed in him; and have been sealed with the Ruach haKodesh who was promised; who is the earnest of our inheritance until the redemption of them that are alive and for the praise of his glory." This verse is loaded. Paul is calling YAHUSHA Torah made flesh.

Remember, Paul makes references or uses terms that will refer you back to the Old Testament. Here again, he is guiding you back to what our life is as we spoke of in the chapter concerning the Son of YAHUAH. Remember, in Deuteronomy chapter 30, Moses is talking to Israel about keeping the law, keeping the Torah. Starting in verse 19, Moses says, "I call the heavens and the earth to record this day against you, that I have set before you life and death, blessing and cursing: therefore choose life, that both you and your seed may live: that you may love YAHUAH ELOHAYKA, and that you may obey **his**

voice and that you may cleave unto him for **He** is your life and the length of your days: that you may dwell in the land which YAHUAH swore to your fathers, to Abraham, to Isaac, and to Jacob, to give them."

Please read the whole chapter of Deuteronomy 30. In his book On Dreams 25:175, Philo calls this a prophecy of the Messiah's second coming. And Paul agrees with this assessment. Paul uses the term 'Word of Truth,' which he repeats in 2 Timothy 2:15, 2nd Corinthians 6:7, and James also uses it in 1:18. We should ask the question just like Pilate asked YAHUSHA "What is truth"?

Paul is pointing us back to Psalms 119:41-48. It is a short psalm, so I will just put the whole of it here. "Let your mercies come also unto me, O YAHUAH, even your yeshu'ah, according to your word. So shall I have wherewith to answer him that reproaches me; for I trust in your word. And take not the Word of Truth utterly out of my mouth; for I have hoped in your judgments. So shall I guard your Torah continually forever and ever. And I will walk at liberty: for I seek your precepts. I will speak of your testimonies also before kings and will not be ashamed. And I will delight myself in your commandments, which I have loved. My hands also will I lift up unto your commandments, which I have loved; and I will meditate in your statutes".

Psalms 119:142 is even more precise as to what the Truth is. It says, "Your righteousness is an everlasting righteousness, and your Torah is the Truth." And again, verse 151 says, "You are near, O YAHUAH; and all your commandments are Truth." So, it is a good practice when reading the letters of the Apostle Paul where appropriate to substitute the word Torah for Truth, and you will have a better understanding of what Paul is teaching. He is teaching Torah.

I realize that many of my readers will want to throw this book in the trash or burn it as an effigy in their front yard. Especially you who believe the law was nailed to the cross and that Paul disparaged the law. However, Paul admitted being a kosher Jew in Acts 25:8, and this was during his third missionary journey. He repeats that he is a kosher Jew where in Philippians 3:2-6 Paul states that he was blameless in the law, so as delicious as a bacon, lettuce, and tomato sandwich is, Paul never ate one. He followed the law. You need to understand the time and the context in which Paul wrote, especially in Romans and Galatians chapter 6, where he talks about the conversion of the believers in Messiah to Judaism. They were doing it to escape persecution, not from the heart. Judaism was legal to practice; however, new religions, such as Christianity, were forbidden.

I realize that I have stepped off a deep cliff here because a lot of people will point to Romans 3, in particular verse 21, which states, "But now the righteousness of YAHUAH without Torah is manifested, being witnessed by the Torah and the prophets" and then in verse 27 Paul asks "Where is boasting then? It is excluded. By what Torah? Of works? Nay; but by the Torah of belief". An excellent example of Torah without belief is found in the Book of Jonah chapter 1. The pagan shipmates of Jonah, without realizing it, engaged in a ceremony ordered in the Torah for the declaration of innocence as prescribed in Deuteronomy chapter 21:7, when they prayed to YAHUAH to not hold them accountable or guilty of Jonah's innocent blood after throwing him overboard. Now, you might say that Jonah was not sinless, after all he was running from YAHUAH, but Jonah had not sinned against the men of the ship, and so after they had thrown him overboard and the seas calmed, they offered a sacrifice unto YAHUAH and made vows. These men practiced the Torah without faith by submitting this simple prayer and offering sacrifices and vows as prescribed in Deuteronomy 21:7. Just as these Shipmates of Jonah were participating in a ceremony; they knew needed to be done to prevent them from coming under some sort of curse from the god of Jonah. During the time of Paul Christianity was an illegal religion, Christians were participating in Jewish ceremony as prescribed by the oral law to prevent their persecution by the government or the religious authority. It is a heart condition that Paul is trying to explain to his listeners.

In Jonah chapter 1:12 says, "And he (Jonah) said unto them, take me up, and cast me forth into the sea; so shall the sea be calm unto you; for I know that for my sake this great tempest is upon you." This act of self-sacrifice is a foreshadowing of YAHUSHA the Messiah; the death of one would save others, as stated in John 11:50, "consider that it is expedient for us, that one man should die for the people, and that the whole nation perish not." YAHUSHA mentions three times the sign of Jonah. Luke 11:29-30 says that Jonah was a sign to the Ninevites, meaning they listened to his message of the coming destruction, turned from their sin, and were saved.

In Matthew 12:39, YAHUSHA says that the sign of Jonah they would receive was that of 3 days and nights in the fish's belly, so shall "the son of Adam be three days and three nights in the heart of the earth." But in Matthew 16, the scribes and the Pharisees came to him, and they wanted a sign from heaven, and he answered and told them, "A wicked and adulterous nation seeks after a sign, and there shall no sign be given unto it, but the sign of the prophet Jonah. And he left them and departed." He did not hint at what sign he was talking about. I always assume that he was talking about the three days and three nights; however, after reading Chapter 1 of Jonah, it is possible that YAHUSHA was also talking about He being the one sacrificed to save many, and by his death, he would lead other nations, the Gentiles, into the worship of the Father.

To understand Paul, we need to know what verses in the Old Testament he is drawing from. What is righteousness? We need to go to Psalms 119, specifically verse 172, which states, "My tongue shall speak of your word; for all your Commandments are righteousness." Remember verse 142 of Psalm 119 reads, "Your righteousness is an everlasting righteousness, and your Torah is the truth." Righteousness in the Strong's Concordance is H6664 from the root of H6663 tsedeq. We all should be familiar with Melchizedek, the King of righteousness, as spoken of in Genesis 14. Knowing that righteousness means Torah and Malik means King, this verse becomes a more meaningful prophecy of the coming Messiah. Psalms 110:4 says, "YAHUAH has sworn, and will not repent, you are a priest forever after the order of Malkiy-Tsedeq, the King of Torah. YAHUSHA the Messiah was and is the living, breathing Torah and, as Paul puts it, the Word of Truth.

Paul taught the Torah. The listeners of Paul's letters would have also been familiar with Deuteronomy 6:25, which states, "And it shall be our righteousness (lawfulness) if we guard to do all these commandments before YAHUAH ELOHAYNU, as he has commanded us." The book of Jubilees tells us in chapter 23:26, "And in those days (these days, the latter days) the children shall begin to study the Torah, and to seek the commandments, and return to the path of righteousness (lawfulness)."

These should give a whole new meaning to the 23rd Psalm as well as Proverbs 8:20, which states, "I lead in the way of righteousness, in the midst of the paths of judgment; that I may cause those that love me to inherit substance and I will fill their treasures." It is interesting that word judgment. The Torah judges us. In conversations past, I have heard people tell me that they are good, meaning that they are righteous, but they do not keep the Torah. My response is if I am speeding down a road without a posted speed limit and a police officer pulls me over. By what rule is he going to find me guilty? How can you claim to be good if you are living according to your own rules? You are only good in your own eyes. Many pedophiles have told me they believed they had harmed no one and could go to church with a clear conscience.

YAHUSHA said in John 5:45, "Do not think that I will accuse you to the Father; there is one that accuses you, even Mosheh, in whom ye trust. For had ye believed Mosheh, ye would have believed me; for he wrote of me". YAHUSHA is confirming that the standard to which we are held is Moses. Jordan Peterson has said, "The Bible is the precondition of the manifestation of the Truth. It is how you know that what you know and then speak is the Truth.

Returning to Romans 3:21, "But now, the righteousness (lawfulness) of Elohim without Torah, is manifested; and Torah and the prophets testify of it." As Andrew Gabriel Roth states in his translation of the Aramaic, "Yeshu'ah qualified as Mashiyach because he fulfilled all Torah and prophetic requirements, and he became torah. Torah is written upon the heart by the Ruach haKodesh; the spirit of Mashiyach is Torah, the spirit of Mashiyach, or the manifestation (Word) of Yahweh became flesh and dwelt among us. Therefore, if we live in Yeshu'ah, we also become Torah." It is evil to assume that Paul brought the Torah down when, in fact, YAHUSHA the Messiah and Paul restored and elevated the Torah to be the foundation of a spiritual dialogue with heaven.

With the idea of Torah being foundational, let us return to the Aramaic Romans 3, starting at verse 22 and ending in verse 28, "Even the righteousness (lawfulness) of Elohim, which is by faith in Yeshu'ah the Mashiyach for everyone and on every one that believes in him; for there is no distinction; for they have all sinned and failed of the glory of Elohim. And they are granted the status of being righteous (lawful) by grace and by the redemption which is in Yeshu'ah the Mashiyach whom Elohim has ordained in advance an atonement by faith in his blood because of our previous sins. In the space which Elohim in his long-suffering gave to us for the manifestation of his righteousness (lawfulness) at the present time, that he might be righteous, and might with righteousness make him righteous who is in the Faith of Our Master Yeshu'ah the Mashiyach. Where then is glorying? It is completely unmade. By what Torah? By that of works? No! But by the Torah of faith. We therefore conclude that it is by faith a man is being made righteous, and not by The Works of Torah" (See section on Works of Torah). In other words, the oral law versus the law of Moses.

An example of works by faith is found in Genesis 15:6, which a lot of people know by heart, which says, "And he (Abraham) believed in YAHUAH; and he counted it to him for righteousness." Abraham believed in the promise YAHUAH made to him, and he obeyed. On that belief, Abraham packed up his wife, family, and whole household and traveled to a land unknown to him.

Without being told, Abraham could have just as easily looked to the horizon, packed up his family and went with the expectation of finding greener pastures, fulfilling the will of YAHUAH without even knowing he was doing so. the Torah is something we hear, believe, and then do. Paul writes on this in Romans 4, where he quotes this passage in Genesis and says, "For if Abraham were justified by works, he has wherefore to glory; but not before ELOHIYM." In Romans 4:4, Paul writes, "Now to him that works is the reward not reckoned of Grace, but of debt. But to him that works not but believes on him justifies the wicked; his belief is counted for righteousness. King David also describes the blessedness of the man, unto whom YAHUAH imputes righteousness without works. Saying. 'Blessed are they whose transgressions are forgiven, and whose sins are covered. Blessed is the man to whom YAHUAH will not impute sin". Paul quotes Psalm 32:1-2, where David recognized unearned forgiveness would come. The point is you must have faith first. Belief in the words of YAHUAH will compel you to act upon that belief. One thing to remember about the Apostle Paul is that he cannot disagree with any of the other Apostles, and he especially cannot be in conflict with the words of his Messiah.

The Apostle James wrote in chapter 2:14, "What does it profit, my brethren, though a man say he has belief, and have not works? Can belief save him? If a brother or sister be naked, and destitute of daily food, and one of you saying to them, depart in peace, be ye warmed and filled; notwithstanding you give them not those things which are needful to the body; what does it profit? Even so belief, if it has not works, is dead, being alone". The prophet Baruch wrote of these works in 2 Baruch 14:12: "For the righteous justly hope for the end, and without fear depart from this habitation, because they have with you a store of works preserved in treasuries." Peter talks about works in 1 Peter 2:12, where we probably get the statement that we are our neighbors' Bibles and they read us daily; it says, "Having your conversation honest among the other nations; that, whereas they speak against you as evildoers, they may by your good works, which they shall behold, glorify YAH in the day of visitation." The prophet Isaiah in 46:12 from the Targum of Isaiah reads, "Hearken unto my Word, ye stout-hearted, that are far from righteousness. My righteousness is nigh, it is not far off, and my salvation shall not tarry: and I will place salvation in Zion, and my glory in Israel".

Paul asks in Romans 3:29-30, "Is he the YAH of the Yahudiym only? Is he not also of the other nations? Yes, of the other nations also: Seeing it is one YAH, which shall justify the circumcision by belief, and uncircumcision through belief", in other words, the motivation behind your actions. Paul then continues and asks in verse 31, "Do we then make void the Torah by belief (the law of Moses)"? Then he answers his question, "Never yea, we establish the Torah." If Torah is Truth and the Word is YAHUAH made flesh, then the WORD of TRUTH which Paul speaks of, in my mind, is the living, breathing Torah, YAHUSHA the Messiah. But do not take my word for it. Let us look at what Paul said. Then, we will look at what Paul read.

From the Aramaic text in Philippians 2, starting in verse 5, Paul writes, "And think you so in yourselves, as Y'shua the Mashiyach also thought; who, as he was in the likeness of Elohim, did not regard it sinful to be co-equal of Elohim; yet disinherited himself and assumed the likeness of a servant, and was in the likeness of men and was found in fashion as a man, and he humbled himself and became obedient to death, even the death of the stake. Wherefore, also, Elohim has highly exalted him and given him a name which is more excellent than all names; but at the name of Yeshua every knee should bow, of being in heaven and on earth and under the earth; and that every tongue should confess that Master YHWH is Y'shua Mashiach to the glory of Elohim, his father". In verse 16, Paul commands that we hold forth this word of life.

Again, Paul points us back to the verses in Deuteronomy 30, where Moses tells the Israelites that the Torah is the word of life. Let's read starting in verse 20, "That you may love YAHUAH and that you may obey **his voice,** and that you may cleave unto him: for he is your life and the length of your days; that you may dwell in the land which YAHUAH swore unto your fathers, to Avraham, to Yitzhak, and to Ya'aqov, to give them." Let us read this from the Targum; "I attest this day, not only you, who are to pass away from this world, but the heavens and the earth, but I have set before you life and death, blessing and its reverse. Choose consequently, the way of life, even the law, that you and your children may live the life of the world to come; that you may love the Lord your God, to obey **His Word**, and keep close to his fear; for the law in which you occupy yourselves will be your life in this world, and the prolongment of your days in the world that comes, and you shall be gathered together at the end of the scattering, and dwell upon the land which the Lord swore to your fathers, to Abraham, Isaac and Jacob, to give it to them".

I would like to address one more place in scripture before leaving the topic of who is making the Covenant and who the Covenant is between. In Exodus chapter 34, after he breaks the two tablets containing the ten commandment Moses takes another two tablets and goes up onto the mount to meet YAHUAH as commanded. In verse 5, it says, "And YAHUAH descended in the cloud, and stood with him (Moses) there, and proclaimed the name of YAHUAH. And YAHUAH passed by before him, and proclaimed, YAHUAH, YAHUAH EL, merciful and gracious, long suffering, and abundant in goodness and truth".

The Targum has this verse in Exodus 34:5 as, "And the Lord revealed himself in the cloud of the glory of His Shekinah and Mosheh stood with Him there, and Mosheh called on the name of the Word of The Lord. And the Lord made his Shekinah pass by before his face, and proclaimed, the Lord, the Lord God, merciful and gracious, long-suffering, and near in mercies, abounding to exercise compassion and Truth; keeping mercy and bounty for thousands of generations, absolving and remitting guilt, passing by rebellions, and covering sins; pardoning them who convert to the law, but holding not guiltless in the great day of judgment those who will not convert; visiting the sins of fathers upon rebellious children upon the third and upon the fourth generation". Who spoke these words? Who is standing on the mount with Moses? Is it YAHUAH, or is it YAHUSHA HAMASHIACH, The Word? Are they the same? Psalm 138:1,2 states, "I will praise you with my whole heart; before the ELOHIYM will I sing praise unto you. I will worship towards your holy Temple and praise your name for your loving kindness and for your

Truth; for you have magnified your word above all your name".

The Word of YAHUAH was operating as a manifestation of YAHUAH and in HIS office of authority throughout the scriptures, not just when he came in the flesh. The disciples knew this and were declaring the good news to their listeners that ELOHIYM had fulfilled his promise of reconciliation in the form of the Messiah. YAHUAH, himself made the way for all to return to Covenant with the groom, the King of the Universe. We have a new song now, in addition to the song of Moses. This new song was promised in Psalm 33:3 and is cited in Revelation 15:3 as the song of the Lamb. Psalm 33:3,4 reads, "Sing unto him (YAHUAH) a new song; play skillfully with a loud noise. For the Word of YAHUAH is right; and all his works are done in truth". I cannot resist adding verse 6, which says, "By the Word of YAHUAH were the heavens made, and all the host of them by the breath of his mouth."

Notice that all his works are done in truth, the truth being the Torah. In science, we have rules of creation demonstrated in sacred geometry, which is the underlying geometry in nature. These rules prove there are mathematical rules governing nature, which indicate a Divine creator of the universe, the WORD of YAHUAH, who not only provided rules of operation to Nature itself but also rules of operation for mankind to provide an orderly existence.

MESSIAH YAHUSHA IS YAHUAH IN THE FLESH

Let this mind be in you, which was also in MASHIACH YAHUSHA: who, being in the form of YAH, thought it not robbery to be equal with YAHUAH: but made himself of no reputation, and took upon him the form of a servant, and was made in the likeness of men: and being found in fashion as a man, he humbled himself, and became obedient to death, even the death of the cross. 2 Philippians 2:5-8

Paul puts it succinctly: YAHUSHA HAMASHIACH is YAHUAH. Again, Paul wrote, "Now concerning spiritual gifts brethren, I would not have you ignorant. Ye know that ye were of the other nations, carried away unto these dumb idols, even as you were led. Wherefore I give you to understand, that no man speaking by the RUACH YAHUAH calls YAHUSHA accursed: and that no man can say that YAHUAH is YAHUSHA, but by the RUACH HA'QODESH". Paul is saying here in 1 Corinthians 12:1-3 that the Holy Spirit will lead you to the knowledge that YAHUSHA is Messiah YAHUAH. I also want to point out that Paul is talking to the lost sheep of Israel who were dispersed among the other nations and ultimately became part of the other nations. He was merely accomplishing the commission given to the disciples by YAHUSHA to find his lost sheep and feed them the good news that a way had been made for them to return to Covenant with YAHUAH, their ELOHIYM.

YAHUSHA himself hints that he is YAHUAH. He never hesitated to act and to speak like YAHUAH, which is why the Jewish leadership sought to kill him. There is a parallel verse to Luke 12:49 where YAHUSHA declares that he has come to send fire to the earth. In 2 Peter 3:5-10 from the Aramaic, YAHUSHA says concerning scoffers in these latter days: "For they willingly forget, that the heavens were of old; and the earth rose from the waters by the word of Elohim. And by means of these waters, the world, which then was being submerged, again perished in the waters. But the heavens that now are, and the earth, are by his **word** stored up, being reserved for the fire at the day of judgment and the perdition of wicked men. And of this one thing, my beloved, be not forgetful: that one day to Master YAHUAH is as a thousand years; and a thousand years, as one day. Master YAHUAH does not delay his promises as some estimate delay; but He is long suffering for your sakes, being not willing that any should perish, but t h a t everyone should c o m e to repentance. And the day of Master YAHUAH will come like a thief; in which the heavens will suddenly pass away; and the elements, being ignited, will be dissolved, and the earth and the works in it will not be found".

Who is Peter saying is coming to rain fire on earth? The Word or Master YAHUAH? Remember, in Luke 12:49, YAHUSHA said he had come to send fire on the earth. There is a parallel verse in Matthew 10:34-39 where He tells them, "Think not that I come to send peace on earth: I came not to send peace, but a sword." This should have brought his listeners back to Exodus 32:28-29, the golden calf episode when Moses had come down off the mountain and found the children of Israel worshiping a golden calf. He made a stand and asked the people whose side they were on. Either you were on the side of YAHUAH or against him. At that, Aaron and the Levites gathered themselves to Moses and were instructed to go throughout the camp and slay every man who had worshiped the calf. They went through the camp and killed the people who were against YAHUAH. "They slayed every man his brother, and every man his companion and every man his neighbor. And there fell that day about three thousand men".

We see YAHUSHA the Messiah again insinuating that he is YAHUAH in Luke chapter 19, starting in verse 8. YAHUSHA is dining with Zakkai at his house, and Zakkai tells YAHUSHA that he gives half of his wealth to the poor. YAHUSHA replies to him in verse 9, "Life has come to this house today, because this man is also a son of Abraham. The Son of Man came to seek and to save that which was lost". What a statement this is. Remember Deuteronomy 32: life equals Torah. YAHUSHA also refers to the Book of Ezekiel chapter 34, especially verse 12. I want to make clear that there is a distinction between YAHUAH and the Creator, his Son, YAHUSHA. The Messiah YAHUSHA was 100% the word of YAHUAH, but YAHUAH is more than his voice. We cannot see YAHUAH, the great I AM and live. Just as Moses was hiding in the cleft of the rock, when he asked to see the full Glory of YAHUAH, Moses only got to see the back of YAHUAH. This incident is found in Exodus 33:23, where it says, "And I will take away my **hand**, and you shall see my back parts; but my face shall not be seen." Interestingly, the hand keeps Moses from seeing YAHUAH; the hand is our shield, protector, and mediator.

YAHUSHA did indeed Proclaim his divinity (John 5:18 and 10:30). "And because of this, the Yehudeans were seeking all the more to kill him, not only because he had loosed the Shabbat by not observing the laws the priests had added to prevent people from breaking the commandments, but YAHUSHA proclaimed that his father was ELOHIYM, equating himself with ELOHIYM. In the footnote to John 5:18, Andrew Gabriel Roth says: "to consider oneself equal to YHWH is a very serious matter. Y'shua spoke of himself as being about his Father's business, of coming in his Father's name; he spoke and taught with authority and performed healings, which made him a formidable opponent to religious tradition. The charge here of Y'shua making himself equal to YHWH is simply Pharisee tradition projecting itself onto Y'shua.

The Ruach haKodesh in MESHIYACH is 'equal' to YHWH, but the Pharisees supposed that Y'shua and his followers equated his Humanity with YHWH". They didn't understand Isaiah 11:1-2 or chapter 63. Isaiah 11:1-2 states: "And there shall come forth a shoot out of the stem of Jesse, and a branch will grow out of his roots, and he shall be at peace, and the spirit of YAHUAH shall rest upon him, the spirit of wisdom and understanding, the spirit of counsel and might, and the spirit of knowledge and the reverence of Yahweh." These same seven spirits are spoken of in The Book of Enoch, chapter 61. They are being poured out upon the earth, over the water, on the days of creation.

In Chapter 93 of the Book of Enoch, verse 12 states: "Afterwards, in the seventh week, a perverse generation shall arise; abundant shall be its deeds, and all its deeds perverse. During its completion, the righteous shall be selected from the everlasting plant of righteousness; and to them shall be given the sevenfold doctrine of his whole creation". Those Spirits rested in YAHUSHA as the Ruach haKodesh which is another name for YAHUAH as Psalm 51:1-11 indicates: "Have mercy upon me, O Elohim, according to your loving-kindness: according to the multitude of your tender mercies, blot out my transgressions, wash me thoroughly from my iniquity, and cleanse me from my sin. For I acknowledge my transgressions; and my sin is ever before me. Against you, you only, have I sinned, and done this evil, in your sight: that you might be justified when you speak, and be clear when you judge. Behold I was shapened in iniquity; and in sin did my mother conceive me. Behold, you desire truth in the inward parts: and in the hidden part you shall make me to know wisdom. Purge me with hyssop, and I shall be clean; wash me, and I shall be whiter than snow. Make me to hear joy and gladness; that the bones which you have broken may rejoice. Hide your face from my sins and blot out all my iniquities. Create in me a clean heart, O ELOHIYM, and renew a right Ruach within me. Cast me not away from your presence and take not your Ruach haKodesh from me". Just as YAHUSHA said in John 17:22,23, "And the glory which you gave me I have given them; that they may be yachad (one), even as we are yachad; I in them, and you in me".

YAHUAH spoke through the spirit of Messiah rather than through his human component. YAHUSHA maintained that his soul would die but that YAHUAH would resurrect it. YAHUSHA believed his spirit was mortal. In Zechariah 12:10, the spirit of YAHUAH is pierced, but they mourned for him as an only begotten son. YAHUAH cannot literally be pierced; therefore, this refers to Messiah, who has the spirit of YAHUAH in him. Again, you must believe that for YAHUSHA to be the perfect sacrifice, he was in the flame that cut the covenant with Abraham.

YAHUSHA confirms it is the Father who is raising the dead in John 5:21, where the Messiah says: "For as the Father raises up the dead and quickens them; even so the son quickens whom he will." We see from this verse that the son has the authority of his Father as the firstborn for both resurrection power and judgment. But what exactly is this resurrection power? Yahusha proclaimed in many places to deliver his believers to eternal life with him in the place where he was going to make room for them. In John 10:28, he stated, "And I give unto them eternal life; and they shall never perish, neither shall any man pluck them out of my hand." Has anyone in the scriptures been given eternal life? We are told in Genesis 5:24 that Enoch "walked with ELOHIYM, and he was not; for ELOHIYM took him." We see that Enoch never died. This is also the case with Elijah, where we learn in 2 Kings 2:10-11 how he was taken up to heaven by a whirlwind.

Let us not confuse the mortal body living in eternity as Enoch and Elijah with the raising of the dead as described in 10 places in Scripture. It is believed that Enoch and Elijah will return as the two witnesses in Revelation and will be killed at that time. Also, remember prophets raised the dead. Elijah raised the widow's Son in 1 Kings 17:17-24. Elisha raised the Shunammite's son in 2 Kings 4:18-37. A dead man came to life when his bones were set on the dead bones of Elisha in 2 Kings 13:20-21. YAHUSHA himself raised a Widow's Son in Luke 7:11-15. He raised the daughter of Jarius in Luke 8:41-56. He also famously raised Lazarus in John 11:1-46. YAHUSHA brought many saints out of their graves at the resurrection, as described in Matthew 27:51-53. More details of Matthew 27:51-53 can be found in the book of Nicodemus.

We see the disciples themselves raising the dead. Peter raises Tabitha in Acts 9:36-51. Paul raised Eutychus in Acts 20:9-12. As miraculous as it is, this raising of mortal bodies is not what YAHUSHA is speaking about in John 10:28. Remember, we are to receive our bright nature upon resurrection. Peter begins his first epistle with, "Kepha, an apostle of

YAHUSHA HAMASHIACH, to the strangers scattered throughout Pontus, Galatia, Cappadocia, Asia and Bithynia, Elect according to the foreknowledge of YAHUAH the Father, through sanctification of the RUACH, unto obedience and sprinkling of the blood of YAHUSHA HAMASHIACH; Grace unto you, and peace, be multiplied. Blessed be YAHUAH and the Father of our ADONAI YAHUSHA HAMASHIACH, which according to his abundant mercy has begotten us anew and to a lively hope by the resurrection of YAHUSHA HAMASHIACH from the dead to an inheritance incorruptible, and undefiled, and that fades not away, reserved in heaven for you."

Paul also preached the promise of eternal life in his epistle to Titus chapter one, where he begins the epistle with: "Paul, a servant of YAHUAH, and an apostle of YAHUSHA HA'MASHIACH, according to the belief of YAHUAH'S elect, and the acknowledging of the Truth which is in the fear of YAHUAH; in hope of eternal life, which YAHUAH, that cannot lie, promised before the world began; but has in due times manifested his word through preaching which is committed unto me according to the commandment of YAHUAH our savior". Paul also wrote of a better resurrection in Hebrews 11:35. After speaking about the prophets raising the dead, he says, "When women received their dead raised to life again; and others were tortured, not accepting deliverance; that they might obtain a better resurrection."

John echoes this belief in the promise of eternal life in 1 John 5:13, where he says, "These things have I written unto you that believe on the name of the Son of ELOHIYM; that ye may know that ye have eternal life, and that ye may believe on the name of the Son of ELOHIYM. " But most famously, John stated in 3:16, "For YAH so loved the world, that he gave his yachiyd (beloved son), that whosoever believes in him should not perish, but have everlasting life." The disciples believed YAHUSHA when he said in John 6:37, 39-40, "That all that the Father gives me shall come to me, and him that comes to me I will in no wise cast out. For I came down from heaven, not to do my own will, but the will of him that sent me. And this is the Father's will which has sent me, that of all which he has given me I should lose nothing but should raise it up again at the last day. And this is the will of him that sent me, that everyone which sees the Son, and believes on him, may have everlasting life: and I will raise him up at the last day". Notice it is YAHUSHA who will be doing the raising of the dead and granting eternal life., thus equating himself with YAHUAH.

In Genesis 18 and 19, Three Angels or three men have come to Moses on the plain of Mamre, and according to the Targum, these Three Angels are each given a task to accomplish. However, the text indicates YAHUAH is one of these entities, and I believe the other two are mere shadows of the one, just as the host of the angels who met Esau as he was coming to meet Jacob in Genesis 32 and 33. It is important to note the three tasks YAHUAH accomplishes during this visitation. The first is to promise the gift of Isaac. The second is to bring salvation to Lot. And the third is to bring judgment on the wicked. Notice how the same tasks are the same for Messiah. First, he promises the gift of the Ruach, which is received on the day of Pentecost. The second is salvation, which is the promise of everlasting life. The third is the promise of the judgment of the wicked on the last day. These promises are all promises only the Most High can deliver.

As a side note, it is interesting to consider the mohar, the bride price, a gift paid by the groom to the bride's Family. The father gave the best part of the mohar to his daughter to help establish her home. Traditionally, this was exchanged or presented when the Ketuvah, marriage contract, was agreed upon by the two fathers. The bride price was given at that time as a down payment as a promise by the groom to return once he had made room in his Father's house for his bride, at which point he would return and gather her to his father's house. YAHUSHA left many gifts with us before he left, but in particular, the Holy Spirit was given to help prepare us for his return.

MESSIAH YAHUSHA IS THE STRONG ARM OR HAND OF YAHUAH

And they that follow truth are hidden, and those that depart from evil become a prey. It is revealed before the Lord that there is no justice, which is evil in His sight. And it is revealed in His sight that there is no man who hath good works, and it is known to Him that there is no man, who would arise and seek after them: therefore, he will redeem them by the arm of His strength, and by the Word of His delight. He will help them. It is revealed that He will work a great salvation for his people; yea, He will render vengeance to his enemies. He is the Lord of retributions, he shall render recompense; vengeance to His enemies, retribution to His adversary; He shall render recompense to the islands.-Targum Isaiah 59:15-18

John knew that the arm or strong right hand would bring Salvation, and he wrote about the Word of YAHUAH appearing on earth in the flesh. John 1:1 in Aramaic uses Miltha instead of the word 'logos' or 'word,' which has no direct English equivalent. It can mean word, manifestation, instance, or substance, among other things. In Andrew Gabriel Roth's English translation of the Aramaic New Testament, he left the word Miltha untranslated. The Book of John chapter 1:1-3 in the Aramaic reads: "In the beginning was the Miltha. And that Miltha was with Elohim. And Elohim was that Miltha. This was with Elohim in the beginning. Everything existed through his hands, and without him, not even one thing existed of the things which have existed".

4 Ezra 3:6 states, "And you led him (Adam) into paradise, which your right hand had planted before ever the earth came forward." Everything was made with YAHUAH's hands. Jeremiah confirms this in chapter 27:5, where YAHUAH tells Jeremiah that he "made the earth, the man and the beast that are upon the ground, by my great power, and by my outstretched arm, and have given it unto whom it seemed meet unto me." I like what Isaiah says in chapter 40:10: "Behold, ADONAI will come with strong hand, and his arm shall rule for him, behold, his reward is with him and his work before him." Is his reward the bride? Is the work that is before him the renewed earth? In Isaiah chapter 52:10, it says: "YAHUAH has made bare his holy arm in the eyes of all the nations, and all the ends of the earth shall see the yeshu'ah of our ELOHIYM."

Let us move to the Book of Job 40:6-9 which says: "Then answered YAHUAH unto Job out of the whirlwind, and said, gird up your loins now like a man: I will demand of you, and declare unto me. Will you also disannul my judgment? Will you condemn me, that you may be righteous? Have you an arm like EL? Or can you thunder with a voice like him?" We can also go to the Book of Psalms in chapter 77:14-15, which says: "You are the EL, that does wonders: you have declared your strength among the people. You have with your arm redeemed your people, the sons of Ya'aqov and Yoceph". Again, in the Book of Psalms chapter 89:10, it says: "You have broken Rachav in pieces, as one that is slain; you have scattered your enemies with your strong arm." Psalms 98:1 says: "O sing unto YAHUAH a new song; for he has done marvelous things: His right hand, and His holy arm, has gotten him the victory." Again, in the Book of Psalms 136:10-12 "To him that smote Egypt in their firstborn; for his Mercy endures forever: and brought out Israel from among them: for his Mercy endures forever. With a strong hand, and with a stretched out arm: for his Mercy endures forever".

Finally, so that I do not belabor this too much, let us read from the Song of Solomon in chapter 8:1, which says: "He shall give you as a brother to me as one laying at the breasts of my mother. When I am finding you in the outdoors, I am kissing You: yea, they are not despising to me. I am leading you, and I am bringing you into my mother's house. She is teaching me. I am giving you wine to drink from the juice of my pomegranate. His left arm is under my head, and his right arm is embracing me. I charge you, O

Daughters of Jerusalem, that you not rouse up the love she desires. Who is this that comes up from the wilderness, leaning on the arm of her darling? I roused you under the apricot tree: there, your mother labored with you; there, she gave birth to you. Place me as a seal upon your heart, as a seal upon your arm that love is as strong as death; jealousy is cruel as the coals thereof are coals of fire, with a blazing flame". The Wisdom of Solomon Chapter 5 verse 16 says more simply: "Therefore shall they (the righteous) receive a glorious kingdom, and a beautiful crown from YAHUAH'S hand: for with his right hand shall he cover them, and with his arm shall he protect them."

YAHUAH, as we see, has a right arm. When you reach out your hand or your arm to do anything, it isn't the arm or the hand that gets credit for whatever creative force it is set out to do, like a handshake, a hug, or a giving of a gift, no, the arm by itself is a part of the body, it is not the whole body, it is only accomplishing the will of the person to whom it belongs. When YAHUSHA states that he is doing the will of the Father, he is doing it as the Father's right hand. The Book of Matthew, chapter 19:16 says: "And behold, one came and said unto him, good rabbi, what good thing shall I do, that I may have eternal life? YAHUSHA answered him and asked why he called him good. There is none good but one, that is YAHUAH". This passage always confused me; was not YAHUSHA good? But now I know by understanding previous chapters and verses that we have gone over. If YAHUSHA is the strong arm, the creative force of YAHUAH, then it makes sense now.

What is good? What makes a person good is not his right hand. Your right hand may write your tithing checks to your church, or your right hand may reach out to do good to somebody, but it is not the hand itself that is good. It is the mind, the Logos, that willed the good action.

YAHUSHA indicates his Father has a hand, and he YAHUSHA is working by that authority in Luke Chapter 11:20. After he has cast out a demon and was accused of doing so by the power of Beelzebub, YAHUSHA says, "But if I with the finger of YAH cast out devils, no doubt the kingdom of YAHUAH is come upon you." The fact that people who witnessed this saw it as miraculous and proof that YAHUSHA was the Messiah is puzzling because no scriptures foretold the Messiah would control demons except maybe Psalm 91. This idea would have to come from David, who was able to soothe King Saul's evil spirit, which plagued him (1 Samuel 16:15). King Solomon, according to a legend contained in the Testament of Solomon, gained control over Beelzebub, the king of demons, and used demons to build the temple. Then you have Psalms 91, which Satan quoted from during the temptation of Christ. This Psalm indicates that the Messiah would have power over demons in that he is protected by a legion of angels while in the flesh. Read Psalm 91 with that in mind.

According to Isaiah 51:5, the arm of YAHUAH shall judge the people. It reads, "My righteousness is near; my yeshu'ah (salvation) is gone forth, and my arms shall judge the people; the isles shall wait upon me, and on my arm they trust." Isaiah 63:1-11, much like Revelation chapter 14, describes the Son of Adam coming to judge the earth and trodding it as one trods a wine press. We know that it is YAHUSHA, the Son of YAHUAH, who will be judging in the end. And Isaiah 63:5 reads, "And I looked, and there was none to help, and I wondered that there was none to uphold: therefore, my own arm brought salvation unto me; and my fury, it upheld me." In the Targum,' my arm' is translated as 'my word'. Both could be interchangeable. The word for arm is H2220 Zeroah, from H2232, which means arm, or figuratively a force - arm or help, a mighty power, strength, or shoulder. YAHUAH often uses the term strong arm when he relates his wondrous deeds.

You will find the phrases outstretched arm, Holy arm, and strong arm when the arm is working as a saving force, another manifestation of YAHUAH. Paul said in 1 Corinthians 12:4-7, "Now there are diversities of gifts, but the same RUACH. And there are no differences in administration but the same YAHUAH. And there are diversities of operations, but the same YAH works overall. But the manifestation of the RUACH is given to every man to profit withal". I know this may seem or will be controversial, but I must put in the quote by Origen where he comments about this verse in 1 Corinthians. He says, "From which it follows that there is no difference in the trinity, but that which is called the gift of the spirit is made known through the Son and operated by God the Father." It is one spirit working in all the different offices. I realize that Tertullian, a contemporary of Origen, is credited with creating the Trinity doctrine. However, He only coined the word Trinity. The idea for three separate entities that make up the "God Head" is not what Tertullian taught. It is the spirit of ELOHIYM operating through various manifestations and offices.

Further down in 1 Corinthians 12:11, Paul says, "But all these works that one and the selfsame RUACH (spirit), dividing to every man severally as he will." In verse 12, it continues, "For us, the body is one and has many members, and all the members of that body, being many, or one body: so also, is MASHIACH." Let us think back to Genesis 1. You have the wisdom of ELOHIYM, the king of the universe who brings forth this idea through his WORD and his hands. Think about what Nikola Tesla said about the universe; he said to think of it in terms of energy, vibration, and frequency. This explains creation as the mind or wisdom of YAHUAH sending his breath (spirit), resulting in vibration that culminates in the frequency or force bringing about creation. Just as we have a thought to convey, we produce breath, which vibrates over our voice box, which then creates sound, thus conveying our thoughts. The vibration or breath and the frequency or word are not separate from our thoughts. Remember Deuteronomy 6:4: "Hear, oh Yashar'el; YAHUAH ELOHAYNU, YAHUAH is one."

The arm or hand of YAHUAH brings Salvation. We will see later that Salvation is also eternal life. In the quote from Isaiah 59:16, as stated above, besides bringing judgment, the arm will accomplish a mighty work of Salvation. In the prophecy of the suffering Messiah in Isaiah 53, verse 1 states, "Who has believed our report? And to whom is the arm of YAHUAH revealed"? The first descriptor of the Messiah is the arm of YAHUAH. In his book Against Marcion, book 4, chapter 10, Tertullian quotes Isaiah 53:12 as "He shall remit to many their sins and shall himself take away their sins." The forgiving of sins is a theme continued from Isaiah 1:18, which reads, "Come now and let us reason together, says YAHUAH; though your sins be as scarlet; they shall be as white as snow; though they be red like crimson, they shall be as wool. If ye be willing and obedient, you shall eat the good of the land: but if you refuse and rebel, you shall be devoured with the sword; for the mouth of YAHUAH has spoken it". The Targum reads, "The Word" of YAHUAH has spoken it.

If anyone wishes to decipher a Bible Code, consider the word 'if.' If you obey, you will receive a blessing, a common theme not only in the Old Testament but also in the back of the book. There, we do not see it as clearly. However, think of the rich young man looking for eternal life, and YAHUSHA gave him the Ten Commandments. The young man told YAHUSHA that he had kept them since his youth. YAHUSHA knew better. YAHUSHA gave the parable of Lazarus and the rich man in Luke 16. YAHUSHA knew this young rich man seeking eternal life had not been generous and supportive of the poor around him as commanded. He did not love his neighbor as himself. YAHUSHA said the whole of The Commandments hangs on that one commandment along with the first; to love YAHUAH with all your heart, with all your might, and with all your soul. So why did the young man go away sad? It could be that he is not going to obtain eternal life because to do so, he needed to care for the people around him, thus spending his wealth.

MESSIAH YAHUSHA IS THE WISDOM OF YAHUAH

"And therefore, we have first to ascertain what the only begotten Son of God is, seeing he is called by many different names, according to the circumstances and views of individuals. For he is termed Wisdom, according to the expression of Solomon; The Lord created Wisdom - "the beginning of His ways, and among His works, before He made any other thing; He founded me before the ages. In the beginning, before he formed the earth, before he brought forth the fountains of waters, before the mountains were made strong, before all the hills, He brought me forth'. He is also styled First-Born, as the Apostle has declared; 'who is the First-Born of every creature.' A first-born, however, is not by nature a different person from the Wisdom, but one and the same. Finally, the Apostle Paul says that 'Christ (is) the power of God and the wisdom of God.' - Origen De Principus, Book 1 chapter 2. Origen [A.D. 185-230-254] is quoting Proverbs 8:22-25, Colossians 1:15, and 1 Corinthians 1:24, respectively.

In the above quote Origen is referring to Wisdom of Solomon 7:25-30 which reads, "For she (Wisdom) is the breath of the power of ELOHIYM, and a pure influence flowing from the glory of EL SHADDAI: therefore, can no defiled things fall into her. For she is the brightness of the everlasting light, the unspotted mirror of the power of ELOHIYM, and the image of his goodness. And being but one, she can do all things: and remaining in herself, she makes all things new: and in all ages entering into holy souls, she makes them friends of ELOHIYM and prophets. For ELOHIYM loves none but him that dwells with wisdom. For she is more beautiful than the sun and above all the order of stars: being compared with the light she is found before it. For after this comes night: but vice shall not prevail against wisdom." Further, in chapter 9 of the Wisdom of Solomon, Wisdom is conflated with the Word when he says, "O ELOHIYM of my fathers, and YAHUAH of mercy, who have made all things with your word. And ordained man through your wisdom, that he should have dominion over the creatures which you have made".

Notice in the above passage from Wisdom 7:26 that wisdom is the unspotted mirror of the power of ELOHIYM and the image of his goodness. If YAHUSHA is the wisdom of YAH and Wisdom is the image of YAHUAH, YAHUSHA's statement in John 5:19 makes sense. he tells the Jews, "Amein, Amein, I say unto you, the Son can do nothing of himself, but what he sees the Father do; for what things so ever he does these also does the likewise." In other words, he is the mirror image of the Father. When you look into a mirror and smile, your image also smiles. Whatever you do while looking into a mirror, your image also does. Therefore, YAHUSHA claims to be wisdom, the mirror image of the Creator in heaven: YAHUAH. Origen in De Principis Book 1 chapter 2:12 says, "For who else was he which is to come then Christ? And as no one ought to be offended, seeing YAHUAH is the father that the Savior is also YAHUAH; for in this way John 17:10 is true". John 17:10 States, "And all mine are yours, and yours are mine; and I am glorified in them." Paul confirms this in Colossians 1:15, 24, which states that YAHUSHA HA'MASHIACH "is the image of the invisible YAH, the first born of every creature." This verse may be referring us back to Psalms 89: 27 which states, "Also I will make him my first born, higher than the kings of the earth."

The writer of Hebrews also states that YAHUSHA, the Messiah, is the reflection of the Father in the opening of the book of Hebrews. I quoted Hebrews 1:3 in the chapter, YAHUSHA is the Son of ELOHIYM. Most Bibles use the quote I cited, which describes YAHUSHA as "the brightness of his (the Father's) glory." Origen, in his Commentary on the Book of John, book 32 (358), quotes this verse as YAHUSHA, 'who being the reflection of his (the Fathers) glory, and the express image of his person".

Enoch was given three parables or visions between chapters 37 and 64. In these chapters, it is apparent that he describes seeing YAHUSHA as the Messiah. Enoch says in chapter 42, "Wisdom found not a place where she could inhabit; her dwelling therefore is in heaven. Wisdom went forth to dwell among the sons of men, but she obtained not a habitation. Wisdom returned to her place and seated herself in the midst of the angels. But iniquity went forth after her return, who unwillingly found a habitation, and resided among them, as rain in the desert, and as a dew in a thirsty land". Wisdom looked for a place on earth, wanting to live among men, but could not find it and returned. Where was iniquity found after her absence? In heaven or on earth, or was it both?

If YAHUSHA the Messiah is the Torah-made flesh, it makes sense Wisdom is Torah. Sirach (Ecclesiasticus) 1:5 seems to agree. It reads, "The Word of EL ELYON is the fountain of wisdom, and her ways are everlasting commandments." Sirach 19:20, "The fear of YAHUAH is all wisdom; and in all wisdom is the performance of the Torah, and the knowledge of his omnipotency." Only YAHUAH is omnipotent, and since He is one, it makes sense that YAHUSHA the Messiah is YAHUAH made flesh through his wisdom. Thought is the first principle of any action; therefore, wisdom would have been there with YAHUAH from the beginning. That thought is made manifest through the word, and since energy is the result of the idea spoken into word, then frequency and vibration would result in the creation through that word or hand. Frequency and vibration in the hands of YAHUAH is a force that can either create or destroy, as Job 40:19 says of the creation of Behemoth: " The chief of the ways of EL; he that made him can make his sword to approach unto him." See also Isaiah 54:16.

I do not want to get into a dialogue about trees; however, I must add the verse from Proverbs 3:18.

Wisdom is the tree of life to them that lay hold upon her, and happy is every one that retains her. In Psalms 1:3, it reads, "And he shall be like a tree planted by the rivers of water, that brings forth his fruit in his season; his leaf also shall not wither; then whatsoever he does shall prosper." I realize some will argue that Psalm 1:1-4 is a prophecy of Joseph of Arimathea, and that could be true if you believe that Joseph of Arimathea was the father of Mary, the mother of YAHUSHA, the Messiah. Even so, Joseph of Arimathea did bring forth fruit in season which did prosper.

At the quote beginning this chapter, Origen used 1 Corinthians 15:24 to show that the mission of the Messiah is to reconcile and deliver the kingdom to the Father. This mission is also stated in John 13:3, which reads, "YAHUSHA knowing that the father had given all things into his hands and that he was come from YAHUAH and went to YAHUAH." 1 Corinthians 15:21 ties this delivery of the kingdom to defeating death and saving mankind from death. This plan of redemption comes from YAHUAH, and the vehicle used to complete it is the manifestation of the word and wisdom of YAHUAH made flesh.

I would caution that wisdom can mean the Spirit of YAHUAH, such as the men who were given the spirit of wisdom to create the Tabernacle, its furniture, and its accoutrement. It can mean obtaining knowledge, such as when Moses was growing up in Egypt, he learned all the wisdom of Egypt. Wisdom can imply shrewdness, craftiness, or even stupidity. For example, when YAHUSHA says in Luke 7:35, "Wisdom is justified by all her children, which is a Hebraism much like the saying 'the acorn doesn't fall far from the tree,' which could mean somebody inherited their stupidity or intelligence depending on the context

.

MESSIAH YAHUSHA AND HIS ELECT AS MESSENGERS

And the Angel of the Lord said to Hagar, "Multiplying, I will multiply your sons, and they shall not be numbered for multitude." And the Angel of the Lord said to her, "Behold, you are with child, and you will bear a son, and you should call his name Ishmael because your affliction is revealed before the Lord. And he shall be like the wild donkey among men: his hands shall take vengeance of his adversaries, and the hands of his adversaries he put forth to do him evil, and in the presence of all his brethren shall be comingled and shall dwell". And she gave thanks before the Lord whose Word spoke to her, and thus said, "You are he who lives and are eternal; who see, but are not seen!" she said, "For behold here is revealed the Glory of the Shekinah of the Lord after a vision." Hagar gave thanks and prayed in the Name of the Word of the Lord, who had been manifested to her saying, "Blessed be you, Eloha, the Living One of all ages who have looked upon my affliction." - The Targum of Jonathan Ben Uzziel on the Pentateuch, Genesis 16.

Notice here that the Angel who appears to Hagar is also the Word of YAHUAH, the Glory of the

Shekinah of YAHUAH, who promises to multiply her seed exceedingly. Is there any other character in The Bible besides YAHUAH who promises to multiply a person's seed? In the previous chapter of Genesis, the Word of YAHUAH had come to Abraham and had promised him seed. In the Book of Judges concerning the story of Samson, we see an angel also doing something that is only attributable to YAHUAH, which is to do wondrously.

In Judges chapter 13, we see an angel of YAHUAH coming to Manoach and his wife. The birth of Samson is foretold; Manoach prepares a meat offering; however, the Angel tells Manoach that he does not eat his food, which is the same thing YAHUSHA tells his disciples in John 4:31 at Jacob's Well on Mount Gerizim when he tells his disciples "I have meat to eat that you know not of." Manoach offers his sacrifice upon a rock. He then asks the Angel his name so that he and his wife could honor him. The Angel replied, "Why ask you thus after my name, seeing it is secret?" The word there for secret is H6383 pili, whose entomology is from H6381 Pala, which means wondrously or, in the case of pili, wonderful. The translation there should be my name is wonderful.

We find in Isaiah 9:6 the prophecy of the coming Messiah, whose name is proclaimed to be wonderful (Pele H6382), whose entomology is also from h6381, which could also mean miracle or miraculous. Psalms 72:18 says, "Blessed be YAHUAH ELOHIYM, the ELOHAI of Yashar'el, who only does wondrous things." Psalms 86:10

says, "For you are great, and do wondrous things: you are ELOHIYM alone." Pala H6381 is also translated as marvelously as in Job 37:5: "EL thunders marvelously (pala) with his voice; great things does he, which we cannot comprehend." After this, the Angel of YAHUAH told Manoach and his wife his name was wondrous; "he then did wondrously" and ascended in a flame of the altar. I have covered the flame or the pillar of fire that led Israel out of Egypt and the fire of Gideon's lamps and how these are manifestations of YAHUAH himself.

If these scriptures aren't apparent enough, then maybe the words of YAHUAH himself may make it more transparent. In Numbers 12, we have YAH admonishing Miriam and Aaron for their arrogant speech against their brother Moses, and it states in verse 5: "And YAHUAH came down in the pillar of the cloud, and stood in the door of the tabernacle, and called Aaron and Miriam; and they both came forth." YAH admonishes them, and then he states in verse 8, "With him (Moses) will I speak mouth to mouth, even apparently, and not in dark speeches; and the similitude, of YAHUAH shall he behold." A similitude is a quality or state of being similar to something.

We see through scripture that YAHUAH is in this flame of fire that led Israel out of Egypt and through the wilderness. The flame of Gideon's lanterns foreshadows the Messiah, the flame that comes in the flesh, as well as the appearance in Judges 13, announcing Samson's birth.

The flame from the altar in which the Angel ascends is a manifestation or similitude of YAHUAH as the Messiah, who stands between us and the Creator of all, who, if we were to see, would kill us. And because of our imperfection, we cannot see him, and he turns his face from us. Only this manifestation, this part of him, allows us to interact with him.

Exodus 29, starting in verse 42, reads, "This shall be a continual burnt offering throughout your generations at the door of the Tabernacle of the assembly before YAHUAH: where I will meet you, to speak there unto you. And there I will meet with the children of Yashar'el, and the Tabernacle shall be sanctified by my glory. And I will sanctify the Tabernacle of the assembly and the altar; I will sanctify also both Aaron and his sons, to minister to me in the priest's office. And I will dwell in the children of Yashar'el, and I will be their ELOHIYM. And they shall know that I am YAHUAH ELOHAYHEM, that brought them forth out of the land of Mitsrayim, that I may dwell among them: I am YAHUAH ELOHAYHEM."

As a side note, I would like you to consider the sacrifice of the red heifer as described in Numbers chapter 19. The ashes of this perfect animal is used to cleanse the temple and the priests. Did YAHUSHA's sacrifice cleanse or sanctify his temple of the renewed covenant?

I often ponder when I come to the subject of Sampson. His birth was foretold by an Angel of YAHUAH; therefore, he must have been expected to do great things. However, he did not live a sinless life in contrast to our Messiah YAHUSHA. So, who was he? Hippolytus, in his book On Christ and Antichrist, paragraphs 14-15, makes the case that Samson is a type of antichrist. Still, I wonder, in light of the manuscript called Joseph's Prayer, which documents Jacob's argument with the Angel Uriel the night before Jacob encountered his brother Esau in Genesis chapter 32:

> "I, Jacob, who speak to you, I am also Israel, I am an angel of YHWH, a ruling spirit, and Abraham and Isaac were created before every work of YHWH; and I am Jacob, called Jacob by men, but my name is Israel, called Israel by YHWH, a man seeing YHWH, because I am the firstborn of every creature which YHWH caused to live.

> When I was coming from Syrian Mesopotamia, Uriel, the Angel of YHWH, came forth and said that, 'I (Jacob/Israel) have come down to the earth and made my dwelling among men, and I am called by the name Jacob'. He envied me and fought with me and wrestled with me saying that his name and the name that is before every Angel was to be above mine. I told him his name and what rank he held among the sons of YHWH. 'Are you not Uriel, the 8th after me? And I, Israel, the Archangel of the power of the Adonai and the chief captain

*among the sons of YHWH? Am I not
Israel, the first minister before the
face of YHWH?' And I called upon my
Elohim by the inextinguishable
name?"*

This passage is quoted by Origen (AD 185 - 253) in
his Commentary on John. Origen introduced the
text as an "Apocrypha presently in use among the
Hebrews." The prayer ran some 1100 lines
originally; however, these are all that remain.
There is much to be said about Uriel and his
struggle with Jacob. In the Book of Enoch 20:2,
Uriel is identified as one of the Angels ruling over
Tartarus, and since Israel overcomes Uriel as
described in Genesis 32:22-32, it could be seen as
an elevation of Israel over all peoples.

In Colossians 1:15, Paul writes of the Messiah
being the image of the invisible YAH, "the firstborn
of every creature:" and then in verse 16, he says,
"for by him were all things created that are in
heaven, and that are in earth, visible and invisible,
whether they be thrones, or dominions, or
principalities, or powers; all things were created
by him and for him." Paul is referring us back to
Deuteronomy 32:8, where it says from the
Septuagint, "When the Most High was
apportioning nations as he scattered Adam's sons,
he fixed boundaries of nations according to the
number of divine sons, and his people Jacob
became the Lord's portion". This translation is
confirmed by Clement of Alexandria (A.D. 150-
215), Novation (A.D. 200-258), and Clement of

Rome (A.D. 35-99); these men all quoted this verse in Deuteronomy 32 and identified these sons of Elohim as angels. In an often-quoted verse in Ephesians 6:12, Paul said, "For we wrestle not against flesh and blood, but against principalities, against powers, against the rulers of the darkness of this world, against spiritual wickedness in high places."

Enoch is shown mountains of power in chapter 52. It says, "These mountains which you have seen, the mountain of iron, the mountain of copper, the mountain of silver, the mountain of gold, the mountain of fluid metal, and the mountain of lead, all these in the presence of the Elect One shall be like a honeycomb before the fire, and like water descending from above upon these mountains; and shall become debilitated before his feet." Daniel 2:35 comes to mind when I read this verse in Enoch in which Daniel describes King Nebuchadnezzar's vision of the statue whose substances are similar and that they were earthly kingdoms. The question becomes, who is ruling these kingdoms, these mountains? Are they ruled over by a spiritual being, like the Angel Uriel? Think of Daniel 10:13. Daniel is in exile, living in Babylon, and he had called YAHUAH for help. An angel finally comes to Daniel, saying, "The prince of the kingdom of Persia withstood me one and twenty days; but, lo, Miyka'el, one of the chief princes, came to help me; and I remained there with the kings of Persia."

I believe that I have adequately covered the concept that YAHUSHA, the Messiah, is the Word and Wisdom of YAHUAH, who created all things, including heaven, which would include angels. In the First Book of Enoch, you find much information about angels and heaven, of which Enoch received a grand tour. Enoch 48:5-6 says of the Son of Adam: "Therefore the Elect and the Concealed One existed in his (the Son of Adam) presence before the world was created, and forever in his presence he existed and has revealed to the qodeshiym and to the righteous the wisdom of YAHUAH TSEVA'OTH; For he has preserved the lot of the righteous, because they have hated and rejected this world of iniquity, and have detested all its works and ways in the name of YAHUAH TSEVA'OTH."

Bear with me. I am not discussing predestination, nor will it be a discussion on reincarnation, the type of which Shirley MacLaine claims, like Hinduism, Sikhism, Buddhism, or Jainism. These Elect are sent to prove their heart for YAHUAH ELOHIYM. They have free will but not the memory of their former greatness. From scripture, it is a one-and-done deal, not a try again until you get it right. Like Paul said man is appointed once to die.

Before talking about Jacob, let us talk about the obvious: John the Immerser. In Luke 1:17, the Angel who speaks to John's father, Zakaryahu, says, "And he (John) shall go before him (YAHUAH ELOHAYHEM) in the spirit and power of Eliyahu, to turn the hearts of the fathers to the children, and the disobedient to the wisdom of the just, to make ready a people prepared for YAHUAH." This

Promise was foretold in Malachi 4:5-6 which says, "Behold, I will send you Eliyahu the prophet before the coming of the great and dreadful day of YAHUAH: and he shall turn the heart of the fathers to the children, and the heart of the children to the fathers, lest I come and smite the earth with a curse."

We all know from 2 Kings chapter 2 that Elijah, like Enoch, never died. And notice the verbiage here in Malachi; it says that I will send Elijah, not the spirit of Elijah. I believe that this is the reason why most people think that it will be Elijah and Enoch who will be the two witnesses that come at the end time, as stated in the Book of Revelation because of what Paul said in Hebrews 9:27, "and as it is appointed unto man once to die, but after this the judgment."

I am aware of John 1:21, where John is asked directly if he is Eliyahu, and he replies, "I am not." However, I would point to Matthew 17:12, where YAHUSHA says, "Eliyahu is come already, and they knew him not, but have done to him whatsoever they will. Likewise, shall also the Son of Adam suffer of them". And verse 13 says, "Then the Talmidiym (apostles) understood that he spoke to them of John the immerser." How did they know that? They, indeed, were aware of the Book of Enoch and all the prophets. In Peter's salutation in 1 Peter chapter 1, he addresses the letter to the "Elect according to the foreknowledge of YAHUAH the Father, through sanctification of the spirit, unto obedience and sprinkling of the blood of YAHUSHA HAMASHIACH." Are they aware that they may be the Elect as mentioned in Enoch 48:5, which says that they were with the Word of YAHUAH from the beginning?

At this point, I will cover some obscure verses that I never really understood. No one can see YAHUAH and live; the only way he could be seen and interact with his creation was to manifest himself in a lesser form, not in his totality. In 4 Ezra 1:39-40, YAHUAH talks to Ezra about the Jews who have refused to follow the commands and statutes of the marriage covenant they had agreed to keep at Sinai. He says, "And now, brother, behold what glory; and see the people that come from the east unto whom I will give for leaders, Abraham, Isaac, and Jacob, Husha, Amoc, and Miykayahu, Yo'el, Ovadyahu, and Jonah, Nachum, and Chabaqquq, Tsephanyahu, Chaggai, Zakaria, and Mal'akiy which is also called an angel of YAHUAH". Now, we have all these prophets sent to us in book form. However, notice the word 'also.' Malachi was also an angel of YAHUAH. By implication, all of them were angels. These angels were sent to minister to us by calling us back to the commands and statutes that will bring us back into covenant with our creator and groom. They experienced persecution for their obeyance to Truth.

Were the prophets the Elect, as mentioned by Enoch, sent to be tested and tried as we are tested and tried? Heaven also must be reconciled back to YAHUAH. Paul said in 1 Corinthians 6:3, "Know ye not that ye shall judge angels"? Paul also wrote in Colossians 1:20, "And, having made peace through the blood of his cross, by him to reconcile all things unto himself; by him, I say, whether they be things in earth or things in heaven." Did Judas Iscariot fail the test? The answer to that question might be a yes since YAHUSHA the Messiah stated that it would have been better if he had never been born. And what about Samson? It was said that he killed more Philistines in his death than he did while he was judging Israel. The idea of the earth as a proving ground for the Elect shines a whole new light on understanding the parable of the talents, does it not? In John 10:34, YAHUSHA quotes Psalm 82:6, "I have said, ye are elohiym; all of you are children of EL ELYON," and he continues in verse 35 saying, "If he (YAHUAH) call them elohiym, unto whom the Word of YAHUAH came, and the scripture cannot be broken; say of him, whom the father has sanctified, and sent into the world you blaspheme; because I said, I am the Son of ELOHIYM"? Remember the WORD came to save the lost sheep of Israel just as all the prophets called Israel to repent their sin and return to the Torah.

This verse in Enoch 48 quoted on page 138 may explain Jeremiah 1:5, where the Word of YAHUAH comes to Jeremiah and says, "Before I formed you in the belly, I knew you; before you came forth out of the womb, I sanctified you, and I ordained you a prophet unto the nations." YAHUAH says in 2 Baruch 23:3, "For as you have not forgotten the people who now are and those who have passed away; so, I remember those who are appointed to come."

I have not come to this conclusion alone of earth being the proving ground for the elect. Origen, in his Commentary on the Book of John Book 13:293, writing of John 4:36, makes the following comment concerning Psalms 126:5, which says: "Those who sow in tears shall reap in joy." Origen says; "This reveals the descent of the more noble souls that come into this life with the saving seeds. They come indeed with groaning as though involuntarily, but they ascend again in joy because they have cultivated well and have increased and multiplied the seeds with which they came."

In Hebrews 13:2, we are told to "be not forgetful to entertain strangers: for thereby some have entertained angels unawares." Hebrews 11, references the sojourning of Abraham in a strange country, and in verse 10, "He looked for a city which has foundations, whose builder and maker is YAHUAH." Further down in verse 13 of chapter 11. It says these (the Patriarchs) "all died in belief, not having received the promises, but having seen them a far off, and were persuaded of them, and embraced them, and confessed that they were strangers and pilgrims on the earth." Interestingly, they were strangers and sojourners on the earth, not just in the land of Canaan or in the land of Egypt. If these, the Elect, are sojourning here on earth from their heavenly home, then verse 15 of Hebrews 11 makes sense, which says, "If they (the Patriarchs) had been mindful of that country from whence they came out, they might have had opportunity to have returned. But now they desire a better country, that is a heavenly".

I believe YAHUSHA also refers to entertaining angels unawares in Matthew 25 after he gives the parable of the ten virgins and the parable of the five talents. He begins in verse 31, telling of his coming into his glory with all his holy angels and sitting upon the throne of glory and gathering all nations to him, then separating the sheep from the goats. Then he will say to the people on his right hand, "Come, Ye blessed of my Father, inherit the Kingdom prepared for you from the foundation of the world: for I was hungry, and you gave me meat: I was thirsty, and you gave me drink: I was a stranger, and you took me in: naked, and you clothed me: I was sick, and you visited me: I was in prison, and you came unto me." The people on his right will say, when did we ever see you in such a state and he replies to them, "I say unto you, and as much as you have done it until one of the least of these my brethren, you have done it unto me." Notice that these little ones will be faced with famine, drought, alienation, destitution, plague, and persecution. It will be up to all of us to help each other through these tribulations, and we do this by following the Word, i.e., the Torah.

This saying of YAHUSHA reminds me of Malachi chapter 3, and I wonder if the disciples thought of it also. In Malachi chapter 3, we see the prophecy of John the Immerser, and then we have a promise from YAH that the Sons of Levy would be purified like a Refiner's Fire and like Fuller's Soap. And they will be purged as gold and silver is purged, and then in verse 4, it says then shall the offering of Yehuda and Jerusalem be pleasant unto YAHUAH. The priests are going to be tried through tribulations. Remember, we are now to be priests and vessels of the Holy Spirit. But verse 6 says, "for I am YAHUAH, and I change not; therefore, ye sons of Ya'aqov shall not be consumed." The earthly body may be consumed, but not the soul, which will live on in eternity. YAHUAH said in Leviticus 11:44, "And ye be holy for I am Holy." Peter reminds us of that in 1 Peter 1:16.

In Matthew 25 YAHUSHA is conveying the same sentiments YAHUAH spoke in Malachi 3. In verse 8 YAH asks the question, "Will a man rob ELOHIYM? And the reply was to ask how they had robbed him. Then he makes the accusation; "Your words have been stout against me, yet you say what have we spoken so much against you? Then, we are told our deeds are being recorded in The Book of Life in heaven. Are these deeds the results of how we behaved during our pressings, trials, and tribulations? When YAH closed a door, did we stand before and claw at it to return or did we walk boldly through the newly opened door like the Philadelphians of Revelation 3? Did we treat others as YAH commanded?

Paul said in Philippians 3:20, "For our conversation is in heaven; from whence also we look for the savior, the ADONAI YAHUSHA HAMASHIACH who shall change our vile body, that it may be fashioned like unto his glorious body, according to the working whereby he is able even to subdue all things unto himself." Remember what they lost during the fall from the book of Adam and Eve, that being their bright nature. Paul says here that we will return to our bright nature at the end of our trials if we endure. Paul here is speaking to believers when he says in Philippians 3:18, "For many walk of whom I have told you often, and now tell you even weeping, that they are the enemies of the cross of MASHIACH; whose end is destruction, whose elohiym is their belly, and the glory is in their shame, who mind earthly things." We are not of earth. It is not the place of our origin. YAHUSHA confirms this in John 17:15-16 where he is praying for his disciples, saying, "I pray not that you should take them out of the world but that you should guard them from the evil one. They are not of the world, even as I am not of the world".

In 2 Corinthians 4:6, Paul alludes to this cosmic exile when, in verse 7, he says we have this treasure, that is the light which has shone out of darkness and into our hearts "to give the light of the knowledge of the glory of YAHUAH in the face of YAHUSHA the Messiah in "earthen vessels," much like Gideon's lamps. Paul then quotes in verse 13 Psalm 116:10; "I believed, therefore have I spoken: I was greatly afflicted." Now, of course, Paul expects us to know Psalm 116. In verse 13 of this Psalm, David says, "I will take the cup of yeshu'ah, and call upon the name of YAHUAH, I will pay my vows unto YAHUAH now in the presence of all his people. Precious in the sight of YAHUAH is the death of his chaciyd (saints)". Now think about the Messiah's statements in Mark

10:39 and Matthew 20:23 of YAHUSHA's conversation with the sons of Zavdiy when they ask that they be set at his right and left hand when he comes into his glory. The MESSIAH's response is to ask them if they would be able to "drink of the cup that I drink of and be immersed with the immersion that I am immersed with." They said that they could, and the response YAHUSHA gives them is interesting because he tells them, "Ye shall indeed drink of the cup that I drink of; and with the immersion that I am immersed withal shall ye be immersed."

I realize that there is a belief, and I used to be there, that in the Garden of Gethsemane, when YAHUSHA is praying and asks that the cup of woe might pass by him, that was a moment of weakness on his part and that he is asking that his suffering may be alleviated. However, there is another way to look at those verses. He knew that his death would bring his disciples and the world tribulation. Tribulation started at his death. When you look at how his disciples and followers, not just his disciples, were tortured and killed for his name, he knew that by drinking this cup of woe, his disciples would also be drinking it. He loved them and wished to spare not just them but us as well.

Let me complete the beautiful scripture in 2 Baruch chapter 23, which I briefly quoted above, where Baruch is lamenting why all this evil is happening to Israel and wants to know why YAHUAH does nothing about it. AHUAH answers Baruch and says, "Why, therefore are you troubled about that which you know not, and why are you ill at ease about things in which you are ignorant? For as you have not forgotten the people who now are and those who have passed away, I remember those who are appointed to come. Because when Adam sinned and death was decreed against those who should be born, then the multitude of those who should be born were numbered, and for that number a place was prepared where the living might dwell, and the dead might be guarded. Before, therefore, the number aforesaid is fulfilled, the creature will not live again, for my RUACH is the Creator of life, and She'ol will receive the dead. And again, it is given to you to hear what things are to come after these times. For truly my redemption has drawn nigh and is not far distant as aforetime".

Where is this land in which we were born? Psalm 87 speaks of Zion, but is it an earthly location? Psalm 87 reads: "His foundation is in the holy mountains. YAHUAH loves the gates of Zion more than all the dwellings of Ya'aqov. Glorious things are spoken of you, O city of ELOHIYM. I will make mention of Rachav (Egypt) and Babel to them that know me; behold Pelehsheth, and Tsor, with Kush; this man was born there. And of Zion it shall be said, this and that man was born in her: and EL ELYON himself shall establish her. YAHUAH shall count when he writes up the people, that this man was born there. As well the singers as the players on instruments shall be there; all my springs are in you "

We know Abraham was not born in Zion, and most people today are not born in Zion. When it states YAHUAH shall count, when he writes up the people, that this man was born there, that's future tense. Speaking of writing up, Enoch 97:15-16 states, 'I have sworn to you, sinners, by the holy and the great one, that all your evil deeds are disclosed in the heavens; and that none of your oppressive acts are concealed and secret. Think not in your minds, neither say in your hearts, that every crime is not manifested and seen. In heaven it is daily written down before EL ELYON. Henceforward shall it be manifested; for every act of oppression which you commit shall be daily recorded, until the period of your condemnation". Our deeds being recorded in heaven is confirmed in Malachi 3:16.

YAHUSHA mentioned the kingdom of YAHUAH often. In the Kailedy chapter 7, YAHUSHAS' disciples question him concerning "the world of spirits wherein lay the kingdom of heaven, and He said, 'it is like a flight of stairs leading from cellar to roof. They who enter the house are given a place on the stairs and may step downwards and back, but never up, though the stair above is not unknown to them. Those on the top stairs are in glorious sunshine, while those at the bottom are in darkness and gloom." The house is a creation. Heaven and Earth are creations.

Paul is intimating this thought in 2 Corinthians 4:16-18 when he says, "Knowing that he which raised up ADONAI YAHUSHA shall raise up us also by YAHUSHA and shall present us with you. For all things are for your sakes, that the abundant grace might through the thanksgiving of many redound to the glory of YAH. For which cause we faint not; but though our outward man perishes, yet the inward man is renewed day by day. For our light affliction, which is but for a moment, works for us a far more exceeding and eternal weight of glory; while we look not at the things which are seen; but at the things which are not seen; for the things which are seen are temporal, but the things which are not seen are eternal". Is he speaking of a fallen time domain? Through YAHUSHA the Messiah and his sacrifice we will be able to live above the ladder or on the roof in the presence of YAHUAH.

Paul continues in 2 Corinthians 5:1, "For we know that if our earthly house of this Tabernacle were dissolved, we have a building of YAH, a house not made with hands, eternal in the heavens. For in this we groan, earnestly desiring to be clothed upon with our house which is from heaven". Our first home was heavenly. We are exiled here on earth, our proving ground, and then as Paul says in 2 Corinthians 5:10, "For we must all appear before the judgment seat of MASHIACH; that everyone may receive the things done in his body, according to that he has done, whether it be good or bad. And continuing in verse 11, he says, "Knowing, therefore, the fear of YAHUAH, we persuade men; but we are made manifest unto you, and I trust also are made manifest in your conscious."

We are all appearing before the judgment seat of Mashiach. In John 5:22, he says, "For the Father judges no man, but has committed all judgment unto the Son." The two are conflated here by Paul.

We are to fear YAHUAH, but it is the Son who is doing the judging. Remember what YAHUAH said to Moses in Exodus 23:20-25: "Behold I send an angel before you, to guard you in the way, and to bring you into the place which I have prepared. Beware of him, and obey his voice, provoke him not; for he will not pardon your transgressions; for my name is in him. But if you shall indeed obey his voice and do all that I speak, then I will be an enemy unto your enemies and an adversary unto your adversaries. For my Angel shall go before you, and bring you in unto the Emoriym, and the Chittiym, and the Perizziym, and the Kena'aniym, and the Yevuciym; and I will cut them off. You shall not bow down to their elohiym, nor serve them, nor do after their works; but you shall utterly overthrow them and quite break down their images. And you shall serve YAHUAH ELOHAYKEM, and he shall bless your bread, and your water; I will take sickness away from the midst of you". Notice this Angel, whose voice we are to obey, is bringing judgment, and YAHUAH will bless you if you obey the Voice of the Angel. Notice he says I will cut them off and utterly overthrow them and that even though we are obeying the voice of this Angel, we are serving YAHUAH. The two, the Angel and YAHUAH, are conflated in this passage.

Philo, On The Cherubim, part 2, page 115, writes, "For our soul understands us without being understood by us, and then it imposes commands upon us which we are necessitated to obey, as servants are compelled to obey a mistress; and whenever it chooses to abandon us and to depart to the Ruler of All Things, it will depart, leaving our house destitute of life. And even if we attempt to compel it to remain, it will disappear; for its nature is composed of substantial parts, such as afford no handle to the body". Does the Elect drink the cup of remembrance and, given a choice, while here on earth to set aside the love we previously held toward our ELOHIYM once embroiled in earthly cares? Or do we endure to the end?

Remember the passage in Jeremiah 31:33 YAHUAH tells Jeremiah that the renewed Covenant or the Torah will be put in our inward parts, that he will write it in Israel's hearts, and that he will be their Elohim and they shall be his people. Psalm 37:31 says, "The Torah of his ELOHIYM is in his heart; none of his steps shall slide'. In John 14:10, YAHUSHA tells his disciples, "Believe you not that I am in the Father, and the Father in me? The words that I speak unto you I speak not of myself: but the Father that dwells in me, he does the works". He is speaking the Father's words. In verse 24, he says, "He that loves me not guards not my words; and the word which you hear is not mine, but the fathers which sent me." Then, he talks about the comforter, the RUACH HAKODESH, the Holy Spirit that is promised to us. The Holy Spirit will be writing the Torah on our hearts.

Just in case you may still be thinking that YAHUSHA the Messiah did not teach Torah, I would have you read chapter 15 of John, starting in verse 10, where he says, "If you guard my commandments, you shall abide in my love; even as I have guarded my Father's commandments and abide in his love." YAHUSHA said in Matthew 5:18, "For amein, I say unto you, till heaven and earth pass, one yod or one tittle shall in no ways pass away from the Torah, till all be fulfilled. The Kailedy expounds on this exchange in Chapter 13, which quotes YAHUSHA, saying, "I have not come to abolish the law or to change the teachings of the prophets but to complete them, adding any necessary clarification and interpreting them to the understanding of men. But the time has come to ask, when will they be put into practice? When will men bring YAHUAH out of the temple and make him a participant in their daily lives? When will men carry these things in their hearts and stop paying them lip service? I say with certainty, so long as earth and the heavens above it remain, not even the smallest particle shall be deducted from the law until the purpose it serves has been completed. Therefore, if anyone try to avoid even the least obligation imposed by the law, or to set aside the slightest of its restrictions, or teach others to do the same, he will be an insignificant thing in the life to come. But whoever lives by them, leading others to do likewise, will achieve the greatest heights of glory". Notice that receiving the life to come is contingent upon performing the Torah. This statement makes it hard to argue that the law of Moses was nailed to the cross. Messiah performed Torah just as prophesied by Micah in Chapter 7:20, and the last I checked, the earth and sky are still with us.

YAHUSHA sends his disciples out on their own to heal and teach the good news that the Messiah had come and was making a way for his people to return to Covenant with their creator, YAHUAH. The story is recorded in Matthew chapter 10, Mark chapter 13, and Luke chapter 21. In Matthew 10:19-20, YAHUSHA tells his disciples, "But when they deliver you up, take no thought how or what you shall speak: for it shall be given you in that same hour what you shall speak. For it is not you that speak, but the RUACH of your father which speaks in you". They would have the law, the Torah, written on their heart. Of course, being raised in the synagogue, they read and heard Moses from their youth. They knew the Torah and trusted YAHUSHA that the Holy Spirit would speak through them.

It is interesting to note how different Luke portrays this. In Luke 21:15, YAHUSHA says, "For I (YAHUSHA himself) will give you a mouth and wisdom, which all your adversaries shall not be able to gainsay nor resist." Even though he was not present with them on their first missionary journey, YAHUSHA said he would give them words and wisdom when the apostles were brought before the authorities.

My hope is that you can see how this Angel who went before Israel into the wilderness and YAHUSHA, who sends his spirit/Word through his disciples, are the same, as well as the Holy Spirit being YAHUAH with us. It gives a complete understanding to Matthew 28:19-20 which says, "Go therefore, make disciples of all nations and immerse them in the name of the Father and the Son and the Ruach haKodesh. And teach them to keep all that I have commanded you. And behold, I am with you all the days until the end of the world." Notice that the word 'name' is singular. According to Isaiah 63:1-11, they are all the same. YAHUSHA had YAHUAH's name in him. YAHUAH is the strong arm from verse 5, and the savior of Israel is the Angel of his presence from verse 9, and in verse 10, it states, "But they rebelled, and vexed his Ruach haKodesh."

Psalms 51 confirms that the Ruach haKodesh is another name for YAHUAH. Verse 6 states, "Behold, you desire truth in the inward parts; and in the hidden part you shall make me to know wisdom." YAHUSHA has his Father's name in him as he said in John 17:11, "And now I am no more in the world, but these are in the world, and I come to you. Holy Father, guard them by your name, the same name which you have given me, that they may be your yachad (one with YAH) as we are". There is no separation between the three. As Philo said, the two are mere shadows of the ONE. The Angel is a manifestation of YAH.

Did the disciples who were given this mission and were told that YAHUSHA would be with them, think of Jacob's vision of the ladder in Genesis 28:12-17? These verses read, "And he dreamed, and behold a ladder set up on the earth and the top of it reached to heaven and behold the angels of ELOHIYM ascending and descending on it. And, behold, YAHUAH stood above it, and said, I am YAHUAH ELOHAI of Abraham your Father, and the

ELOHAI of Yitzhak: the land whereon you lie, to you, will I give it, and to your seed; and your seed shall be as the dust of the earth, and you shall spread abroad to the west, and to the east, and to the north, and to the south: and in you and in your seed shall all the families of the earth be blessed. And behold I am with you and will guard you in all places whither you go and will bring you again into this land; for I will not leave you until I have done that which I have spoken to you of". YAHUSHA had told them they had been given a rung on this ladder, as I quoted earlier from the Kailedy. But notice Jacob had seen angels, and YAHUSHA is telling his disciples it is men who are given rungs.

The ladder is between earth and heaven. Jacob beheld YAHUAH above the ladder, and angels were ascending and descending. Along with earth, heaven is a creation. The pastor of Hermas writes in The Pastor, Book Second - Commandments: "First of all, believe that there is one Elohim who created and finished all things, and made all things out of nothing. He alone is able to contain the whole, but himself cannot be contained". This idea of the disciples being part of the Elect from the Book of Enoch may explain Psalm 82:1-8 which reads, "Elohim stands in the assembly of the mighty; he judges among the elohiym. How long will you judge unjustly, and accept the persons of the wicked? Defend the poor and fatherless: do justice to the afflicted and needy. Deliver the poor and needy; rid them out of the hand of the wicked. They know not, neither will they understand; they walk on in darkness; all the foundations of the earth are out of course. I have said, ye are elohiym, and all of you are children of EL ELYON. But ye shall die like men and fall like one of the princes. Arise, O ELOHIYM, judge the earth; for you shall inherit all nations." Who but YAHUSHA the Messiah inherits the earth? Who is he judging but the heavens and the earth? Who is he talking about that will die like men? We all here on earth die, so it cannot be us that Psalm 82 speaks of. What is this assembly of the mighty?

Enoch 61:10-12 states, "Then YAHUAH seated upon the throne of his glory the Elect One; who shall judge all the works of the holy, in heaven above, and in a balance shall he weigh their actions. And when he shall lift up his countenance to judge their secret ways in the word of the name of YAHUAH TSEVA'OTH, and their progress in the path of the righteous judgment of EL ELYON; they shall all speak with united voice; and bless, glorify, exalt, and praise, in the name of YAHUAH TSEVA'OTH". And it is interesting to add versus 13 which says "He (the Elect One who is judging) shall call to every power of the heavens, to all the holy above, and to the power of ELOHIYM. The Keruviym, the Seraphiym, and the Ophaniym, all the angels of power, and all the angels of YAHUAH, namely of the Elect One, and of the other power, who was upon the earth, over the water on that day." This other power would be from Genesis 1:1, the breath of YAHUAH, the Holy Spirit.

Is this heavenly judgment portrayed in The Book of Enoch what Isaiah talks about in 24:21? From the Targum; "And it shall come to pass at that time that YAHUAH shall punish the mighty host that is dwelling in power, and the kings, the sons of man who are dwelling upon the earth." Notice that the mighty host who is dwelling in power is separate from the Kings. In that statement, the kings are sons of men, the host is different from the kings. In verse 22, the text states that these being punished "shall be utterly gathered for the prison, and they shall be shut up in the dungeon, and after many days they shall be remembered." Is this what John is referring to in Revelation 20:7, where he says, "And when the thousand years are expired, Satan shall be loosed out of his prison?" Are the four angels who are released from their prison under the Euphrates River, as mentioned in Revelation 9:14, angels who were judged in Enoch 61? Did this judgement take place prior to Genesis? Does Genesis 1 describe the first flood making Noah's flood the second?

There are numerous verses concerning our tribulation, our crushing, and our refinement with fire, which I believe is intended to return us to the commandments and statutes of our Creator and allow us to live in his presence. This is confirmed in Deuteronomy 8:2, which says, "And you shall remember all the way which YAHUAH ELOHAYKA led you these forty years in the wilderness, to humble you, and to prove you, to know what was in your heart, whether you would guard his commandments, or no." Are the Angels the Elect?

Is the earth their proving ground? The writer of Hebrews 2:9 says that YAHUSHA tasted death for every man; however, the Greek word there is Strong's Concordance G3956 Pas, which includes all forms of declension: apparently a primary word, all, any, every, the whole. Interestingly, the writer did not use the word oudeis or anthropos, which means man. Remember, heaven must also be reconciled, so YAHUSHA tasted death for all or the whole of creation.

In the book of Jubilees chapter 10:8-10, we are shown the demons' role in our temptation. In chapter 10, YAHUAH has agreed to imprison all the demons (disembodied spirits of the fallen angels' earthly children). However, the chief of the demons argues that he would be unable to tempt and try man if he had no demons under his control. YAHUAH agreed and allowed 10% of the demons to remain free under the control of the chief of the demons. How exactly do they tempt us? The early church writers spent much of their time preaching on the weakness of the flesh.

The Kailedy gives a little bit more insight into the temptation of Christ. It says, "He went out into the wilderness bordering Jordan, uncertain about his next move. While there, hungry, and thirsty, he fought with himself (his flesh), resisting the temptation to go down among the habitations of men and use his powers for selfish ends". Imagine if you were hungry in the wilderness and could turn stones into bread, would you? Would you call a legion of angels to minister to you? Would you go down and show your powers as the Creator of all things and take over the Nations? He could have but resisted those temptations.

YAHUSHAS' mission was explained in Leviticus chapter 17, where we see the Commandment to consume no blood. It reads, "For the soul of the flesh is in the blood: he and I have given it to you upon the altar to make atonement for your souls; for it is the blood of him that makes an atonement in the soul." The blood of YAHUSHA, the Messiah, the spotless lamb, will save your soul once you have accepted it, bringing you back into Covenant. The same Covenant that was given to Israel on Mount Sinai.

In The Book of Enoch, you have the Elect, then The Elect One, which is interchangeable with the Son of Adam. YAHUSHA, the Messiah, identified himself as the Son of Man or the Son of Adam about 80 times, depending on the translation you are reading. Where did this title come from? I believe that YAHUSHA was hearkening his listeners and future readers back to the Book of Enoch, which his listeners would have all been familiar with. In chapter 48, in verse 1, Enoch says, "In that place, I beheld a fountain of righteousness, which never failed, encircled by many springs of wisdom. Of these, all the thirsty drank, and were filled with wisdom, having their habitation with the righteous, the Elect, and the holy. In that hour was this Son of Adam invoked before YAHUAH TSEVA'OTH, and his name in the presence of the Ancient of Days. Before the sun and the signs were created, before the stars of heaven were formed, his name was invoked in the presence of YAHUAH

TSEVA'OTH. A support shall he be, and he shall be the light of nations. He shall be the hope of those whose hearts are troubled. All, who dwell on earth, shall fall down and worship before him; shall bless and glorify him, and sing praises to the name of YAHUAH TSEVA'OTH".

These images are manifestations Enoch, John, and Daniel saw: creations as a conveyance of YAHUAH, as a way of interacting with his creation without destroying it. You cannot pick up an ant without killing it. The ant, allowed to crawl onto our hand, can have no concept of who or what we are no more than the seven Blind Men shown an elephant could completely comprehend the whole animal. The best way to have any meaningful interaction with ants would be to become an ant. But is it YAHUAH that is the only one interacting with creation?

Enoch 48:5-6 says of the Son of Adam: "Therefore the Elect and the Concealed One existed in his (the Son of Adams) presence before the world was created, and forever in his presence he existed and has revealed to the qodeshiym and to the righteous the wisdom of YAHUAH TSEVA'OTH; For he has preserved the lot of the righteous, because they have hated and rejected this world of iniquity and have detested all its works and ways in the name of YAHUAH TSEVA'OTH." The word qodeshiym comes from Strong's Concordance word H6944 qodesh, which means set apart. Qodeshiym would then mean the set apart ones: the Patriarchs, prophets, disciples, and us when we make the choice to set ourselves apart and dedicate our lives to the word of YAHUAH, YAHUSHA the Messiah.

The scriptures are replete with how the patriarchs, prophets and disciples were tried. Abraham searched for the Creator and found him. Abraham was told to leave his country and go to a land unknown to him, which he did. YAHUAH closed a door and Abraham packed up his family and walked through the new door that YAH had opened for him, not knowing where he was going. His Son Isaac was tried. However, you do not see that in the canonized scripture. You must go to the book of Jubilees, of which more copies were found among the Dead Sea Scrolls than Genesis. In that, we are told that Ishmael was boasting of his circumcision to his brother Isaac, and Ishmael bragged that his was a better sacrifice because he was 13 when he was circumcised: he had a choice and suffered more pain. He suffered for ELOHIYM, whereas Isaac had no choice: he was just eight days old when circumcised.

During this argument with his brother, Isaac made a boast, saying that he would lay down his life for his ELOHIYM if asked. ELOHIYM heard that boast and considered it. Would Isaac lay down his life for him? In the story, which is very good, and I would recommend anybody to read it, they were met with many temptations along the way to the sacrifice. Satan appeared to each person who traveled with Abraham (Isaac, Ishmael, and Eleazar) in different disguises, even as a roaring river, trying to keep them from accomplishing the mission. Once on the mount, Isaac asks his father to bind him tightly so that the knife would not miss its mark because he was afraid that he would move at the last minute possibly breaking a bone thus ruining the sacrifice.

We are told in Genesis 22:11-12 an angel of YAHUAH called unto Abraham out of the heavens and said, "Lay not your hand upon the lad, neither do you anything unto him: for now, I know that you fear ELOHIYM, seeing you have not withheld your son, your yachiyd (beloved son) from me."

Who is speaking here? An angel of YAHUAH who says you fear ELOHIYM, and you have not withheld your Son from me. Who had ordered this trial? Was it the Angel or ELOHIYM? In Genesis 22:1 we are told that "Elohim did try Abraham." I believe it's clear from the text they are the same because further down in verse 15, it says, "And the angel of YAHUAH called unto Abraham out of heaven the second time, and said, by myself have I sworn, says YAHUAH, for because you have done this thing, and have not withheld your son, your yachiyd: that in blessing I will bless you." The Targum of Jonathan Ben Uzziel reads "by My Word have I sworn to you."

As a side note, the commandment concerning vows is contained in Numbers 30. It is not clear that if Abraham had heard of Isaac's vow, he could have annulled it, considering Isaac's age, which is unclear how young he was. Still, it appears that Abraham could have negated Isaac's vow by the fact that YAHUAH commended Abraham for not withholding Isaac from completing his vow. It also gives a whole new meaning to James 5:12, which states, "But above all things, my brethren, swear not, neither by heaven, neither by the earth, neither by any other oath: but let your yea be yea; your nay be nay; lest ye fall into condemnation."

Consider the three men Abraham saw in Genesis 18 before the destruction of Sodom and Gomorrah. Everyone agrees these men were angels. However, the text indicates that one of these individuals or angels was YAHUAH. Philo comments concerning this incident in his book On Abraham, 24:119, "When therefore, the soul is shone upon by God as if at noonday, and when it is wholly and entirely filled with that light which is appreciable only by the intellect, and by being wholly surrounded with its brilliancy is free from all shade or darkness, it then perceives a threefold image of one subject, one image of the living God, and others of the other two, as if they were shadows irradiated by it." What Philo is saying here is much like what Paul was trying to explain to his listeners concerning Messiah, which I have covered in Messiah as the Son. If you are drinking milk, you will see these three angels as separate: the Father, the Son, and the Holy Spirit. However, once you eat meat or get to the meat of the issue, you will see them as the same.

In Hebrews 5:12, after he has been making the case that YAHUSHA was Mashiyach, the Son of ELOHIYM, the writer tells his listeners, "For when for the time you ought to be teachers, you have need that one teach you again for which be the first principles of the Oracles of YAHUAH; and are become such as have need of milk and not of strong food." The Aramaic of Hebrews 5:12 gives us a better rendering of what was said there; it reads, "For you should be teachers, seeing that you have been long in the doctrine. But now you need to learn again the first lines of the beginning of the word of Elohim, and you have need of milk, and not of strong food". Something you can do, which is a fun exercise, is to look at the Hebrew characters that make up the word Bere'shiyth (Genesis), the first word of the Book of Genesis. The Hebrew symbols there spell out the prophecy of the coming and suffering Son of ELOHIYM, who will conquer all. And here in Hebrews 5:12, we are being told to go back and look at that and see it with eyes to see. The writer in Hebrews 5:14 declares, "But solid food is for the perfect, who by practice have their senses exercised to the discerning of good and evil." In other words, practice what you preach, and by that practice, you will be made perfect.

In Genesis 31, we have another issue of wondering who is speaking. In verse 3, YAHUAH tells Jacob to return to the land of his fathers, and then in verse 11, it says, "And the angel of ELOHIYM spoke unto me in a dream, and then in verse 13, the angel says, "I am the Elohim of Beyt-El, where you anointed the pillar, and where you vowed a vow unto me." Again, we have an episode where an angel is speaking as YAHUAH. Remember the words of YAHUSHA the Messiah when he said that he does not speak his own words but the words of his Father. Jacob made a vow to the entity above the ladder who spoke to him. Jacob identified him in Genesis 28:16; after Jacob woke from his sleep, he said, "Surely YAHUAH is in this place, and I knew it not."

We have a similar incident in Judges chapter 6 when YAHUAH appears to Gideon, and Gideon receives his Commission. Verse 11 says, "There came an angel of YAHUAH, and sat under an oak." Then, verse 12 says, "And the angel of YAHUAH appeared unto him and said to him YAHUAH is with you. And then, in verse 14, it says, "And YAHUAH looked upon him, and said, go in this your might, and you shall save Yashar'el from the hand of the Midyaniym." I could go on because it interchanges throughout the chapter between verses 11 and verses 24, where you have the Angel of ELOHIYM who had come and was sitting under an oak tree speaking with Gideon; however, when he speaks, Gideon is telling us that it is YAHUAH who is speaking, and it's very telling in verse 23 because Gideon has acknowledged that he has seen an angel of YAHUAH face to face and is afraid he will die. YAHUAH says to Gideon, "Peace be unto you; fear not, you shall not die." Approximately 34 verses tell us, "You cannot see My face, for no man can see my face and live" (Exodus 33:20). Everybody was clear as to the consequences of seeing YAHUAH

However, they are not seeing the totality of YAHUAH. They are only seeing a manifestation created by YAHUAH to be able to interact with his creation so that they would not die. Remember the scene on Mount Sinai, which had to have been a multi-sensory experience for the Israelites. They saw the voice; they witnessed and heard the lightnings, thunderings, fire, and smoke. The energy, frequency, and vibration experienced drove the Israelites away. Years ago, I had a Jewish friend tell me that the Jews reject YAHUSHA, the Messiah, because they do not need a mediator. However, after this experience, they appointed Moses as their mediator because they were afraid that if YAHUAH spoke to them again, they would die.

In Judges 2:1, "An angel of YAHUAH came up from Gilgal to Bokiym and said (to Gideon), I made you to go up out of Mitsrayim, and have brought you unto the land which I swore unto your fathers; and I said, I will never break my Covenant with you." Steven confirms that this Angel is doing all the action, the work of YAHUAH during the exodus. Acts chapter 7 records Stephen saying, "This Mosheh whom they refused, saying, who made you a ruler and a judge? the same did YAHUAH send to be a ruler and a deliverer by the hand of the Angel which appeared to him in the thorn bush". And again, Steven says in verse 38 of Acts chapter 7 that it was "the angel which spoke to him (Moses) in Mount Sinai." Exodus chapter 3 in verse 2 tells us that the Angel of "YAHUAH appeared unto Moses in a flame of fire out of the midst of a thorn bush." In Exodus 14:19, "the angel of ELOHIYM went before the camp of Yashar'el, removed and went behind them; and the pillar of cloud went from before their face, and stood behind them."

We know from Exodus 14:24 that it was YAHUAH himself who went before them by day in a pillar of a cloud; the verse reads, "And it came to pass, that in the morning watch, YAHUAH looked unto the host of the Mitsrayim through the pillar of fire and of the cloud and troubled the host of the Mitsrayim." In Exodus 32:34, YAHUAH tells Moses to go and lead the people to where he had spoken to him about and says again, his Angel shall go before him. Then YAHUAH says something interesting: "Nevertheless, in the day when I visit, I will visit their sin upon them." Isn't it YAHUSHA HAMASHIACH who will be judging? Further, in Exodus 33:2, YAHUAH reminds Moses that his Angel will go before them and drive out the people living in Canaan.

Notice that the Angel of YAHUAH appears in Numbers 22 to the ass of Bil'am, and it is YAHUAH who opens the mouth of the ass and allows it to speak. Then further, the Angel of YAHUAH tells Bil'am to go with the men because, at this point, he is afraid and is going back home. The Angel tells Bil'am to go with the men but only "speak the word that I shall speak to you that you shall speak." Now, when he gets to Balaq, who is requesting that Bil'am curse the Israelites, Bil'am tells Balaq in Numbers 23:15, "Stand here by your burnt offering while I meet YAHUAH yonder. And YAHUAH met Bil'am and put a word in his mouth". Here, again, is another example that leaves the reader to wonder just who is doing the talking. Is it the Angel or YAHUAH? The idea of YAHUSHA as an angel becomes more straightforward when you understand that YAHUAH cannot appear to us in his totality because it would kill us.

Let me be very clear. YAHUSHA, the Messiah, was not created. He was brought forth as a means to interact with a fallen world. Like Paul says in Colossians 14:15, "In whom (YAHUSHA) we have redemption through his blood, even the forgiveness of sins; who is the image of the invisible YAH, the firstborn of every creature." It is the firstborn's duty to guide the family, to keep the family business going. Could Paul be harkening his listeners back to Psalm 89, which says in verse 27, "Also I will make him my firstborn, higher than the kings of the earth"? I know people will say this song is about David. But he was never made higher than the kings of the earth. His horn (kingdom) was never set in the sea, and his right hand in the rivers. This Psalm is talking about the Messiah.

MESSIAH YAHUSHA IS LORD OF THE HOST

YAHUAH, you are the Lord alone; you made heaven and the heaven of heavens and all their positions, the earth and all that is on it, and the sea and all that is in them. You give everything life, and the armies of the heavens do obeisance to you.
- 2 Esdras 19:6 (Septuagint)

The song of Debra, found in Judges 5:2-31 is sung by the judge Deborah and Barack after Israel was delivered from Yaviyn, king of Canaan, and particularly the defeat of Ciycera, the captain of King Yaviyn's host. This song gives a very brief summary of Israel's conquests, and then it details this most recent conflict between Israel and Canaan. Judges 5:4 reads, "YAHUAH, when you went out of Se'iyr when you marched out of the field of Edom, the earth trembled, and the heavens dropped, the clouds also dropped water." Further, in verse 18, you see an interesting detail. It reads, "Zevulun and Naphtaliy were a people that jeopardized their lives unto the death in the high places of the field. The kings came and fought, then fought the kings of Kena'an in Ta'anak by the waters of Megiddo; they took no gain of money. They fought from heaven; the stars in their courses fought against Ciycera. The river of Qiyshon swept them away, that ancient river, the river Qiyshon. O my soul, you have troddened down strength". Did YAH march out of Edom? Did the stars engage in battle? Let us return to the Prayer of Joseph and Jacob's ladder.

In the prayer of Joseph, Jacob is telling Uriel, the archangel, that he, Jacob himself, was an archangel, "the power of the Lord and the chief captain among the sons of YAH." In the vision of the ladder, Jacob sees YAHUAH standing at the top of the ladder and angels ascending and descending. Is this the heavenly host? In Isaiah 54:5, we are told, "Your maker is your husband; YAHUAH TSEVA'OTH is his name; and your Redeemer the Holy One of Yashar'el; The ELOHAI of the whole earth shall he be called." The Septuagint in 2 Esdras 19:6 reads, "And Esdras said: 'You yourself are the Lord alone; you made heaven and the heaven of heavens and all their position, the earth and all that is on it, the sea and all that is in them, and you give everything life, and the armies of the heavens do obeisance to you." In Genesis 2:1 it reads, "Thus the heavens and the earth were finished, and all the hosts of them." The word host is the Hebrew word H6635 Saba, a mass of persons organized for war (an army).

Again, in Genesis 31, we have the Angel of YAH, or YAH himself, speaking to Jacob and telling him to return home. Jacob leaves Laban, his father-in-law. Laban chases Jacob and overtakes him at Gal'ed. After their confrontation and covenant-making, Jacob goes on his way. In chapter 32 of Genesis, we see the heavenly host: it starts in verse 1, "And Ya'aqov went on his way, and the angels of ELOHIYM met him. And when Ya'aqov saw them, he said, this is ELOHIYM's host; and he called the name of that place Machanayim". In the book of Jasher, we have this story in chapter 32. At this point in the story, Jacob has heard that Esau is coming to meet him with an army of 400 men and is praying to YAHUAH for protection. It reads starting in verse 27, "And YAHUAH heard the prayer of Ya'aqov on that day, and YAHUAH then delivered Ya'aqov from the hands of his brother Esau. And YAHUAH sent three angels of the angels of heaven, and they went before Esau and came to him".

Each of these three angels appeared separately to Esau as a host of 2,000 men, "riding upon horses furnished with all sorts of war instruments, and they appeared in the sight of Esau and all his men to be divided into four camps, with four chiefs to them" (verse 29). These angel camps attack Esau and his men in waves, telling them they are the "servants of Ya'aqov who is the servant of ELOHIYM." Esau tells them that he is just coming to see his brother, whom he has not seen in 20 years, but each Angel of the host tells him as their reply that since Esau is the brother of Jacob, he will not be killed. Is this the host that Jacob sees in Genesis 32? And is it also what Zechariah sees in Zechariah 1?

During the reign of King Darius (550-486 BC), Zachariah is shown a vision of a rider on a red horse, and this man stands among Myrtle trees. Pomegranates are of the order of Myrtle. In the Wisdom of Solomon 18:24, we are told that in Aaron's long garment was the entire world. We are given a description of Aaron's garment in Exodus 28. At the top of Aaron's head, you have the NAME of YAHUAH, then you have the ephod, which has the four rows of stones, which is the glory of the Father, and at the bottom of the robe, pomegranates and bells. The famous inventor Nicholas Tesla said that to understand the operation of the world, think about energy, vibration, and frequency. You would have YAHUAH at the head, representing the energy force, and the bells would represent the frequency and vibration that created the world. Because of that, pomegranates would represent the peoples (seeds) of the world. Between the head and feet are the stones which represent the Patriarchs, the sons of Jacob. Much like the ladder Jacob saw.

If the rider of the red horse from Zechariah 1 who stands amongst myrtle trees, are the trees representative of the world? Notice what he says in Zechariah 1:10, "These are they (the red, speckled and white horses) whom YAHUAH has sent to walk to and fro through the earth. And they answered the Angel of YAHUAH that stood among the Myrtle trees and said, "We have walked to and fro through the earth, and behold, all the earth sits still, and is at rest." Notice it is the Angel of YAHUAH who is standing among the myrtle trees. Red, black, white, and spotted horses appear again in Zechariah Chapter 6, pulling chariots out from between two mountains of brass. Zechariah is told these horse-driven chariots represent the four spirits of heaven "which go forth from standing before the ADONAI of all the earth (verse 5). Remember, mountains can represent kingdoms.

This phrase 'walking to and fro in the earth' is repeated in Job 1:6 which reads, "Now there was a day when the sons of ELOHIYM came to present themselves before YAHUAH, and Satan came also among them. And YAHUAH said unto Satan, from whence come you? Satan answered YAHUAH and said, from going to and fro in the earth, and from walking up and down in it". I wonder if this Grove of Myrtle trees is not the grove that Abraham planted in Be'er Sheva in Genesis 21:33; the Targum states that Abraham planted a garden, a paradise, at this well of the seven lambs. I also must wonder if these seven lambs are representative of the seven Holy Angels "who watch" whom Enoch names in chapters 20 and 40.

Do these verses in Zechariah and Genesis give context to the words of YAHUSHA in Matthew 25:31-32? These verses read, "When the Son of Adam shall come in his glory, and all the Holy Angels (host) with him, then shall he sit upon the throne of his glory; and before him shall be gathered all nations; and he shall separate them one from another, as a shepherd divides his sheep from the goats." Notice that he comes with his holy angels, and the people shall be gathered from all the nations before him. This gathering of YAH'S people is reminiscent of Enoch 47:1, which states, "In that day the prayer of the Holy and the righteous, and the blood of the righteous, shall ascend from the earth into the presence of YAHUAH. In that day shall the holy ones

173

assemble, who dwell above the heavens, and with united voice petition, supplicate, praise, laud and bless the name of YAHUAH, on account of the blood of the righteous which has been shed". It appears that Enoch is seeing a resurrection of the dead ascending to meet Angels descending with YAHUSHA and his bride from heaven.

In the Book of Joshua chapter 5, the Israelites are readying themselves to cross the Jordan to inhabit the land of Canaan, and Joshua is confronted by a man with a drawn sword in his hand. Joshua asks this man whether he is for them or against them, and in verse 14, the man replies, "Nay; but as captain of the Host of YAHUAH am I now come. And Yahusha (Joshua the son of Nun) fell on his face to the earth, and did worship, and said unto him, what says my lord unto his servant? And the captain of YAHUAH's Host said unto Yahusha, lose your shoe from off your foot; for the place whereon you stand is holy. And Yahusha did so." Notice how this man said the same thing to Yahusha, son of Nun, as the Angel in the burning bush spoke to Moses.

In Exodus 7:4, YAHUAH tells Moses, "But Pharaoh shall not hearken unto you, that I may lay my hand upon Mitsrayim, and bring forth my armies, and my people, the children of Yashar'el, out of the land of Mitsrayim with great judgments." Notice that 'my armies' are different from 'my people,' the children of Israel. Some will point to Numbers and the census to show that the people are counted and separated by fighting age. Or Exodus 12:17 which says, "And you shall guard the Feast of Matzah; for in this selfsame day have I brought your armies out of the land of Mitsrayim; therefore, shall ye guard this day in your generations by an ordinance forever." Israel did not leave Egypt armed. It was not until after they gathered all the weapons of the fallen Egyptian army, which had washed up along the Reed Sea, that they became armed. But this is a commandment later given to Yashar'el to celebrate the Feast of Matzah. I do not believe the Angelic host would need to be reminded to celebrate any of YAHUAH'S appointed times. However, the armies of Israel would.

Further down in Exodus 12, in verse 41, it says, "And it came to pass at the end of the 430 years, even the selfsame day it came to pass, that all the hosts of YAHUAH went out from the land of Mitsrayim." Remember, YAHUAH had promised to go before Israel to defeat the people inhabiting Canaan.

In 2 Samuel 5:24, the Angelic host is not seen but heard. As King David prepares to battle with the Philistines, he inquires of YAHUAH and is told in verse 23, "You shall not go up, but fetch a compass behind them, and come upon them over against the Mulberry trees. And let it be, when you hear the sound of their going in the tops of the Mulberry trees, that then you shall bestir yourself; for then shall YAHUAH go out before you, to smite the host of the Pelishtiym. And David did so, as YAHUAH had commanded him; and smote the Pelishtiym from Geva until you come to Gezer".

2 Kings chapter 7 tells the story of the four leprous men outside the city gates of Shomeron in Israel. Ben Hadad, king of Aram, had laid siege to the city, and these leprous men decided to go to the Arammiym

camp rather than die in the city gates. They rose at twilight to go into the enemy camp, and nobody was there when they came to the utmost part of the camp. It says in 2 Kings 7:6, "For ADONAI had made the host of the Arammiym to hear a noise of chariots, and a noise of horses, even the noise of a great host, "so they fled for fear of what they had heard.

In the previous chapter of Second Kings, we are shown this host when the prophet Elisha prayed to YAHUAH that his servant's eyes be opened because he was very fearful of this Arammiym host that had come to fetch Elisha to take him captive. In 2 Kings 6:17, it states, "And Eliysha prayed, and said, YAHUAH, I pray you, open his eyes, that he may see. And YAHUAH opened the eyes of the young man, and he saw; and behold, the mountain was full of horses and chariots of fire round about Eliysha". Just like it says in Psalm 34:7, "The angel of YAHUAH encamps round about them that fear him and delivers them."

I would just like to remind the reader here of the host that King David heard was riding atop mulberry trees. Again, are these the same trees from Zachariah 1, which were planted by Abraham? And who is this rider of the red horse? I realize that most of you at this point have already turned to Revelation chapter 6, where the lamb is opening the seals and the second seal releases the red horse, and in verse 4, it reads, "And power was given to him that set there on to take peace from the earth, and that they should kill one another; and there was given unto him a great sword." Remember, in Zachariah, the earth is at peace or rest.

So, at this opening of the second seal, the rider is commanded to remove peace from the earth".

The first seal, which is opened from Revelation chapter 6, releases the white horse, "and he that sat on him had a bow; and a crown was given unto him; and he went forth conquering, and to conquer." This rider looks like the rider described in Revelation chapter 19. However, this rider only has a bow and no arrows. He has one crown. Therefore, I believe this could be a false messiah. The false Messiah will look a lot like our true Messiah. How else could the elect be fooled by him? I do understand there is a belief this rider released by the first seal is the Messiah. I could also agree with this. At the end, YAHUSHA will deliver up all the kingdoms to his father, explaining the many crowns seen later in Revelation chapter 19.

The rider on a white horse in Revelation 19, verses 11-12, is, "Called Faithful and True, and in righteousness he judges and makes war. His eyes were as a flame of fire, and on his head were **many** crowns; and he had a name written that no man knew, but he himself". And further down in verse 14, it states, "And the armies which were in heaven followed him upon white horses, clothed in fine linen, white and clean." Can this rider be the same described in 2 Maccabees (a Chronicle of the Jewish victories against Antiochus Epiphanes, who ruled the Seleucid Empire between 175-164 BC?

In chapter 3, starting in verse 24, Heliodorus was given a warrant by the king to execute a search of the Temple and confiscate any treasure there that was not legal for the priest to have, in other words, to loot the treasury of the Temple. Starting in verse 24, when Heliodorus went to execute the decree at the Temple, he presented himself with his men at the treasury. It states, "YAHUAH TSEVA'OTH, and the prince of all power, caused a great apparition, so that all that presumed to come in with him (Heliodorus) were astonished at the power of ELOHIYM, and fainted, and were sore afraid. For there appeared unto them a horse with a terrible rider upon him, and adorned with a very fair covering, and he ran fiercely and smote at Heliodorus with his four feet, and it seemed that he that sat upon the horse had complete harness of gold. Moreover, two other young men appeared before him, notable in strength, excellent in beauty, and comely in apparel, who stood by him on either side, and scourged him continually, and gave him many sore stripes".

Heliodorus barely made it out of the Temple with his life. And when he reported his failed mission to the king, he said in verse 38, "If you have any enemy or traitor, send him thither, and you shall receive him well scourged, if he escapes with his life; for in that place, no doubt; there is an especial power of ELOHIYM. For he that dwells in heaven has his eye on that place and defends it; and he beats and destroys them that come to hurt it".

Who were these two men accompanying the rider of the white horse? The image of this rider on the white horse defending the Temple reminds me of Messiah's transfiguration as recorded in Matthew chapter 17. It is Moses and Isaiah who appear with YAHUSHA the Messiah. Are these the same two men accompanying the rider from Maccabees? Are they also going to be the two witnesses as recorded in the Book of Revelation chapter 11, where we are told in verse 4 that these two witnesses are the two Olive trees and the two menorahs standing before the YAH of the earth? Notice the word 'and' here. There are two menorahs and two olive trees. Are these men? Remember Enoch chapter 48:5, which states, "Therefore the elect and the concealed one existed in his (YAHUAH TSEVA'OTH) presence, before the world was created and forever."

After this episode from chapter three of 2 Maccabees, the Angelic host is seen again in chapter 5 by the population in Jerusalem. 2 Maccabees 5:1-3 reads, "About the same time Antiochus prepared his second voyage into Mitsrayim; and then it happened that through all the city, for the space almost of forty days, there were seen horsemen running in the air, in cloth of gold, and armed with lances, like a band of soldiers, and troops of horsemen in array, encountering and running one against the other, with shaking of shields, and multitude of pikes, and drawing of swords, and casting of spears, and glittering of golden ornaments, and harness of all sorts. Wherefore every man prayed that that apparition might turn to good", which it did.

The next event in which we see the Angelic host did not turn out so well. In A.D. 66, three and a half years before the destruction of the Temple in Jerusalem, an Angelic host was seen again in Jerusalem and the surrounding cities. These sightings were documented by historians Josephus (a Jewish historian

A.D. 37-100) and the Roman historian Tacitus (c. A.D. 56-120). Josephus writes of the Angelic Army, "I suppose the account of it would seem to be a fable, were it not related by those that saw it, and were not the events that followed it of so considerable a nature as to deserve such signals; for, before sun setting, chariots and troops of soldiers in their armor were seen running about among the clouds and surrounding of cities. Moreover, at that Feast which we call Pentecost, as the priests were going by night into the inner court of the Temple, as their custom was, to perform their sacred ministrations, they said that, in the first place, they felt a quaking, and heard a great noise, and after that they heard a sound as of a great multitude, saying, 'let us remove hence". There were other signs and portends which preceded and proceeded the sighting of this angelic host of which Josephus sadly reports "many had not the eyes to see nor the minds to consider and did not regard the denunciations that God made to them." (Wars 6.5.3)

Tacitus records the sighting of the angelic host in his Histories: "Prodigies had occurred, but their expiation by the offering of victims or solemn vows is held to be unlawful by a nation which is the slave of superstition and the enemy of true beliefs. In the sky appeared a vision of armies in conflict, of glittering armor. A sudden lightning flash from the clouds lit up the Temple. The doors of the holy place abruptly opened, a superhuman voice was heard to declare that the gods were leaving it, and in the same instant came the rushing tumult of their departure. Few people placed a sinister interpretation upon this. The majority were convinced that the ancient scriptures of their priests alluded to the present as the very time when the Orient would triumph and from Judea would go forth men destined to rule the world" (Histories, Book 5, v. 13).

This angelic army would have a commander in chief such as seen by Yahusha ben Nun before crossing into the Promised Land as well as Jacob returning to Canaan. Does this appearance of the Host of YAHUAH fulfill several prophecies given by the Messiah YAHUSHA himself?

In 2 Thessalonians 1:7, Paul said, "And to you who are troubled rest with us, when ADONAI YAHUSHA shall be revealed from heaven with his mighty angels, in flaming fire taking vengeance on them that know not YAHUAH and that obey not the Besorah of our ADONAI YAHUSHA HAMASHIACH." Neither Josephus nor Tacitus identified the head of this angelic host. However, the heavenly host depicted fulfills many of the prophecies made by YAHUSHA, the Messiah, before his death.

In Matthew 24, YAHUSHA gives many details concerning the end times. But could they be double prophecies? Solomon tells us in Ecclesiastes 1:9 from the Septuagint, "What is that which has happened? It is that which will happen! And what is that which has been done? It is that which will be done. And there is nothing new under the sun". In Matthew 24, there is a litany of prophecies given. But first, I believe there is a foreshadowing of things to come when Matthew 24:1-3 tells us that YAHUSHA departed from the Temple with his disciples telling them on the way that there would be not one stone left upon another of this Temple, that it would all be thrown down. Then he sat upon the Mount of Olives.

According to eyewitnesses, the Shekinah Glory removed itself from the Temple and rested on the Mount of Olives, where it remained for three and a half years, from late spring of A.D. 66 to about December of A.D. 69, some eight months before the Temple was destroyed. According to Eusebius in his book Proof of the Gospel, there's a passage that says, "Believers in Christ congregate from all parts of the world, not as of all time because of the glory of Jerusalem, nor that they may worship in the ancient temple at Jerusalem, but... that they may worship at the Mount of Olives opposite to the city, whither the glory of the Lord migrated when it left the former city". (Book VI, chapter 18).

We are told in Zechariah 14:4 that upon the Messiah's return, his feet shall stand upon the Mount of Olives. I think it's important to note that during those three and a half years, the leadership, the priesthood, could have returned to the Torah, repented of their iniquity, and called the people to do the same, and YAHUAH would have returned to them just as he said in Jeremiah 3:14, Malachi 3:7 and Hosea 5:15. Remember Nineveh from the Book of Jonah.

It appears that these eyewitnesses who lived and wrote at the time of these occurrences indicate that YAHUSHA the Messiah is also YAHUAH TSEVA'OTH. I do not want to be accused of being a preterist, someone who believes that all prophecies, especially those of the Book of Revelation, have been fulfilled, and nothing is left to be done regarding prophecy. I am not saying that at all. Just like YAHUSHA said, look for the sign of Daniel, the abomination that would make the altar abominable. That happened during the time of Antiochus IV. It happened at the time before the fall of the second Temple. Their Messiah had come. They had 40 years to repent and accept that their Messiah had come, and they did not. Instead, they continued to make animal sacrifices that were not necessary any longer. Therefore, we must guard against the pollution of our own Temple.

The writer of Hebrews confirms that animal sacrifices were no longer needed when, in Hebrews 10:4, he says, "It is not possible that the blood of bulls and of goats should take away sins." This verse refers to Jeremiah 6:20, Isaiah 1:11-15, and Amos 5:21-23. Then Psalm 40:6-7 is quoted, "In sacrifice and offering you would have no delight, but a body have you prepared me. In burnt offerings and sacrifices for sin you have had no pleasure. Then said I, Lo, I come; in the rolls of the cepher it is written of me, to do your will, O YAH". Of course, we are expected to know the whole of Psalm 40, which should bring the listener to Jeremiah 31 and other psalms about this new song that the Elect will learn, as spoken of in the Book of Revelation, chapter 5, and chapter 14. This new song will speak of YAHUSHA, who has redeemed us with his blood, and only the 144,000 can learn.

Jeremiah 31 is not just a prophecy of the days when the Torah will be written in our inward parts. It is also a prophecy of the coming Messiah. Verse 22 speaks of a woman who will bring forth or cast forth a man and that the whole land of Judah and the cities thereof will discuss this event. The house of Israel and the house of Judah will again go into captivity and "be sewn with the seed of man and with the seed of beast" (Jeremiah 31:27). "It will be in those days they shall say no more, the fathers have eaten a sour grape, and the children's teeth are set on edge. But every one shall die for his own iniquity; every man that eats the sour grape, his teeth shall be set on edge" (verses 29 and 30). Everyone now is responsible for their own salvation. There is no more being accountable for the father's sins to the third and fourth generations. Verse 31-34 says that after those days will, the renewed covenant be cut. When "They shall teach no more every man his neighbor; saying know YAHUAH; for they shall all know me, from the least of them and to the greatest of them, says YAHUAH; for I will forgive their iniquity, and remember their sins no more." Do all men know YAHUAH? Do all men have the Torah written on their hearts? Are we no longer in need of teachers? So, as Solomon said, what has been done will happen again, only this time, as the Book of Revelation says, all the kingdoms of the world will come under the reign of Messiah our King.

In Matthew 24, the disciples have asked a specific question: when will this Temple be destroyed? YAHUSHA gives a list of things that are going to happen. He says many will come in my name, and there will be the release of the red horse with the command to bring wars and rumors of wars, and nation will rise against nation. There will be famines, pestilence, and earthquakes in diverse places, and then he says that is just the beginning. Afterwards, the followers will be afflicted and killed. There will be many false prophets. Transgression of the Torah will abound, and the love of many will fail. Then he says that those who endure to the end shall be saved. We see these events occurred before the destruction of the Temple.

Reading Josephus's History of the Jews and the gospel's accounts of the crucifixion of Mashiach, you could tick off many items on that list YAHUSHA gave his disciples, for the followers of Messiah tribulation began at the arrest. When you read the disciples' stories of their travails and martyrdoms you see that they endured many tribulations as they searched out the lost sheep of the tribes who had been dispersed centuries before and to give them the good news that their awaited Messiah had come.

Matthew 24:30 says, "Then shall appear the sign of the Son of Adam in heaven; and then shall all the tribes of the earth mourn, and they shall see the Son of Adam coming in the clouds of heaven with power and great glory." According to Josephus, this sign or wonder did occur during Pentecost, an appointed time of YAHUAH when all the males were expected to be in Jerusalem at the Temple. Now, the Elect, the disciples, did leave Jerusalem around or right after the martyrdom of James, the brother of YAHUSHA, the Messiah.

We know the disciples were headquartered in Pella. In Hugh Smith's History, we read the following: "Under the reign of Vespasian, Rome declared war against the Jews, because of their repeated revolts and

General Titus besieged the city of Jerusalem in 70 A.D. Approximately eleven hundred thousand Jews perished in the six-month siege. The church there escaped the horrors of the siege by following the instruction of Christ in Matthew 24 and fleeing to the mountains beyond the Jordan. This timely retreat was made to the small town of Pella".

The account Josephus gives of this siege is beyond imagination concerning the horrors committed not just by the Romans but by the citizens of Jerusalem against one another, leading up to the destruction of the temple. In his Church History, the bishop of Caesarea (Circa A.D. 260-340) wrote, "But the people of the church in Jerusalem had been commanded by a revelation, vouchsafed to approved men there before the war, to leave the city and to dwell in a certain town of Peria called Pella. And when those that believed in Christ had come thither from Jerusalem, then, as if the royal city of the Jews and the whole land of Judea were entirely destitute of holy men, the judgment of God at length overtook those who had committed such outrages against Christ and his apostles, and totally destroyed that generation of impious men" (3.5.3). The Romans who had laid siege on the city merely sat outside the walls of Jerusalem and waited while the people inside destroyed themselves with their civil wars. There is a modern maxim attributed to Napoleon, which states to never interfere with an enemy while he is in the process of destroying himself. The siege of Jerusalem in A.D. 70 may have inspired that maxim.

Knowing that this prophecy of YAHUSHA occurred clears up a couple of statements he made to the disciples, which are troublesome to me. For instance, in the gospel of Mark 9:1, YAHUSHA tells his disciples, "Amein I say unto you, that there be some of them that stand here, which shall not taste of death, till they have seen the kingdom of YAHUAH come with power." All the Gospels record this statement YAHUSHA made to his disciples. Now we all know that right after this statement is the transfiguration where he takes Kepha, Ya'aqov, and Yahuchanon up to a high mountain where they see the Transfiguration of Messiah, whom Eliyahu and Mosheh accompany. It is possible that they witnessed the kingdom of heaven, given the possibility that Eliyahu and Mosheh, as well as Kepha, Ya'aqov, and Yahuchanon, were elected from the foundation of the world.

However, that explanation fails to clear up Mark 14:61-62 which occurs just before the crucifixion. When being questioned by the high priest, YAHUSHA "held his peace and answered nothing. Again, the high priest asked him, and said unto him, are you HAMASHIACH, the SON of the BLESSED? And YAHUSHA said, "I am; and you shall see the Son of Adam sitting on the right hand of power and coming in the clouds of heaven". Clement of Alexandria [A.D. 153-193-217] in Fragments from Cassiodorus page 574 says concerning this passage, "But powers mean the holy angels. Further, when he says at the right hand of God, he means the selfsame [beings] by reason of the equality and likeness of the angelic and holy powers, which are called by the name of God. He

187

says, therefore, that he sits at the right hand; that is, that he rests in preeminent honor". This thought reminds me of Philo's image of the three men or angels who visited Abraham at the tent of Mamre, where the three become one, and the two other angels are mere shadows of YAHUAH. The same could be said of the three angels who approached Esau whom were seen as a host of 2,000.

All the apostles anticipated the return of YAHUSHA, the Messiah, within their lifetimes. The Gospel of John 21:22-23 states, "YAHUSHA said unto him, if I will that he tarry till I come, what is that to you? Follow me. Then went this saying abroad among the brethren, that that Talmidiy should not die: yet YAHUSHA said not unto him, he shall not die; but, if I will that he tarry till I come, what is that to you"? According to the above listed accounts of the angelic host being seen in the surrounding cities of Jerusalem it is possible the Disciples seen the angelic host being led by the Messiah YAHUSHA. This host led by a captain acting under the command of the Most High ELOHIYM, fulfills many New Testament scriptures:

1. Matthew 10:23, "But when they persecute you in this city, flee ye into another; for amein, I say unto you, Ye shall not have gone over the cities of Yashar'el, till the son of Adam is come." See also Mark 9:1, Mark 14:61-62 and John 21:23, as covered above.

2. Matthew 24:30, "Then shall appear the sign of the Son of Adam in heaven and then shall all the tribes of the earth mourn, and they shall see the Son of Adam coming in the clouds of heaven with power and great

glory." in Mark 14:62, YAHUSHA tells the high priest that he would see the "Son of Adam sitting on the right hand of power and coming in the clouds of heaven."

3.   Mark 8:38, "Whosoever, therefore, shall be ashamed of me and of my words in this adulterous and sinful nation; of him also shall the Son of Adam be ashamed, when he comes in the glory of his Father with the holy angels." see Matthew 16:27 as well as 1 Thessalonians 1:7 which has been covered above. This supernatural specter appears to be the Messiah coming to his kingdom. This was seen by many people around the cities of Judea, accompanied by lightning resembling fire, and by those who had seen it as an army.

Another heavenly occurrence was observed approximately 1500 years later over the skies of Nuremberg, Germany, in 1561. There was a Celestial phenomenon that was recorded in a broadsheet which reads:

In the morning of April 14, 1561, at daybreak, between 4 and 5 am, a dreadful apparition occurred on the sun, and then this was seen In Nuremberg in the city, before the gates and in the country – by many men and women. At first there appeared in the middle of the sun two blood-red semi-circular arcs, just like the moon in its last quarter. And in the sun, above and below and on both sides, the color was blood, there stood a round ball of partly dull, partly black ferrous color. Likewise, there stood on both sides and as a torus about the sun such blood-red ones and other balls *in large number, about three in a line and four in a square, also some alone. In between these globes there were visible a few blood-red crosses, between which there were blood-red strips, becoming thicker to the rear and in the front malleable like the rods of reed-grass, which were intermingled, among them two big rods, one on the right, the other to the left, and within the small and big rods there were three, also four and more globes. These all started to fight among themselves, so that the globes, which were first in the sun, flew out to the ones standing on both sides, thereafter, the globes standing outside the sun, in the small and large rods, flew into the sun. Besides the globes flew back and forth among themselves and fought vehemently with each other for over an hour. And when the conflict in and again out of the sun was most intense, they became fatigued to such an extent that they all, as said above, fell from the sun down upon the earth 'as if they all burned' and they then wasted away on the earth with immense smoke. After all this there was something like a black spear, very long and thick, sighted; the shaft pointed to the east, the point pointed west. Whatever such signs mean, God alone knows. Although we have seen, shortly one after another, many kinds of signs on the heaven, which are sent to us by the almighty God, to bring us to repentance, we still are, unfortunately, so ungrateful that we despise such high signs and miracles of God. Or we speak of them with ridicule and discard them to the wind, in order that God may send us a frightening punishment on account of our ungratefulness. After all, the God-fearing will by no means discard these signs, but will take it to heart as a warning of their merciful Father in heaven, will mend their lives and faithfully beg God, that He may avert His wrath, including the well-deserved punishment, on us, so that we may temporarily here and perpetually there, live as his children. For it, may God grant us his help, Amen. By Hanns Glaser, letter-painter of Nurnberg*

In 1566 over Basel, Switzerland, a similar phenomenon occurred and was recorded in a pamphlet as follows:

It happened in 1566 three times, on 27 and 28 of July, and on August 7, against the sunrise and sunset; we saw strange shapes in the sky above Basel. During the year 1566, on the 27th of July, after the sun had shone warm on the clear, bright skies, and then around 9 pm, it suddenly took a different shape and color. First, the sun lost all its radiance and luster, and it was no bigger than the full moon, and finally it seemed to weep tears of blood and the air behind him went dark. And he was seen by all the people of the city and countryside. In much the same way also the moon, which has already been almost full and has shone through the night, assuming an almost blood-red color in the sky. The next day, Sunday, the sun rose at about six o'clock and slept with the same appearance it had when it was lying before. He lit the houses, streets and around as if everything was blood-red and fiery. At the dawn of August 7, we saw large black spheres coming and going with great speed and precipitation before the sun and chattered as if they led a fight. Many of them were fiery red and soon crumbled and then extinguished.

Did these people witness the war in heaven as described in Revelation 12:7-11? Was Satan and his angels cast out of heaven? Is it a coincidence that before this event, German astronomer Nicholas Copernicus (2/19/1473 to 5/24/1543) wrote Revolutions of the Celestial Spheres, published just before his death, which influenced German astronomer Johannes Kepler (12-27-1571 to 11-15-1630), who became the key figure in the 17th-century Scientific Revolution, which dethroned the holy scriptures as the source of truth? Is it a coincidence that in 1878, German engineer Carl Humann started dismantling the altar of Zeus from the abandoned city of Pergamum and eventually took it to Berlin? The altar was stored until 1910 when a museum was built for the altar's display. Because of World War I, the museum was not opened for visitors until 1930, when it was displayed with a reconstruction of the Ishtar gate of ancient Babylon, otherwise known as the Gate of hell. Coincidence? I think not. Three years later, Adolf Hitler became Chancellor of Germany, and the third iteration of the Roman Empire, otherwise known as the Third Reich, rose from the ashes. Most believe the Axis powers won that war, World War II. However, a study of the United States Project Paperclip proves we might have won the battle but lost the war. But that is something that you need to study for yourself.

In conclusion, it occurred to me that some would read this and conclude that I am conflating YAHUAH TSEVA'OTH with the Nephilim from the Old Testament, spoken about in Genesis chapter 6. I want to clarify that I am not drawing any kind of comparison. In Genesis 6, angels left their heavenly estate, came to earth, and mated with human women who gave birth to Nephilim, i.e., giants. Now, these children were not meant to be, so that when they died, their spirits remained here on earth and became demons. I have spoken about these. After the flood, YAHUAH agreed with Noah to chain them all up. However, the leader of these demons bargained with YAHUAH to leave some, and according to the book of Jasher, 10% remained on earth so that man could be tried or tempted.

We get more details of this fall from The Book of Enoch. You will not be able to understand Genesis 6 or even the whole of scripture without reading The First Book of Enoch. I am saying there is a significant difference between Jacob, Abraham, Isaac, and all the Elect who existed in the presence of YAHUAH TSEVA'OTH before the world was created, as mentioned in Enoch 48, and these fallen ones. These angels who left their heavenly home and came to earth did so without the permission of YAHUAH. If they had waited, he would not have been so angry as never to grant them forgiveness. They did not wait, like Abraham and

Sharah who not wait for YAHUAH to deliver her the promised child; thus, we have Ishmael.

The difference between these Fallen ones and our Patriarchs is that of their offspring: some were not meant to be, and the others were fully human. Those who waited were sent, tried, and overcame to the end of their lives. I do understand that there is a belief out there that Genesis 6 is merely talking about the sons of Seth coming down from the mountain and having sex with Caine's daughters. But that makes no sense to me, and it does not solve the issue of where all these giants mentioned in the Old Testament come from.

Enoch tells us in chapter 54 that there is a place prepared for the host of Aza; he has an army. I imagine his host is organized much like YAHUAH's host, as we are told in 1 Samuel 22, 2 Samuel 18, First Chronicles 13, 27,29, and 2 Chronicles 1 and 17. Satan's host would also have its own captain. All sin is attributed to Aza. In Leviticus 16:8, YAHUAH gives instructions for the sacrifice of Yom Kippur. Two goats are brought before the priests for sacrifice, of which lots are cast, one being sacrificed to YAHUAH, and the other is led out to Aza in the wilderness. In chapter 69, Enoch lists five watchers/angels who precede these fallen ones from Genesis 6 and are present in Genesis 3. The one who seduced Eve is listed. Now you must ask how this temptation in the Garden of Eden, the seduction of Eve which caused the fall of mankind, occurred. This entity, we learn from the First Book of Adam and Eve, took over the body of the snake who allowed this entity to speak through him. The snake's sin for which he was punished was to let evil abide in him. More important for the topic is this Angel who prevailed upon the angels, as mentioned in Genesis 6, to leave their heavenly abode and come to earth to take wives.

The Hebrew word for scapegoat in Leviticus 16:18 is H5799 Azazel, which comes from H5795 ez, which means she-goat. However, that word comes from the primitive root word H5810 Azaz, which means harden, impotent, prevail, strengthen as in self, or be strong. The other word that forms scapegoat, H5799 Azazel, is H235 Azal, which is a primitive root word that means to go away, hence, to disappear. So, what we have here is not the word scapegoat. Instead, it is the name of an entity that was impudent and turned away from his creator, who also prevailed upon his friends to turn away from their creator and leave their heavenly home. Therefore, all sin is attributed to him.

Enoch names the Angel who "pointed out evil counsel to the sons of the holy angels and induced them to corrupt their bodies by generating mankind." Here, we see these angels who were led astray have a problem figuring out how to accomplish the deed of procreating with human women. They were taught by another angel how to change their bodies to accomplish the deed. Like YAHUSHA, the Messiah, said in Matthew 22:28, angels were not given wives. He was quoting Enoch chapter 15. Therefore, the children who were created by this unholy union had no place for their souls to go once they died.

According to Enoch, these spirits remain on earth as demon spirits "who shall cause lamentation. No food shall they eat; and they shall be thirsty; they shall be concealed, and shall rise up against the sons of men, and against women; for they come forth during the days of slaughter and destruction". So, a lesson here would be that just because you can do it does not mean you should. But the most important lesson here is that you wait on YAHUAH ELOHIYM. From the Kolbrin bible chapter 15 of The Voice of EL, there are many I am statements made by ELOHIYM. Here are two of them: "I am the EL of consciousness, the listener in the silences." And "I am the EL of silences." We are to be quiet and wait.

2 Thessalonians 2:13 will make sense now. It reads, "We are bound to give thanks always to YAH for you, brethren beloved of YAHUAH because YAH has from the beginning chosen you to yeshu'ah through sanctification of the RUACH and belief of the truth'. Remember, truth and life equal Torah. I do not believe in predestination, so let us clear that up. However, we are chosen, as Paul says from the beginning, to go on this sojourn here on earth to prove our hearts to Elohim. As YAHUSHA said, if you love me, you will keep my commandments (John 14:15). As you continue to read in John 14, there is an 'and' after verse 15. So, it all reads, "If you love me, guard my commandments. **And** I will pray to the Father, **and** he shall give you another comforter, that he may abide with you forever". So, you do not get that Holy Spirit until you have met the prior conditions: to love YAHUSHA the Messiah, and because you love YAHUSHA, you will commit to guard his commandments, then He will pray for you. Men are appointed once to die, Hebrews 9:27, and it is up to us to choose whether we

obtain eternal life or participate in the second death (Revelation chapters 20 and 21).

Paul mentions the elect again in 2 Timothy 2:10: "Therefore I endure all things for the elect's sakes, that they may also obtain the salvation which is in MASHIACH YAHUSHA with eternal glory." The Hebrew word yeshu'ah means salvation. In the Aramaic, the word salvation means life. When you see the word salvation in your text, you can translate it as eternal life or Torah in other places. But to my point, Paul here in 2nd Timothy is talking to the Elect, and it is the Elect, according to Enoch, who resided in the presence of YAHUAH from the beginning. Turn to your scriptures and read the fourth book of Psalms, Chapters 90 through 106. Now, you will see that this book talks about YAHUAH TSEVA'OTH, the Lord of The Host who has prepared his throne in the heavens. Remember, the heavens are a creation, and Psalm 103:20 tells the angels to "bless YAHUAH, ye his angels, that excel in strength, that do his commandments, hearkening unto the voice of his word. Bless ye YAHUAH, all his hosts; Ye ministers of all Ministers of his, that do his pleasure".

MESSIAH YAHUSHA IS OUR JUDGE AND HIGH PRIEST

Here now, O Yahusha the high priest, you, and your fellows that sit before you; for they are men wondered at; for, behold, I will bring forth my servant the BRANCH. For behold the stone that I have laid before Yahusha; upon one stone shall be seven eyes; the whole I will engrave the graving thereof, YAHUAH TSEVA'OTH, and I will remove iniquity of that land in one day. In that day, says YAHUAH TSEVA'OTH, shall you call every man his neighbor under the vine and under the fig tree. - Zechariah 3:8- 10

What exactly does it mean to be the judge and high priest? As we seen from the previous chapter YAHUAH, Lord of The Host, led his people in battle. He and his host went out into battle before King David. During the time of Yahusha ben Nun, YAHUAH went before the Israelites defeating the peoples of Canaan. The Host went before Jacob as he was coming home from Haran with his wives and children. YAHUAH and his host went before the Israelites during the time of Judge Deborah. The judges were all military leaders for Israel. Jacob, during his battle with the Angel Uriel, called himself 'a chief captain" among the angels.

When I see the word captain, I usually think of a commissioned officer in the military. A captain is not the highest rank; however, he is the highest-ranking company officer, leading anywhere from 60 to 200 enlisted soldiers. However, when interpreting the Bible, we need to see how the Bible uses the word captain. We see in The Book of Numbers chapter 2 that after each male was counted, there was named a captain over the whole of each of the twelve tribes. Then we see later that there are appointed under these princes i.e., tribal leaders, captains of thousands and of hundreds. In 1 Chronicles 27:1, we see the leaders described as "the chief fathers and captains of thousands and hundreds, and their officers that serve the king in any matter of the courses." This description is repeated in 1 Chronicles 29:6. In 1 Samuel 18:13, King Saul makes David a captain over a thousand men. There are numerous scriptures where we see the phrase captains over thousands and captains over hundreds. But are any of these Chief captains, as Jacob called himself during the fight with the angel Uriel?

In 1 Samuel chapter 8, we learn that after Samuel was old, he made his sons judges over Israel, and because they were not righteous men, Israel requested to have a king because they wanted to be "like all the nations; and that our king may judge us, and go out before us, and fight our battles". In 1 Samuel 9:16, Samuel is told to anoint Saul Captain over Israel. This anointing made him king over all twelve tribes. In this instance, Captain equals king, and because he is King over all the tribes of Israel, it would be a chief captain, right? Because the king is the ultimate judge, he is what we today would consider our commander-in-chief who leads our nation into battle.

However, when considering Uriel and Jacob, let us not forget Deuteronomy 32:8, where YAHUAH divided the nations amongst his angels. Israel was just one of many nations. Let us consider the rider of the white horse in Revelation chapter 6 who is given one crown, then remember the words of YAHUSHA the Messiah when he says in several places that he is sent to gather the lost sheep of Israel and that they will be gathered out of many nations. While gathering these sheep, is our Messiah conquering these nations only to deliver them up to the Father, as Paul states in 1 Corinthians 15:24?

I have not forgotten what Isaiah 43:10-11 says, "Ye are my witnesses; and my servant whom I have chosen: that ye may know and believe me, and understand that I am he: before me there was no El formed, neither shall there be after me. I, even I, am YAHUAH, and besides me, there is no yeshu'ah (salvation)". Isaiah 46:9 says, "Remember the former things of old: for I am EL, and there is none else. I am ELOHIYM, and there is none like me." These verses leave no doubt in the readers or the listeners' minds concerning a plurality of YAHUAH.

The Pharisees wanted to destroy YAHUSHA because he made himself equal to YAHUAH, a sin worthy of death. He had admitted to being the Son of ELOHIM (Matthew 27:43 and John 10:36), which I covered already. Remember, in Mark 14:62, YAHUSHA said, "I am: and you shall see the Son of Adam sitting on the right hand of power and coming in the clouds of heaven." The high priest tore his clothing at this and said, "What need we any further witnesses?" The words "I am' in this verse is the Aramaic 'ena na' which indicates that YAHUAH is speaking through him. Also, remember John chapter 10, the Yahudiym took up stones to stone him after he had said that he and the Father were one, and then in verse 36, YAHUSHA says he is the Son of Elohim.

In Mark chapter 3, YAHUSHA heals, on the Sabbath, the man with the withered hand, hearkening back to Exodus 4:6-7 where YAHUAH made Moses put his hand to his bosom. When he took it out, it was leprous, then YAHUAH had Moses repeat the process, and when Moses brought out his hand again, it was healed. Remember, this was a sign Moses was to show the Israelites living in Egypt to prove to them that YAHUAH had sent him. The Pharisees would have recognized this as a sign that the Most High ELOHIYM sent YAHUSHA. It should be noted at this point that YAHUSHA, the Messiah, was not a lawgiver. But neither was Moses to be honest. Most all the Ten Commandments that were written on stone tablets by the hand of YAHUAH were clearly given prior to Noah's flood. Therefore, YAHUSHA was the man whom YAHUAH chose to reveal his Torah.

All of Judea were looking for a prophet like Moses as promised in Deuteronomy 18:18, who would deliver them their physical kingdom. It is obvious to me that they had no faith that YAHUSHA could deliver Israel from Roman rule. Hence, Caiaphas' counsel in John 18:14. The chief priests and scribes sought to kill YAHUSHA because they feared the people (Luke 22:2). Because the people were astonished by YAHUSHA's doctrine (Mark 11:18), the Pharisees feared the challenge YAHUSHA posed to their authority. These chief priests and scribes were afraid the people would Proclaim YAHUSHA king, resulting in Rome coming in force and squashing what they perceived as a rebellion in Judea. How is it that these Pharisees disregarded the prophecies of the suffering messiah?

YAHUSHA, in Luke chapter 11, proclaimed that he was a greater prophet than Jonah and a greater one than the greatest King, King Solomon. I covered Jonah concerning his sign. Besides being in the belly of the whale for three days, he was thrown overboard and killed, or so the men thought, to save the many men on the ship. However, I cannot think of a single prophet who brought a nation to repentance and a foreign nation at that. Jonah would have been aware of the prophecy of Isaiah telling how the King of Assyria, who resided in Nineveh, would be brought up by YAHUAH against Israel. Once you know this, it is easy to understand why Jonah did not want to go to Nineveh. He knew these people would be used to destroy Israel, and he was sent to save them, to bring them to repentance. Jonas's anger is understandable when Nineveh repented, and their destruction did not come. YAHUSHA was sent to redeem the descendants of Adam if they recognized his divinity, accepted his blood, and sacrifice, thus bringing us to repentance so that we may covenant with YAHUAH, our Father.

With that said, you can see how bold of a statement YASHUAH made, saying that he was greater than Jonah and King Solomon. King Solomon was endowed with the wisdom of YAH. YAHUSHA stating that he is better than Solomon should make one wonder about wisdom. If Solomon was full of YAHUAH'S wisdom, then to be greater than Solomon would be claiming to be wisdom itself. Hearing this statement of YAHUSHA, the Pharisees would understand that he is equating himself with the wisdom of the Most High ELOHIYM, which would be equating himself with YAHUAH.

In The Book of Mark chapter 2, before YAHUSHA healed the man's withered hand, his disciples were admonished for gathering grain into their hands and eating on the Sabbath as they were on their way to synagogue. In verse 28, YAHUSHA says, "For the son of Adam is Lord of the Sabbath." The word Sabbath is G4521 sabbaton in the Strong's Concordance. This word can also be used in the plural form. Therefore, what YAHUSHA, the Messiah, is really saying is that he is Lord of the feasts, all the Sabbaths. YAHUAH instructs the Israelites to keep **HIS** feasts in Leviticus chapter 23, and then the times of these Feasts are given. The party invitation was or has been given, and it is up to us to meet or appear at the time indicated on that invitation.

It would be terribly impolite for us to receive a birthday party invitation for a specific date but then decide to show up at a date and time that is more to our liking. This is what we do as Christians. Read Leviticus chapter 23 to see if you are attending the correct party.

YAHUSHA calls himself Lord again in John 13:13, where he says, "You call me Rabbi and Adonai: and you say well; for so I am." Rabbi means teacher, and Adonai means Lord. In the Aramaic, he says, "I am master and Lord". He quotes Psalm 41:9 about one of his betraying him, then says, "I tell you before it come, that, when it is come to pass, you may believe that I am he." Like Paul, YAHUSHA expected his disciples to know the rest of this Psalm. The last Psalm of book one is about a blessed man who is hated and reviled. This blessed man dies after being betrayed by a friend but will be raised up and set before YAHUAH'S face forever. YAHUSHA is directly telling his disciples he is fulfilling this prophecy.

I wonder if YAHUSHA, the Messiah, when he tells his disciples they speak well by calling him rabbi is intimating the fulfillment of the prophecy from Zechariah Chapter 3:3 where his name appears. I used to think that the Yahusha spoken of there is Yahusha ben Nun, the deliverer of Israel from the Book of Joshua. However, Yahusha ben Nun was never a priest. He was a warrior and Israel's military leader. From scripture, Yahusha ben Nun was never promised a priesthood or that he would judge the world. If you go to Zechariah 3:6, the verse begins, "And the angel of YAHUAH protested unto YAHUSHA." But the word there for protest can also mean to repeat. The Most High is repeating the promise he had made to YAHUSHA. The bargain was, "If you will walk in my ways, and if you will guard my watch, then you shall also judge my house, and shall also guard my courts, and I will give you places to walk among these that stand by."

Keep in mind that in Zechariah 4:7, it is the mountain being addressed there, not Zerubbabel, again reminding us that mountains are not merely a land feature. Is this chapter in Zechariah about how the belief came about that the Messiah would be a king and priest? Notice that Yahusha will judge his house, which means he is a military leader. And he shall guard my courts, meaning that he will be set up in the temple. This king and priest took on our infirmities (Isaiah 53:4) by clothing himself in filthy garments (Zechariah 3:3-4).

What does all this mean? What is he talking about when YAHUAH says to YAHUSHA, guard my watch, judge my house, guard my courts, then He will be placed among these that stand by? I believe I have established that to judge means to militarily lead. But what about the priesthood and the affairs of the temple? Consider also that Moses was not the High Priest, that office went to Aaron and his sons. Let us examine the administration of the second temple. First was the high priest, his deputy and then his two attendants. There existed a Priestly guard which consisted of three priests: one to guard the chamber of the flame, the second guarded the chamber of the hearth and the third guarded the chamber of the abtinas (attic).

The affairs of the temple were managed by a board of 15 appointed officers. These officers oversaw the following duties:

1. Officer in charge of the seals given in exchange for money to purchase sacrifices.
2. Libations
3. The selection of priests of the day.
4. Nests of fowls for sacrifices.
5. Health department.
6. Digging wells.
7. Announcements (Temple crier).
8. Gates, opening and closing.
9. Wicks for the candle sticks
10. Music leader
11. Musical instruments
12. Preparation of the showbread
13. Incense
14. Curtains
15. Vestments

Besides these Priestly duties toward the operation of the Temple itself you had 21 Levites whose jobs it was to guard specific locations on the temple grounds. These locations were as follows:

1. The five gates at the Temple mount entrances.
2. The four corners of the mount enclosure.
3. The five important gates of the court.
4. The four corners within the court.
5. The chamber of sacrifice.
6. The chamber of Curtains.
7. Behind the Holy of Holies.

Then there was a captain of the Guard who saw that every man was alert, chastening a priest if found asleep at his post, and sometimes even punishing him by burning his shirt upon him, as a warning to the others. Notice how this captain of the Guard comes with fire and burns those who are asleep on the job.

Did the high priest oversee all these jobs? Are these similar jobs Moses was to delegate (Exodus 18:21)? Did Moses follow the advice of Jethro, his father-in-law? If he appointed these men, did he relegate authority to them? I am not sure that he did because later YAHUAH himself told Moses to appoint leaders. Was Moses King and priest as well as a prophet, and mediator who stood between the people and YAHUAH'S wrath?

Do we see the office of the high priest in Exodus 17? During Israel's first battle after the Exodus, you see Moses positioned on a hill sitting on a rock. Beside Moses are two attendants, his brother Aaron and their nephew Chur, who eventually must hold up Moses's arms because of weariness. Meanwhile, Yahusha, Moses's deputy, is leading the battle against the Amalekites. Is this an image of the kingdom of Heaven, i.e., The Rock, his prophet, the two witnesses, and a commander-in-chief?

Throughout his ministry, YAHUSHA spoke and performed deeds equating himself with YAHUAH, making himself even greater than Moses. In Matthew 9:6, YAHUSHA boldly proclaims that you may know that the "Son of Adam has power on earth to forgive sins." Since only YAHUAH can forgive sins, then YAHUSHA cannot merely be a son, but ELOHIYM himself and the Pharisees recognized this and cried blasphemy when

YAHUSHA forgave a man's sins after healing him in Mark chapter 2.

In Isaiah 43:25, YAHUAH says, "I, even I, am He that blots out your transgressions for my own sake and will not remember your sins." Isaiah 1:18 in the Targum states, "Then, when you return to the law, you shall pray before me, and I will grant your petition, sayeth the Lord. Though your sins be stained as with dye, they shall be white as snow; though they be crimson, they shall be white as snow". Psalm 130:4 says, "But there is forgiveness with you, that you may be feared." Daniel 9:9, 'To ADONAI ELOHAYNU belong mercies and forgivenesses, though we have rebelled against him". Isaiah 55:7, "Let the wicked forsake his way of wickedness, and the man of violence his thoughts, and let him return to the worship of YAHUAH and he will have mercy upon him; and to our ELOHIYM, for he will abundantly pardon."

I could go on, but the point is made, YAHUSHA created quite the stir when he stated in Matthew 12:31-32 that sins against the RUACH HAKODESH wouldn't be forgiven and "whoever speaks a word against the Son of Adam, it shall be forgiven him" hearkening us back to Isaiah 48:16,17 which reads,, "Come ye near unto me (EL), hear ye this; I have not spoken in secret from the beginning; from the time that it was, there am I: and now ADONAI YAHUAH, and his RUACH, has sent me. Thus says YAHUAH, your Redeemer, the Holy One of Yashar'el; I am YAHUAH ELOHAYKA, which teaches you to profit and leads you by the way that you should go." Who has YAHUAH and his spirit sent? It has to be an angel who prepares the way.

The writer of Hebrews chapter 10 speaks of this judgment when he says that transgressors of the Torah of Moses died without mercy by two or three witnesses. There was no mercy given to people who transgressed the law, remember the man who was found gathering wood on the Sabbath. Then the writer of Hebrews asks, "How much more sorer punishment, suppose you, shall he be thought worthy, who has trodden underfoot the Son of ELOHIYM, and has counted the blood of the covenant, wherewith he has been sanctified, an unholy thing, and has done despite unto the Spirit of Grace. For we know him that has said, vengeance belongs unto me, I will recompense, says YAHUAH". The writer quotes YAUAH's words in Deuteronomy 32:35-36, those who bring to nothing this grand and wondrous work YAHUAH accomplished in the death and resurrection of YAHUSHA HAMASHIACH.

The Pharisees had accused YAHUSHA of demon possession and using that power to heal, thus grieving the Holy Spirit YAHUAH himself. YAHUSHA is Torah in the flesh, the Word, and he laid down his life so that we may enter into covenant with him. He will be the one who will judge by the law, and since he is the judge, he also is the sole authority that can forgive. The Pharisees correctly perceived these statements as Divinity statements YAHUSHA made in both word and deed. However, they would have been better served had they remembered Exodus 23:20-22 which I will repeat here: "Behold, I send an angel before you to guard you in the way, and to bring you into the place which I have prepared. Beware of him, and obey his voice, provoke him not; for he will not pardon your transgressions: for my name is in him. But if you shall indeed obey his voice and do all that I speak, then I will be an enemy to your enemies and an adversary to your adversaries". YAHUAH is speaking through this angel. It is his voice that they heard. Again, the text changes from the Angel shall go, to I YAHUAH will cut off enemies and bless Israel for their obedience to him. When YAHUSHA forgave sins, he was signaling that he was this angel from Exodus 23 leading the way to eternal life and speaking YAHUAH'S words.

212

MESSIAH YAHUSHA IS THE LIGHT OF THE WORLD

In the beginning ELOHIYM created the heavens and the earth. And the earth was without form and void; and darkness was upon the face of the deep. And the RUACH ELOHIYM moved upon the face of the waters. And ELOHIYM said, let there be light and there was light and ELOHIYM saw the light, that it was good and ELOHIYM divided the light from the darkness. Genesis 1: 1-4

The sun, moon and stars were not created until the 4th day, so what is this light? It can be none other than the Messiah himself. And the Darkness was divided from the light. Keep in mind the next action of ELOHIYM was to create the firmament which divided earth from heaven thus limiting access to heaven and to earth. Remember what the writer said in Hebrews 5:12 when he told the

Hebrews that they should go back to the beginning of the scriptures to learn the meat of the issue. He scolded them because they needed a teacher to teach them the first principles: the truth of Genesis 1:1-4: YAHUSHA is the light of the world.

YAHUSHA stated that he was the light of the world in John 8:12. Also, in John 1:4-5 when speaking of the beginning, John reminds us the Word was the "light of men. And the light shines in darkness; and the darkness comprehended it not". Luke, in chapter 1:78-79 states, "Through the tender mercy of our YAHUAH where by the dayspring from on high has visited us, to give light to them that sit in darkness and in the shadow of death, to guide our feet into the way of peace." So here, the light is equated with wisdom, the knowledge of the Torah.

Luke further states in 11:35, "Take heed therefore that the light which is in you be not darkness. If your whole body therefore be full of light, having no part dark, the whole shall be full of light, as when the bright shining of a candle gives you light". Again, light is the wisdom or knowledge of the Torah. And remember that YAHUAH promised to walk in us. This is possible if we accept that YAHUSHA HAMASHIACH is YAHUAH made flesh, the WORD of YAHUAH, which made all things that are made, thus making him Torah itself, the living breathing WORD of ELOHIYM, the light which dwells in us, if we accept it; that being truth/Torah.

Let us consider the parable of the ten virgins, which YAHUSHA the Messiah told in Matthew chapter 25. Verse 1 from the Aramaic, reads, "Then let the kingdom of heaven be likened to those ten virgins who took their lamps and went out for the meeting of the bride and the bridegroom." Now, the bride is not mentioned in the Greek manuscripts. However, according to the new Greek English Interlinear New Testament by Robert Brown and Philip Comfort (United Bible Society 4th edition, Nestle-Aland 26th edition), some ancient Greek texts agree with the Peshitta. Without the bride, the passage allows for the virgins to marry one man, which would have been against YAHUSHAS' teaching from Matthew 19:3-8. These ten virgins are not the bride. Psalm 45 should come to mind. Remember that these were the top 40 of their day; everybody could sing the songs. This song tells of the queen who sits at the right hand of ELOHIYM, and she will be accompanied by "the virgins her companions."

This parable could be hearkening his listeners to the prophecy in Zechariah 8:23, which states, "Thus said YAHUAH TSEVA'OTH; in those days it shall come to pass, that ten men shall take hold out of all languages of the nations, even shall take hold of the skirt of him that is a Yahudiy, saying, we will go with you: for we have heard that ELOHIYM is with you." Remember, at this time, Israel, the ten northern tribes, were divorced from YAHUAH and spread to the four corners of the earth, making them the other nations. Again, in Acts 2:5, "And there were dwelling in Yerushalayim Yahudiym, devoted men, out of every nation under heaven." This idea of these 10 men taking hold of the skirt of a Jew brings to mind the woman with the issue of blood who in Matthew 9:20 was cured after touching YAHUSHA the Messiah's tsiytsith (fringes of his garment). And also, Matthew 14:36 where the men of Kinneroth asked YAHUSHA that they might only touch the tsiytsith of His garment: "And as many as touched were made perfectly whole".

YAHUSHA the Messiah would have worn tsiytsith on his garment as commanded by YAHUAH to Moses in numbers 15:38-41 which reads, "Speak unto the children of Yashar'el, and bid them that they make them tsiytsith in the borders of their garments throughout their generations, and that they put upon the tsiytsith of the borders a ribbon of blue: and it shall be unto you a tsiytsith, that you may look upon it, and remember all the commandments of YAHUAH, and do them; and that ye seek not after your own heart and your own eyes, after which you used to go a whoring; that ye may remember, and do all my commandments, and be holy unto your ELOHIYM. I am YAHUAH ELOHAYKEM, which brought you out of the land of Mitsrayim, to be your ELOHIYM: I am YAHUAH ELOHAYKEM." These people who are touching the fringes of the Messiahs garment and being healed by them, I believe are remembering and acknowledging the commandments of YAHUAH and are healed through the power of YAHUSHA the Messiah, the living breathing commandments of YAHUAH.

Let us return to the parable of the 10 virgins. These ten virgins had lamps. Proverbs 6:23 says, "The Commandment is a lamp; and the Torah is light; and reproof of instruction are the way of life." So again, when YAHUSHA says he is the way, the Truth, and the life, he talks about the light, the eternal life promised in the Torah. The Truth and the Commandment is a lamp that lights the way. Think again of Gideon's lamps. YAHUSHA is the living, breathing Torah made flesh. He is the lamp, and his spirit is the light, the flame that is within. But what is the oil?

The Song of Solomon 1:3 tells us, "Because of the savor of your good ointments [oils], your name is as ointment poured forth, therefore do the damsels love you." The creator's name is a touchy subject, but you must know your creator's name. In numerous places, YAHUAH said of the Messiah that his name would be in him. In John 17:6, YAHUSHA said, "I have manifested your name unto the men which you gave me out of the world: yours they were, and you gave them me; and they have guarded your word." the word there for manifest is G5319 phaneroo, which means to render apparent (literally or figuratively), appear, manifestly declare. (make) manifest, show self. YAHUSHA the Messiah declared the name of the creator. He spoke it and made it apparent to all who heard and saw him in both word and deed. He is declaring himself to be the Word of YAHUAH. I also understand that oil is created by crushing fruit or nuts. Therefore, oil could also represent our crushing, i.e., our trials and tribulations. Remember, YAHUAH wants us to have a contrite, humble heart, and I do not believe you can get one without trials and tribulations.

YAHUSHA reminds us again he is the light of the world in John 9:5. It should also bring to mind Revelation 21:24, which states, "And the nations of them which are saved shall walk in the light of it: and the kings of the earth do bring their glory and honor into it." The light of it is explained in verse 23: "And the city had no need of the sun, neither of the moon, to shine in it: for the glory of YAHUAH did lighten it, and the Lamb is the light thereof." Matthew 4:16 speaks of the town of Bethlehem, the place of Messiah's birth; a great light sprung up from there. And we see an example of that light in Matthew 17 at the Transfiguration, where his face did shine as the sun, and his raiment was white as the light. Here, John conflates the two. Remember Hebrew poetry: the same thing is said twice differently, so the Glory of YAHUAH is the light of the Lamb". Also consider Exodus 34:29-35. After coming down from Mount Sinai with the two tablets of the testimony Moses's face shone. Just like we will shine after receiving our bright nature from living in the presence of the true light of the world.

MESSIAH YAHUSHA IS THE ANGEL WHO PREPARES THE WAY

On that day there shall be no light nor cold weather nor frost. It shall be for one day - and that day is known to the Lord - and not a day and not a night, and at evening time there shall be light.

And on that day living water shall come forth from Jerusalem, half of it into the first sea and half of it into the last sea; even in summer and spring it will be sea.

And the Lord will become king over all the earth; on that day the Lord will be one and his name one. Zechariah 14: 6-9

The heavenly habitation where YAHUSHA the Messiah has gone to prepare a place for his people is spoken of in Revelation 21:23–27, which tells us of this city that will be coming down from heaven which will not need the light of the sun or the moon because the glory of YAHUAH will lighten it, "and the lamb is the light thereof". It speaks of the nations who will come and walk in the light: the kings of the earth will bring their glory and honor into it. The gates will not be shut at all because there will be no night. Then, in verse 27, it says, "And there shall in no wise enter into it anything that defiles, neither whatsoever works abomination, or makes a lie; but they which are written in the Lamb's Cepher (book) of Life". I believe John here in Revelation is paraphrasing Isaiah 60:19-21 which reads, "The sun shall be no more your light by day; neither for brightness shall the moon give light unto you; but YAHUAH shall be unto you an everlasting light, and your ELOHIYM your Glory. Your sun shall no more go down; neither shall your moon withdraw itself; for YAHUAH shall be your everlasting light, and the days of your mourning shall be ended. Your people also shall be all righteous; they shall inherit the land forever, the branch of my planting, the work of my hands, that I may be glorified."

Remember, YAHUSHA is the angel in the pillar of fire, a great light by day and night, who went before Israel to find places in the wilderness to camp (Deuteronomy 1:33). YAHUSHA told his followers that he would make room for them in his Father's house. Enoch was given three parables or visions between chapters 37 and 64. In these chapters, it is apparent that he is describing YAHUSHA as the Messiah. In Enoch 39, Enoch is shown heavenly habitations of the righteous, which "were under the wings of YAHUAH TSEVA'OTH." YAHUSHA's listeners would have been aware of Enoch's vision and would have had it in mind in John 14:1, when YAHUSHA stated, "Let not your heart be troubled, ye believe in YAH, believe also in me. In my Father's house are many mansions: if it were not so, I would have told you. I go to prepare a place for you. And if I go and prepare a place for you, I will come again, and receive you unto myself; that where I am, there you may be also."

Let us look at 2 Baruch chapter 4. It is a short chapter, so I will put it all right here, "And YAHUAH has said unto me: this city shall be delivered up for a time, and the people shall be chastised during a time, and the world will not be given over to oblivion. Do you think that this is that city of which I said: on the palms of my hands have I graven you? This building now built in your midst is not that which is revealed with me, that which was prepared beforehand here from the time when I took counsel to make paradise, and showed it to Adam before he sinned, but when he transgressed the commandment, it was removed from him, as also paradise. And after these things I showed it to my servant Abraham by night among the portions of the victims. And again also, I showed it to Mosheh on Mount Sinai when I showed to him the likeness of the Tabernacle and all its vessels. And now behold, it is preserved with me, as also paradise. Go, therefore, and do as I command you". In Revelation 21:2, John sees the holy city, A Renewed Jerusalem coming down from YAHUAH out of heaven prepared as a bride adorned for her man. This city, according to Baruch, this New Jerusalem, was removed along with Paradise from Adam and is being reserved in heaven, as Enoch observed.

Baruch has quoted from Isaiah 49:16, but I will begin in verse 14 which states, "But Tsiyon said, YAHUAH has forsaken me, and my ADONAI has forgotten me. Can a woman forget her sucking child, that she should not have compassion on the son of her womb? Yea, they may forget, yet will I not forget you. Behold, I have graven you upon the palms of my hands; your walls are continually before me. Your children shall make haste; your destroyers and they that made you waste shall go forth of you." Isaiah chapter 49 is another instance where you are not sure who is speaking. Once you have considered that YAHUSHA is the hand of YAHUAH it becomes clear that it is YAHUSHA who says in Isaiah 49:5, "And now, says YAHUAH that formed me from the womb to be his servant, to bring Ya'aqov again to him", then we will have no question as to the identity who the servant is in verse 6. who will be restoring the preserved branches of Israel. Further, in verse 6, it leaves no doubt as to who the subject is of Isaiah chapter 49, where it says, "I will also give you for a light to the other nations, that you may be my yeshu'ah unto the end of the earth." Isaiah was a prophet in Judah who prophesied to the people of Israel. He was not given to the other nations to prophesy.

In Second Corinthians 5:1, Paul says, "For we know that if our Earthly House of this Tabernacle were dissolved, we have a building of YAH, a house not made with hands, eternal in the heavens." The Messiah is called in these chapters of Enoch, the chosen, the anointed, the righteous one, the Son of Man, and the elect one. Enoch 45:3-6 says, "In that day shall the Elect One sit upon a throne of Glory and shall choose their conditions and countless habitations, while their Spirits within them shall be strengthened, when they behold my Elect One, for those who have fled for protection to my holy and glorious name. In that day I will cause my Elect One to dwell in the midst of them; will change heaven; will bless it, and illuminate it forever, I will also change the earth, will bless it and cause those whom I have elected to dwell upon it". Noticed that YAHUAH is changing heaven and earth, not creating a new heaven and earth.

Enoch chapter 51:1-3 says, "In those days shall the earth deliver up from her womb, and She'ol deliver up from hers, that which it has received; and destruction shall restore that which it owes. He shall select the righteous and holy from among them, for the day of their yeshu'ah has approached. And in those days shall the Elect One sit upon his throne, while every secret of intellectual wisdom shall proceed from his mouth, for YAHUAH TSEVA'OTH has gifted and glorified him". When YAHUSHA says that he will prepare a place for his followers, numerous examples come to mind that of Baruch, of Enoch, of the angel in the flame that led Israel through the wilderness. YAHUSHA's listeners would have recognized this statement of YAHUSHA to be a declaration of his divinity.

Psalm 103:9 also speaks of this heavenly Kingdom where we will be living. This verse reads, "YAHUAH has prepared his throne in the heavens; and his kingdom rules over all." Keep in mind that heaven is also a creation; ELOHIYM created the heavens and the

Earth (Genesis 1:1). Daniel 7:27 reads, "And the kingdom and dominion, and the greatness of the kingdom under the whole heaven, shall be given to the people of the qodeshiym (set apart ones) of EL ELYON, whose kingdom is an everlasting kingdom, and all dominions shall serve and obey him." Finally let's go to Zachariah 14:9 which reads, "And YAHUAH shall be king over all the earth; in that day shall there be one YAHUAH and his name one", because as Paul says in 1 Corinthians 15:24, "Then comes the end, when he (YAHUSHA) shall have delivered up the Kingdom to YAHUAH, even the Father; when he shall have put down all rule and all authority and power"

.

MESSIAH YAHUSHA IS THE BREAD OF LIFE

YAHUSHA said, "I tell you with certainty, he who follows my cause wholeheartedly will gain eternal life, for I have the bread of immortality. The bread I give forms part of my being, and I share it for the good of the world. Many have the grains, but these are yet to be ground and baked. Unless, therefore, you can partake of my substance and become like me you cannot gain immortality in glory. Yet what I can do you can do also, what I have become you can become, I do not ask men to follow a path I would not travel myself, neither is there anything in me not inherent in you. As I am, I am the True Food of men and the power of life flowing in me is their true drink, no. I come with special gifts and authority from above, clothed with the living spirit, and I express life as I do because of the powers within me. So it will be with those who partake of my bread". - The Kailedy chapter 12

YAHUSHA said in John 6:35, "I am the bread of life." And he repeats that in verse 48. Remember what the writer of Hebrews said in 2:3 (from the Aramaic) when he asked how we will escape retribution if we hate the things that are our life? That points us back to Deuteronomy 32:47, which teaches that Torah is life. When YAHUSHA tells those listening to his teaching in John 6:56, "He who eats my body and drinks my blood abides in me and I in him." These statements made in the synagogue at Capernaum caused not only the Jews to murmur against YAHUSHA but some of his disciples as well. In John 6:66, we are told that many of his disciples had gone back and walked no longer with him. But remember what Peter told the savior when YAHUSHA asked if they would go as well. Peter's reply was to ask the question, "To whom would we go?" Because it is YAHUSHA, the Messiah, who has the words of eternal life.

The imagery of consuming the flesh and blood of YAHUSHA the Messiah should bring to mind Ezekiel 2:9-3:15 where the prophet ate a Torah scroll. This scroll was a book of lamentation and mourning, dire warnings to be delivered to Israel, words of the prophet which, if Israel had heeded, would have saved their lives. Ezekiel wrote that the scroll tasted as sweet as honey. We are told in Psalm 19:10 that YAHUAH's Torah and judgements are sweet as honey. This is also reminiscent of Revelation 10:9, which tells of John being given a little book by an angel who told him to eat it. John reports the book tasted as sweet as honey but caused his stomach to become bitter. Life equals Torah (the first 5 books of the Bible), the Word of YAHUAH, which is ingested and becomes part of our innermost being. It is sweet, especially when you first come into the truth; it is exciting when you learn of the life to come and the promises that it holds. However, as you walk in the way of Truth and the path of that walk becomes narrow and lonely, it is bitter, and to overcome, you must always keep those promises ever before you because it means your life.

In the Targum, Deuteronomy 30:20 commands us to "love the Lord thy God, and keep close to his fear; for the law in which you occupy yourselves will be your life in this world and the prolongment of your days in the world that comes, and you shall be gathered together at the end of the scattering, and dwell upon the land which the Lord swore to your fathers, to Abraham, Isaac, and Jacob to give it to them." This verse speaks of another life to come, promised to Adam and his descendants. Pursuing the law determines the life you will inherit.

MESSIAH YAHUSHA IS THE WAY AND THE TRUTH

The Deliverer comes to take men to their places of labor and will ease their burdens there, but He cannot undertake the whole of the task. He will initiate the rule of God, but cannot force it upon men. He will teach them to judge the underprivileged justly and to deal harshly with the arrogant. The rich will be less rich and the poor less poor. He will point the feet of man towards the path of perfection but cannot carry them along it. Earthly Kings can drive men to fulfill their tasks, but no one can be driven along the path to glory, only those who guide and lead can take men this way.
- The Kailedy chapter 12

I have covered and will continue to repeat what Truth is. Psalms 119:142,151, which explicitly tells us Truth is Torah. And John was very explicit in 1 John 3:4, where he says, "Whosoever commits sin transgresses also the Torah: for sin is the transgression of the Torah." 3 Ezra 4:38-40 says, "As for the Truth, it endures, and is always strong; it lives and conquers forever more. With her, there is no accepting of persons or rewards; but she does the things that are just, and refrains from all unjust and wicked things; and all men do well like of her works. Neither in her judgment is any unrighteousness; and she is the strength, kingdom, power, and majesty, of all ages. Blessed be the ELOHIYM of Truth".

Psalms 26 states that we are to walk in the Truth. To walk in the Truth would imply a path we are to follow. Psalms 119 teaches us the way. Verse 1 states, "Blessed are the undefiled in the way, who walk in the Torah (Truth) of YAHUAH. Blessed are they that guard his testimonies, and that seek him with the whole heart. They also do no iniquity: they walk in his ways". This idea that Torah is the way is restated in verse 30, which says, "I have chosen the Way of Truth: your judgments have I laid before me."

The way is walking out the Torah in your life as YAHUSHA walked the Torah. In Mark 12, even the Pharisees and the Herodians acknowledged that YAHUSHA walked the walk of what he was teaching. In Mark 12:14, the Pharisees tell YAHUSHA, "Rabbi, we know that you are true, and care for no man; for you regard not the person of men but teach the Way of ELOHIYM in Truth." Remember Deuteronomy 30:19, where Moses admonished the Israelites by saying, "I call the heavens and the earth to record this day against you, that I have set before you life and death, blessing and cursing; therefore, choose life that both you and your seed may live."

YAHUSHA reminds us what is at stake, that is eternal life. In Matthew 7:12-14 YAHUSHA told us, "All things whatsoever you would that men should do to you, do you even so to them: for this is the Torah and the prophets. Enter ye at the narrow gate, for wide is the gate, and broad is the way that leads to destruction, and many there be which go in thereon; because narrow is the gate, and troublesome is the way which leads to life, and few there be that find it". YAHUSHA admitted that he was that gate when he said in John 10:7,11; "I am the door of the Sheep, I am the good shepherd."

Ezra is told by the angel about the way in 4 Ezra 7:6-13: "A city is built, and set upon a broad field, and is full of all good things: the entrance thereof is narrow, and is set in a dangerous place to fall, like as if there were a fire on the right hand, and on the left a deep water; and there is but one path between them, even between the fire and the water, so small that there could be one man go there at once. If this city now were given unto a man for an inheritance, if he never shall pass the danger set before it, how shall he receive this inheritance? And I said, it is so ADONAI. Then said he to me, even so also is Yashar'el's portion. Because for their sakes I made the world: and when Adam transgressed my statutes, then was decreed that now is done. Then were the entrances of this world made narrow, full of sorrow and travail: they are but few and evil, full of perils; and very painful. For the entrance of the elder world were wide and sure, and brought immortal fruit. If then they that live labor not to enter these straight and vain things, they can never receive those that are laid up for them". This should bring to mind Mark 9:22. YAHUSHA is asked to cast out a demon and asks the youth's father how long the demon had been with him, and the father answered, "And oft times it has cast him into the fire, and into the waters, to destroy him."

Psalm 16:11 says, "You will show me the path of life: in your presence is fullness of joy; at your right hand there are pleasures forevermore." The writer of Hebrews agrees with these statements of YAHUSHA/angel. Hebrews 12:4 reads, "Ye have not resisted unto blood, striving against sin." This world is fleeting, and it is essential to strive to live out the Torah because it will lead to a prolongment of our life to come. Since we allow it to be written on our hearts, it becomes a heart condition instead of a ritual we are obligated to do. If you love YAH with all your heart and soul, you want to do the things that please him and not just pay lip service.

In Hebrews 12:6-7, "For whom YAH loves he chastens, and scourges every son whom he receives. If ye endure chastening, YAH deals with you as with sons; for what son is he who the father chastens not"? We do not want to be the bastard sons who are not chastened, who, as in the Wisdom of Solomon 5:5-7 weary themselves in "the way of wickedness and destruction, yea, we have gone through deserts, where there lay no way: but as for the Way of YAHUAH, we have not known it. What has pride profited us? Or what good has riches with our vaunting brought us? All those things are passed away like a shadow, and as a post that hasted by". These had erred from the "way of truth."

Solomon would have known about the way of Truth from Psalm 119:1-3 which states, "Blessed are the undefiled in the way, who walk in the Torah of YAHUAH. Blessed are they that guard his testimonies, and that seek him with the whole heart. They also do no iniquity: they walk in his ways". In verse 30 of the same Psalm, it says, "I have chosen the way of Truth: your judgments have I laid before me. I have stuck unto your testimonies: O YAHUAH, put me not to shame. I will run the way of your commandments when you shall enlarge my heart". In The Pilgrim's Progress by John Bunyan, Christian left the city of Destruction, his hometown, and followed the way to that narrow gate, that gate being YAHUSHA the Messiah, the Torah made flesh.

One could also think of Bi'lam's donkey when thinking of the way. This story is recorded in Numbers chapter 22. Bil'am was told not to go to Balaq, but he did anyway, and the anger of YAHUAH was kindled against him. An angel stood in Bi'lam's way for an adversary against him and drove him into a very narrow path between two walls, which caused Bi'lam's foot to be crushed. See how YAHUAH drove Bil'am into the narrow path causing him to acquiesce to the will of the Father. I also like this story because it shows us that YAH will accomplish his will because of or despite us.

YAHUSHA himself does one better when talking about the way in Luke chapter 10 with the parable of the Good Samaritan. A young lawyer had asked the Messiah

233

what one must do to obtain eternal life. YAHUSHA's answer was, "What is written in the Torah? How read you? The young lawyer gives him the first commandment, which is to love "YAHUAH ELOHAYKA with all your heart, and with all your soul, and with all your strength, and with all your mind and your neighbor as yourself" from the Shema in Deuteronomy 6:3-9 and Leviticus 19:18. In Matthew 22:40 YAHUSHA had given these same Commandments as being the greatest commandments and further stated that "on these two commandments hang all the Torah and the prophets." However, in Luke 10, the young lawyer is sarcastic and asks, "And who is my neighbor?" YAHUSHA is reminding them of Exodus chapter 23:4, where it says, "If you meet your enemy's ox or his ass going astray, you are to bring it back to him." The Targum adds to this verse, "You shall relinquish at once the dislike of your heart against your enemy and help him."

YAHUSHA the Messiah said in Matthew 5:44: "But I say unto you love your enemies, bless them that curse you, do good to them that hate you, and pray for them which despitefully use you, and persecute you. This statement is a confirmation of Jeremiah 39:39 from the Septuagint in which YAHUAH tells the Israelites: "And I will give them another way and another heart, to fear me all the days, both for their own good and for that of their children after them." YAHUSHA demonstrated how to walk in the Torah.

What you see in the parable of the Good Samaritan is the priest and the Levite walking along in the way and finding a man beaten, stripped of his clothing, and left half dead along the path. These holy men leave the path or the way to avoid being defiled by the blood of this stranger, whose blood would have ruined the sacramental or ritual cleansing they had undergone as prescribed by the law, thus causing them inconvenience for seven days of purification if it turned out the man was dead lying there. In contrast, the Good Samaritan did not stray from his path but stopped and helped the man in spite of the inconvenience. He took the man to an inn and left money for his care. He waylaid his journey, laid out some cash, and promised to return to check on him and pay more if needed. This stranger stopped the progress of his journey twice for a fellow traveler who needed help.

Matthew 5:44-48 reads, "But I saying unto you, love your enemies, bless them that curse you, do good to them that hate you, and pray for them which despitefully use you, and persecute you; that you may be the children of your father which is in heaven: for he makes his sun to rise on the evil and on the good, and sends rain on the just and on the unjust. For if you love them which love you, what reward have you? Do not even the publicans the same? And if ye salute your brethren only, what do you more than others? Do not even the publicans so? Be ye therefore perfect, even as your Father which is in heaven is perfect."

In Matthew 8, YAHUSHA heals a leper after touching him. This simple act of reaching out and touching this leper caused YAHUSHA to become unclean, but he did it anyway because of his compassion and mercy. This image is an incredible example of how badly YAHUAH wants to interact with his creation despite our filthiness.

Psalm 25:10 tells us, "All the paths of YAHUAH are mercy and truth unto such as keep his covenant and his testimonies." Psalm 26:3, "I have walked in the Truth. Psalm 86:11: "Teach me your way, O YAHUAH; I will walk in your Truth; unite my heart to fear your name." Psalm 51:6 tells us that YAHUAH desires that Truth be in our inward parts. According to Jeremiah 31:31-33, we are promised, "Behold, the days come, says YAHUAH, that I will cut a renewed covenant with the house of Yashar'el, and with the house of Yahuda; not according to the covenant that I cut with their fathers in the day that I took them by the hand to bring them out of the land of Mitsrayim; which my covenant they broke, although I was a husband unto them, says YAHUAH: but this shall be the covenant that I will cut with the house of Yashar'el; after those days, says YAHUAH, I will put my Torah in their inward parts, and write it in their hearts; and will be there ELOHIYM, and they shall be my people." "Those days" in Jeremiah 31 refers to the beginning of chapter 30 of Jeremiah, where verse 3 says, "And I will cause them to return to the land that I gave to their fathers, and they shall possess it." Judah was in the land when YAHUSHA walked the earth in the flesh. Remember Acts 2:5 states, "There were dwelling at Yerushalayim Yahudiym, devoted men, out of every nation under heaven" who received the Holy Spirit, which allows the Torah to be written in our hearts. I have covered this. We have a choice. YAHUSHA stands at the door knocking, and all we must do is open it and accept his offer of eternal life by entering into Covenant with him, which means accepting the terms of that covenant and receiving the Holy Spirit which is YAHUAH dwelling in us.

Let us finish with what it means to be perfect. In 2nd Samuel 22:31-33 we are told, "As for ELOHIYM, his way is perfect; the Word of YAHUAH is tried: he is a buckler to all them that trust in him. For whom is ELOHIYM, save YAHUAH? And who is a rock, save our ELOHIYM? ELOHIYM is my strength and power: and he makes my way perfect." 1 Kings 8:61 reads, "Let your heart therefore be perfect with YAHUAH ELOHAYNU, to walk in his statutes, and to guard his commandments, as at this day". From the Septuagint Psalms 14:1,2 reads, "O Lord, who shall sojourn in your covert? And who shall encamp on your holy mountain? One who walks spotless and practices righteousness. Who speaks truth in his heart; he who did not beguile with his tongue nor did evil to his fellow and did not take up reproach against his next of kin." Psalm 18:30 repeats 2 Samuel 22:31. And I will finish with Psalms 19:7-9 which reads, "The Torah of YAHUAH is perfect, restoring the soul: the testimony of YAHUAH is sure, making wise the simple. The statutes of YAHUAH are right, rejoicing the heart; the Commandment of YAHUAH is pure, and enlightening the eyes. The fear of YAHUAH is clean, enduring forever; the judgments of YAHUAH are true and righteous altogether."

MESSIAH YAHUSHA IS THE TRUE VINE

Behold the days come, says YAHUAH, that I will raise unto David a righteous Branch and a King shall reign and prosper, and shall execute judgment and justice in the earth. In his days Yehudah shall be saved, and Yashar'el shall dwell safely; and this is his name whereby he shall be called, YAHUAH TSIDQENU (YAHUAH our righteousness). – Jeremiah 23:5,6

Jeremiah made this prophecy some 600 years before the birth of our Messiah. The word Jeremiah uses for branch is H6780 samah, a sprout or bud that grew. This same word is used by Isaiah (4:2), "in that day shall the branch of YAHUAH be beautiful and glorious, and the fruit of the earth shall be excellent and comely for them that are escaped from Yashar'el. "

Isaiah prophesied in 11:1-3, "And there shall come forth a rod out of the stem of Jesse, and a Branch (H5342

Neser) shall grow out of his roots (H8328 sheresh); and the spirit of YAHUAH shall rest upon him, the spirit of wisdom and understanding, the spirit of counsel and might, the spirit of knowledge and the fear of YAHUAH; and shall make him of quick understanding in the fear of YAHUAH and he shall not judge after the sight of his eyes, neither reprove after the hearing of his ears". This verse in Isaiah usually comes to mind when we read John 15:5, where YAHUSHA said, "I am the vine, and you are the Netzariym. Whoever abides in me and I in him, this man will produce plentiful fruit because without me you are not able to do anything". In verse 1 of John 15, he says, "I am the True Vine, and my father is the husbandman."

When you look at the words used in the previous verse in Isaiah 11 you see that it is a stem or a rod that comes out of the root of Jesse. And it is the neser which grows out of this stem meaning that there is a difference between the actual main stem of this vine and the actual branches which grow out of it. The early church followers of YAHUSHA the Messiah were called Netzariym (branches). The Father, the husbandman is doing the trimming and the grafting of this plant working from the true vine.

In most verses where the word Vine is used, it does appear that it is talking about the church. Three or four vines are distinguished in the scriptures. There is the vine of Sibmah (Moab), as seen in Isaiah 16:9. There is the vine of Sodom in Deuteronomy 32:32. Psalm 80:8 is the vine of Israel. There is also in 2 Kings 4:39 an old vine that produced gourds which poisoned the pot the men were eating from. Then there is the vine in the Book of Jonah, which YAHUAH provided to Jonah for shade, which produced a cucumber. Then, in Isaiah 14:29, we see the root of the serpent, which "shall bring forth a cockatrice, and his fruit shall be a fiery flying serpent." Do these vines represent people, governments, or systems of belief? Or all of the above? I wonder about the old vine which produced gourds. Is it representative of the fallen ones from Genesis 6? And the vine who shaded Jonah, a representative of the Watchers.

In Ezekiel 17, we see a parable of an eagle who takes the cedar from Lebanon and transplants it into another land, where it becomes a willow, a spreading vine of low stature that produces branches and sprigs. We know that branches represent people, but do the trees represent a system of belief? In Job 13:27, the same root word, H8328 seres, is used but is translated as heel. It reads, "You put my feet also in the stocks, and look narrowly upon all my paths; you set a print upon the heels (seres) of my feet." This statement by Job indicates a solid foundation, such as a core belief.

There are Vines that poison the pot, the vine of Sodom, which would be like the vine of Moab. Remember the story of Bil'am of Be'or. In the book of Numbers, starting in chapter 22, Balaq, ruler of Moab, had joined forces with the people of Midyan, the sons of Abraham and Katurah, his last wife. All parties are related; Moab was Lot's son. Lot was Abraham's nephew. They could all claim to be of the Seed of Abraham. Just something to consider when you read the conversations about patronage between YAHUSHA and the Pharisees and Sadducees, they could claim kinship with Abraham but not be sons of Jacob.

After Bil'am blesses Israel, he leaves and returns home. In Numbers 25, we are told that Israel joined himself to Ba'al of Pe'or, and the anger of YAHUAH was kindled against Israel. Philo, in The Changes of Names 18:107, tells us Ba'al of Pe'or means "lord of the gap," according to Philo, that translates to the "mouth above the skin, "meaning a mind overwhelmed by the body senses. And so, we are told in the book of Jasher chapter 85, starting in verse 52, that while Israel was living in the plane of Moab, they approached and began communicating with the people of Moab.

Before leaving for home, Bil'am advised Balaq to kindle YAH's anger against Israel. Bil'am knew that if Balaq could cause Israel to break the Commandments, then he and his army could just stand back and watch as Israel was destroyed through their separation from YAHUAH because if you are not living within the law, you cannot receive His blessings. You are going to receive his curses.

The book of Jasher tells us that Moab "took all their daughters and their women of beautiful aspect and comely appearance and dressed them in gold and silver and costly garments. And the children of Moab seated those women at the door of their tents so that the children of Israel might see them and turn to them, and not fight against Moab". It worked, and they started committing whoredom with these women, succumbing to fleshly desire. This sexual seduction of Israel culminates with Phineas, the son of Eleazar, the son of Aaron, the priest, who sees one of the sons of Israel bring one of these women of Moab into the tent, and he stabs both through with a spear, ending this plague on Israel.

Moab cannot be the True Vine because of their separation from YAHUAH and causing others to be separate from him. What is the true vine? In Genesis 49:10-11 Jacob prophesies over his son Judah, telling his sons that the scepter (ruler) and priest (Torah giver) will not depart from him until Shiloh comes and "unto him shall the gathering of the people be." Besides tranquility, Shiloh can also mean His gift. Remember Zechariah 8:23, the ten men or tribes who will join themselves to Judah to receive salvation through the Torah. Verse 11 states Judah will bind his "foal to the vine, and his ass's colt unto the choice vine."

If Shiloh is translated as the gift, YAHUSHA, the gathering is to him and not Judah. Judah will bind his foal and colt to the choice vine, which has sprouted from the root of Jesse. The true vine cannot be the ten tribes of Israel because they are gathering to Judah. When YAHUSHA, a descendant of Jessie, King David's father, of the tribe of Judah, came riding into Jerusalem on the ass's colt, it fulfilled the prophecy in Zechariah 9:9, which states, "Rejoice greatly, O daughter of Tsiyon; shout, O daughter of Yerushalayim, behold your King comes unto you: he is just, and having salvation; lowly, and riding upon an ass." Verse 10 continues, "And I will cut off the chariot from Ephrayim, and the horse from Yerushalayim, and the battle bow shall be cut off; and he shall speak peace unto the heathen; and his dominion shall be from sea even to sea, and from the river even to the ends of the earth." You can see that this prophecy is about a coming Messiah. But it is a prophecy of a peaceful Messiah, not one that comes to conquer. Notice that the battle bow shall be cut off, and he shall speak peace unto the heathen. Remember, Shiloh can also be translated as tranquility or peace. It can mean both here, a gift of peace.

I have covered The Prophecy of the Messiah in Isaiah 53. In verse 2, the Messiah is called a tender plant and a root that sprouts from dry ground. This Choice Vine cannot be Israel. Hosea tells us in chapter 10 in verse 1 that Israel is an empty vine. "He brings forth fruit unto himself; according to the multitude of his fruit he has increased the altars; according to the goodness of his land they have made goodly images. Their heart is divided; now shall they be found faulty; he shall break down their altars, he shall spoil their images". Like all the prophets in Hosea chapter 14, there is a plea to Israel to return to YAHUAH as was all the prophet's message: A call to repent is a call to return to Torah. Hosea 14:4 says, "I will heal their backsliding; I will love them freely; for my anger is turned away from him. I will be as the dew unto Yashar'el: he (Israel) shall grow as the lily and cast forth his roots as Lebanon. His branches shall spread, and his beauty shall be as the olive tree, and his smell is Lebanon. They that dwell under his shadow shall return; they shall revive as the grain and grow as the vine". This describes a people who have returned to the law and have been healed of their backsliding.

Hosea 14:9 says, "Who is wise, and he shall understand these things? Prudent, and he shall know them? For the ways of YAHUAH are right, and the just shall walk in them; but the transgressors shall fall therein". We will be dwelling under the vine of Israel once it has been healed of their backsliding and make their heart wholly committed to YAHUAH divided no more. Unfortunately, today, Judaism no more abides by the Torah than Christians do. John, Paul, and YAHUSHA himself condemned Judaism because they were not following the TORAH. They were following oral traditions much like those set forth in the Community Rules, which were found among the Dead Sea Scrolls. Now, they follow the Midrash and the Talmud, and I am not sorry to say it is not Torah. Paul called the followers of Judaism enemies of the entire world. (2 Thessalonians 2:15) YAHUSHA called them the synagogue of Satan (Revelation 3:9).

John, throughout his gospel, called all who opposed YAHUSHA Jews, thus making it not about ethnicity. John and the disciples were descendants of Jacob. In John 8:44, he quotes the Savior, telling the Jews, "Ye are of your father the devil, and the lusts of your father ye will do. He was a murderer from the beginning and abode not in the Truth, because there is no truth in him." Remember Truth equals Torah. It is interesting to know that during this conversation with the Pharisees in John 8 they call him in verse 48 a Sumerian who has a devil. Yahusha answers concerning that he does not have a devil. He does not answer the accusation of being a Samaritan. I never thought of it before, but if you study the entomology of the word Samaritan, you will see that its primitive root is Hebrew and not just the place name, but it also means to guard. And what does a Good Shepherd do but guard his sheep?

When I covered the works of Torah, I described who the Netzarim were or are still. They do not call themselves that anymore. They should. The early followers of the Messiah were Netzariym, as indicated in Acts 24:5. They met the definition of who the remnant would be, which is described in Revelation 12:17 as those who "guard the commandments of YAHUAH and have the testimony of YAHUSHA HA'MASHIACH".

When Joseph moved his family back to Galilee into the city of Nazareth (Matthew 2:23), YAHUSHA became YAHUSHA the Netseriy, indicating the one spoken of in Isaiah 11:1. Isaiah is the only prophet who used the word H5342 Neser to describe the coming Messiah. Also, John 19:19 tells us that "Pilate wrote a title and put it on the cross. And the writing was, YAHUSHA THE NATSERIY AND KING OF THE YAHUDIYM". That would have looked like this:

Yahusha

Ha'netseriy

V'melek

Ha'Yahudiym

Do you see why the Priests were so upset with Pilate's sign? This sign spelled out the Tetragrammaton, the name of YAHUAH. I wonder if the Pharisees thought of Psalms 96:10. Tertullian (A.D. 145 - 220) quotes Psalm 96:10 as reading, "Say among the heathen that YAHUAH reigns from the tree".

In Luke 23:31, when YAHUSHA is being led to his crucifixion. Some women are lamenting him, and he turns to them and tells them that they need to be more concerned about themselves and their children. He quotes Hosea 10:8, and then in verse 31, he says, "For if they do these things to a green tree what shall be done to the dry?" He is referring to Ezekiel 20:47, which is a clear Messianic claim. In this chapter of Ezekiel, the green tree represents the righteous, and the dry trees are the unrighteous. In this chapter, Ezekiel is told to prophesy against the forest of the South, Jerusalem, and Judea, that YAHUAH will destroy it with a fierce fire that will also destroy the green trees. The righteous one will be killed. In Exodus 15:23-26 when Israel comes to Marah, they have no drinkable water due to its bitterness. YAHUAH instructs Moses to cast a tree into the waters, which makes them sweet or drinkable. This is considered a miracle within a miracle - bitter waters made sweet by a bitter tree. This tree used is a rhododaphne, described in Shemoth Rabba as a tree that grows beside water and bears flowers resembling lilies of a bitter taste. This miracle in a miracle should put us to mind of the miracle of Mercy and Grace both of which we receive from YAHUAH, neither of which we are deserving.

Then we have the wood of the sacrifice which Isaac carries on his back up the mountain. YAHUSHA the Messiah is the Tree of Life. If Adam and Eve had eaten from this tree while in their sin, they would have obtained eternal life and remained sinful eternally. They were forbidden entry back into the garden to keep them from eating from this tree. Quoting from an unknown biblical source, Barnabas (A.D. 100), in his Epistle Chapter 12, quotes the MESSIAH who is responding to the question given him by the disciples concerning his return (same as Matthew 24). YAHUSHA answers them, "When a tree shall be bent down, and again arise, and when blood shall flow out of wood." This should bring to mind Habakkuk 2:11-12, "For the stone shall cry out of the wall, and the beam out of the timber shall answer it. Woe to him that builds a town with blood and establishes a city by iniquity!" Remember, YAHUSHA died because it was better that one man die than to lose the nation (John 18:14).

Paul answers my question concerning who the branches are. He says in Romans 11:16, from the Aramaic, "For, if the first fruits (are) Set Apart, then the rest of the dough (it came from is) also; and if the root is set apart, then also the branches." YAHUSHA the Messiah is the rod that sprang from the root and creates the branches which grow from him. Did Paul recall all the prophecies of the Messiah? Was he thinking of Zechariah as well as Isaiah?

Zechariah 3 tells us YAHUSHA will be the high priest and king. He is called YAH's servant, the Branch. YAHUAH states further in verse 9, "For behold the stone

248

that I have laid before YAHUSHA; upon one stone shall be seven eyes; behold, I will engrave the graving thereof, say YAHUAH TSEVA'OTH and I will remove the iniquity of that land in one day.

MESSIAH YAHUSHA IS THE ROCK OF SALVATION

And Yahusha wrote these words in the Cepher of the Torah of ELOHIYM, and took a great stone, and set it up there under an oak, that was by the sanctuary of YAHUAH. And Yahusha said unto all the people, behold, this Stone shall be a witness unto us; for it has heard all the words of YAHUAH which he spoke unto us: it shall be there for a witness unto you, lest ye deny your ELOHIYM. -Joshua 24:26,27

Notice how this rock heard all the words of YAHUAH. I wonder if this verse in Joshua 24 came into the minds of the Jews when they were told by YAHUSHA the Messiah in John 5:30, "I can of my own self do nothing; as I hear, I judge; and my judgment is just; because I seek not my own will, but the will of the Father who has sent me".

When thinking about the treatment our Messiah received from the Jews, Pharisees, and Sadducees, Habakkuk 2:9-14 comes to mind. It reads, "Woe to him that covets an evil covetousness to his house, that he may set his nest on high, that he may be delivered from the power of evil! You have consulted shame to your house by cutting off many people and have sinned against your soul. For the stone shall cry out of the wall, and the beam out of the Timber shall answer it. Woe to him that builds a town with blood and stablishes a city by iniquity! Behold, is it not of YAHUAH TSEVA'OTH that the people shall labor in the very fire, and the people shall weary themselves for very vanity? For the earth shall be filled with the knowledge of the glory of YAHUAH, as the waters cover the sea." Remember the words of the High Priest Caiaphas in John 11:50 when he said, "Nor consider that it is expedient for us, that one man should die for the people, and that the whole nation perish not."

The Stone in Habakkuk 2:11, crying from the wall, reminds me of the vision given to the Shepherd of Hermes. In this book, which was written around A.D. 160, Hermes is given a vision of six angels who are building a building of stone. These angels carry stones from the field that have been weathered/polished with time and harsh conditions. These stones are placed in the wall. However, some are discarded and thrown back into the field because they are not a good fit. They are thrown back into the world for more polishing or tribulation. The Shepherd is told that this is the church being built and the foundation; the cornerstone is the Word of YAHUAH, whom the builders rejected (Psalm 118:15). The Builders here are Judaism who failed to accept this stone into their religious system.

They were and still are looking for a messiah to restore their power. YAHUSHA, the promised suffering Messiah (Isaiah 53), arrived and was rejected by those who used religion/ oral law to rule the people.

Let us talk about Matthew 16:18, where YAHUSHA the Messiah said, "And I say also unto you, that you are Kepha, and upon this Rock I will rebuild my called-out assembly; and the gates of She'ol shall not prevail against it." Yes, Kepha means rock; however, YAHUSHA uses a play on words. Peter, in the Strong's Concordance is G4074 which means a (piece of) rock (larger than G3037). G3037 is lithos, which means stone (literally or figuratively): - (mill-, stumbling-) stone. The Rock on which the church will be built is G4073, Petra, which means a (mass of) rock. If you look at the Bible usage for Petra, it is always used to indicate a foundation on which you build a house or a Doctrine. YAHUSHA is telling Peter in Matthew 16:18 you are a little rock, but I will build my assembly of called out ones on this big rock, this foundation stone, meaning himself.

Yes, it does appear that Peter obtained the keys to the kingdom at that time, and church legend has it that Peter was the first Bishop of Rome. That is patently wrong. Archaeologically, there is no proof of Peter having been buried in Rome. Two graves have been exhumed with no bones. According to Irenaeus (A.D. 120- 202) in Against Heresies 3.3.3, it was Linus, whom Paul consecrated, was the first bishop of Rome and confirms that this Linus is the same one mentioned in 2 Timothy 4:21. Tertullian (A.D. 145-220) in Prescription of the Heretics 32 claims Clement was a Bishop of Rome appointed by Peter.

When Ignatius (A.D. 30-107) wrote his Epistle to the Romans, he addressed it to the entire congregation, not a specific leader. He addressed it "to those who are united, both according to the flesh and spirit, to every one of his Commandments, who are filled inseparably with all the grace of God." Eusebius and Origen also confirm that Clement of Rome is the same as Paul mentioned in Philippians 4:3. Hegesippus, a second-century historian, also listed Clement among the popes.

It is clear from the reading of Acts 15 that Peter and James were the elders in charge of the congregation in Jerusalem. If you read Clement's Recognitions, you would see Peter never traveled so far away from Jerusalem that he could not return for the feasts. The temple was still standing, so all Torah followers were required to be at the temple in Jerusalem for the three major feasts. Therefore, it is possible that Peter may have visited Rome and appointed Clement as a bishop over a congregation there, but he would not have stayed long enough to be a bishop himself.

Therefore, in Matthew chapter 16, the rock spoken of is YAHUSHA himself. And that would have drawn the listeners back to Deuteronomy 32 in the song of Moses, which says, in verse 4, "He is the Rock, his work is perfect; for all his ways are judgment; an EL of Truth and without iniquity, just and right is He. Verse 18 says, "Of the Rock that beget you you are unmindful, and you have forgotten EL, that formed you." And verses 30-31 say,

"How should one chase a thousand, and two put ten thousand to flight, except their rock had sold them, and YAHUAH had shut them up? For their rock is not as our Rock, even our enemies himself being judges. For their vine is of the vine of Cedom.". I had to get that vine in there to remind you that vine can mean doctrine. Also, in these verses, YAHUSHA says he is renewing his called-out assembly, which could also be translated as qodeshiym, his set apart ones, in other words, establishing prophets. This statement of YAHUSHAs` in Matthew 16 is quite the Divinity statement.

In Ephesians chapter 4, Paul builds upon this idea of renewing the called-out assembly. Modern church doctrine calls it the five-fold ministry. In verses 4–6, Paul establishes there is no trinity as taught today when he says, "There is one body, and one Ruach, even as ye are called in one hope of your calling; One YAHUAH, one Belief, one immersion, one YAH and Father of all, who is above all." Then, in verse 11, Paul gives the list of what today is taught as offices of the church. However, it could be argued these are not offices but gifts, as stated in verse 8 when Paul quotes Psalms 68:18, "When he ascended up on high, he led captivity captive, and gave gifts to men." "Paul expects us to know that Psalm, so he did not add the rest of that verse which says, "You have received gifts for men; yea for the rebellious also, that YAH ELOHIYM might dwell among them." What else could those gifts David references here be but the Torah, which, if we obey, allows YAH to live among us? If Torah is truth, and we stand in truth, then Exodus 33:21 places us next to YAHUAH. Exodus 33:21 reads:

"And YAHUAH said, Behold, there is a place by me, and you shall stand upon a rock." That rock is the rock of salvation, YAHUSHA the Messiah, the living breathing word of YAHUAH.

These gifts of the Holy Spirit are five, the number of books Moses gave us. They also correspond to the appointed times or Feasts of YAHUAH. These festivals are gifts of YAHUAH:

1. Apostles: The sent one, Moses, who received instruction for the Passover, which encompasses Matzah and First Fruits.
2. Prophets: The Torah and the Holy Spirit were received on Pentecost, allowing for prophesying the Kingdom of heaven.
3. Evangelists: The Feast of Trumpets, which calls us, the sheep, out to him.
4. Pastors: Yom Kippur, or the day of Atonement, is a time of spiritual reflection and growth.
5. Teachers: The Feast of Weeks is a time for teaching and learning Torah in fellowship with one another.

YAHUSHA's followers who heard his statement in Matthew 16 may have thought of Isaiah 8:14, which says, "And he shall be for a sanctuary; but for a stone of stumbling and for a rock of offense to both the houses of Yashar'el, for a gin and for a snare to the inhabitants of Yerushalayim." Isaiah 17:10 says, "Because you have forgotten the ELOHAI of your yeshu'ah and have not been mindful of the Rock of your strength, therefore shall you plant pleasant plants, and shall set it with strange slips." The Targum of Isaiah translates verse 10 as, "Because thou hast forsaken the God of thy salvation, and thou hast not remembered the fear of the Mighty One, whose Word was thy support; therefore, thou hast planted a choice plant, and hast multiplied despicable works." Rock and Word could be interchangeable. Isaiah 51:1 states, "Harken to me, ye that follow after righteousness, ye that seek YAHUAH; look unto the Rock whence ye are hewn, and to the hole of the pit whence ye are dug."

Most interestingly is Isaiah 48:21, where Isaiah refers to Moses splitting The Rock and causing the water to gush out, easing the thirst of Israel. However, in the Targum Isaiah, this is a future event. It reads. "He will not suffer them to thirst in the desert; he will guide them; he will cause water to flow for them from the rock; yea, he will cleave the rock, and the waters shall gush out." This makes it clear that the scene in Exodus chapter 17 of Moses smiting the rock is a prophecy of the Messiah. Paul confirms this when citing this event in 1 Corinthians 10:4; he says, Israel "did all drink the same spiritual drink; for they drank of that spiritual Rock that followed them, and that Rock was MASHIACH." It appears Paul is conflating the Rock with the pillar of fire. There is also the image of Moses on Mount Sinai being hidden in the cleft of The Rock and protected from death by the Hand of YAHUAH when he is allowed to see YAH'S Glory. The hand protected him from seeing YAHUAH'S face, which would have caused death. YAHUAH's hand was removed after YAH had passed, allowing Moses to see his back parts. But notice that

Moses was standing on the rock when he received the instructions to see YAHUAH'S glory. Also, Moses was sitting on a rock in Exodus 17 during Israel's battle against the Amalekites.

The fourth book of Psalms begins with "a prayer of Moses the man of ELOHIYM." This prayer appears to run from Psalms 90 through to Psalm 100. In Psalm 92:1, Moses sings, "YAHUAH is upright: He is my Rock, and there is no unrighteousness in him." In Psalm 18, David confirms this in verses 2 and 31, when he sings, "For who is ELOAH save YAHUAH? or who is a rock save our ELOHIYM"? And further, verse 46 says, YAHUAH lives; blessed be my Rock; and let the ELOHYIM of my YAHUAH be exalted". Maybe it is just me, but I see the similarity between this verse, Psalms 18:46, and Psalms 110:1. Remember the question YAHUSHA poses to the scribes and Pharisees in Matthew 22:41, Mark 12:25 and Luke 20:30-43 where he quotes Psalm 110:1. Who was David talking about when he says, "YAHUAH said to my ADONAI? David again repeats this in Psalm 18:46 when he says, "Blessed be my Rock; and let the ELOHYIM of my YAHUAH be exalted." David also refers to his Rock of salvation in Psalms 61 and 62.

Let us return to Jacob's Ladder in Genesis 28. In verse 17, Jacob exclaims that this place is the Gate of Heaven. YAHUSHA the Messiah stated that he was the gate, i.e., the entryway to the kingdom of heaven that no man may come to the Father except through him (John 14:6). Jacob then takes the stone he had used for a pillow, set it up for a pillar, and poured oil upon it, thus anointing it. In verse 22, he states, "This Stone which I have set for a pillar, shall be ELOHIYM'S house." The word there for pillar is masseba H4676, which means something stationed, i.e., A column or (memorial stone); by analogy, an idol: - garrison, (standing) image, pillar.

In 2nd Samuel 18:18, we are given an example of a memorial stone when Absalom, who had no son, reared up a pillar in the Kings Valley, "for he said, I have no son to keep my name in remembrance, and he called the pillar after his own name." YAHUSHA said in John 5:43, "I am come in my father's name," making him a standing Stone calling people to remember his father.

Notice that Jacob anoints the stone with oil for the first time while he is on his way to his uncle Laban's house in Haran to escape the anger of Esau. Jacob makes a vow to YAHUAH in Genesis 28, starting in verses 20-22, saying, "If ELOHIYM will be with me, and will guard me in this way that I go, and will give me bread to eat, and raiment to put on, so that I come again to my father's house in peace; then shall YAHUAH be my ELOHIYM. And this stone, which I have set for a pillar, shall be ELOHIYM'S house; and of all that you shall give me, I will surely give the 10th unto you".

We know the story: Jacob obtains wives and children and is returned to his land as promised. In Genesis 35, YAHUAH reminds Jacob of the vow he owes him. Jacob orders his household to put away their strange gods, be clean, and change their garments. They return to Bethel, where ELOHIYM appeared to Jacob (Genesis 35:9). Jacob is reminded of his new name, Israel, and vows that the land promised to Abraham and Isaac would go to his seed. "And ELOHIYM went up from him to the place where he talked with him. And Ya'aqov set up a pillar in the place where he talked with him, even a pillar of stone; and he poured a drink offering there on, and he poured oil there on and he called the place where ELOHIYM spoke with him Beyt-EL".

In Exodus chapter 30, YAHUAH gives Moses the recipe for the holy anointing oil, which the Tabernacle and all its furniture and sacred pieces were to be anointed with, as well as the high priest. This instruction is repeated in Exodus chapter 40. Later, in 1 Samuel 9:16-10:1, we see that the kings of Israel were ordered to be anointed with oil, much like the priests. In 1 John 2:27, we read, "But the anointing which you have received of him abides in you, and you need not any man teach you (Jeremiah 31:31-34); but as the same anointing teaches you of all things, and is Truth, and is no lie, and even as it has taught you, you shall abide in him; that, when he shall appear, we may have confidence, and not be ashamed before him at his coming".

According to John, we receive anointing from YAHUSHA the Messiah, a prophet like Moses, as instructed in Leviticus 8:30, which states "And Mosheh took of the anointing oil, and of the blood which was upon the altar, and sprinkled it upon Aaron and his garments and upon his sons and upon his son's garments with him, and sanctified Aaron, and his garments and his sons, and his sons' garments with him." By accepting the sacrifice of the blood of YAHUSHA, the Messiah, and the oil of his name, we become anointed Tabernacles containing the Holy Spirit of YAHUAH. Remember Song of Solomon 1:3, "Because of the savor of your good ointments your name is as ointment poured forth, therefore do the damsels love you."

YAHUSHA told us he was the bread of life. Remember, the unleavened wafers were anointed with oil. (Exodus 29:2, Leviticus 2:4; 7:12, and Numbers 6:15). In Mark 6:13, we see the 12 apostles sent out by YAHUSHA, and we are told that they cast out many devils and anointed with oil the many who were sick and healed them. Was this a foreshadowing of the coming Holy Spirit who would write Torah on our hearts, making us temples or oil-anointed pillars of stone to be set into the church? We like Simon Peter, whose name means small stone, are small stones set upon the immense cornerstone who is YAHUSHA the Messiah.

Is the anointing that YAHUSHA brings the removal of the burden of Ashshur, as mentioned in Isaiah 10:27? YAHUAH TSEVA'OTH tells Israel, who is living in Tsiyon, "It shall come to pass in that day, that his (Ashshur) burden shall be taken away from off your shoulders, and his yoke from off your neck, and the yoke shall be destroyed because of the anointing." Is the anointing the power to tread upon serpents and scorpions? Is this what YAHUSHA meant when he said in Matthew 11:28-30, "Come unto me, all ye that labor and are heavy laden, and I will give you rest. Take my yoke upon you and learn of me; for I am meek and lowly in heart: and you shall find rest for your souls. For my yoke is easy, and my burden is light". He is quoting Jeremiah 6:16, which states, "Thus says YAHUAH, stand ye in the ways, and see, and ask for the ancient paths, where is the good way, and walk therein, and you shall find rest for your souls."

Is the anointing of YAHUSHA the one mentioned in Ezekiel chapter 16? YAHUAH is reminding Israel of the Covenant they entered into on Mount Sinai. This is very much marriage language where he is telling them that he had found them polluted in their blood and that He spread his skirt over them. Remember the Book of Ruth. Ruth asks Boaz to cover her to become her redeemer/husband. YAHUAH covered Israel's nakedness and entered into a covenant, a marriage covenant. In Ezekiel 16:9, YAHUAH tells them, "Then I washed you with water; yea, I thoroughly washed away your blood from you, and I anointed you with oil." There you have the baptism of salvation, right? And the anointing of oil. What is the oil? Remember the parable of the sleeping ten virgins. They all had lamps and oil. Some had more oil than others.

Is the oil a product of our crushing tribulation, or is it the name? How can you truly know anyone if you do not know their name? Remember the battle that Jacob had with Uriel. It was vital for him to know his name. Remember Moses when he was going to Egypt? He requested YAH's name so that he could tell the leaders of Israel who had sent him. Whose name was he to come in? It was important.

When I was baptized the first time, I was baptized in the name of the Father, the Son, and the Holy Spirit, which are not names but titles. When I came to the truth, I felt the compulsion to become baptized in the name of the creator of all things, YAHUSHA, the

Messiah, and the creator of heaven and earth, YAHUAH. I did this to receive the promised anointing of the Holy Spirit. Of course, that is what I believe; you must come to your own conclusions, to true knowledge, not **your** truth but **the** Truth. And the only way to come to truth is through studying the word. And not just to open the Bible to a random passage or do a little word study, which is all good. No, I am talking about picking it up, opening to page one, Genesis 1:1, and reading some every day until you reach Revelation 22:20. All the answers are in your Bible.

The best version of the Bible is the one you will read. Before you begin, pray, and ask the Holy Spirit to guide you in truth and knowledge. However, there is one translation whose stated purpose is to not offend anyone who picks it up to read. For instance, personal pronouns have been removed as well as the fact that Mary, the mother of our Messiah, was a virgin. The Bible should be offensive. It should convict you of your sins. It is in scripture where we learn exactly what sin is, so that we will turn from our sinful life and turn to YAHUAH and walk in his ways. And once you have read that one, then read another translation. Once you have come into truth you will know the truth and have no need of any man to guide you. You will not have to be taught by any man. Just as John 2:26-27 says, "These things have I written unto you concerning them that seduce you. But the anointing which ye have received of him abides in you, and you need not that any man teach you; but as the same anointing teaches you of all things, and is truth, and is no lie, and even as it has taught you, you shall abide in him". It is up to us to remove the stone of offense (Isaiah 8:14) or The Stumbling Stone as Paul calls it in Romans 9:33 as well as Peter in 1 Peter 2:8. Remember Jacob (Genesis 29) who rolled back the stone which covered the well so that all the sheep of his uncle Laban could access the water. Even so, we must roll back the rock of offense that blocks our access to Living Water. And remember that YAHUSHA, the Messiah, removed the stone of death, which blocks our access to live in the presence of the Father. In John 11:39, the stone was taken away from the tomb; it was not merely rolled back. "But let us not be like Martha, who would have hindered the removal of the stone from the tomb entrance for fear of her brother Lazarus' stink. YAHUSHA asked Martha in John 11:40, "Said I not unto you, that, if you would believe, you would see the glory of YAHUAH?" And that is what happened to Lazarus when he was raised from the dead and walked out of that tomb. He walked into the presence of the glory of YAHUAH, his Messiah YAHUSHA

.

MESSIAH YAHUSHA MESSIAH IS OUR SALVATION

"Blessed is Master YHWH the Elohim of Israel,
Who has visited his people and wrought salvation to it.
And he has raised up a horn of salvation for us in the
house of David his servant,
As he spoke by the mouth of his Set Apart prophets who
were from old,
That he would save us from our enemies and from the
hand of all who hate us
And he has shown his mercy to our fathers and has
remembered his Set Apart Covenant,
And the oaths that he swore to Awraham our father that
he would give to us.
That we would be delivered from the hand of our enemies,
and we might serve before Him without fear
All the days of our days of ritual purity In Separateness
and Righteousness
And to you, my child, will be the prophet of the Most High,
for you will go before the face of Master YHWH to prepare
His way.
So that He will give the knowledge of life to his people in
the forgiveness of their sins,
By the kindness of the mercy of our Elohim By which will
visit us from a ray above.
To enlighten those who are in darkness
And sit in the shadows of death that he might direct our
feet in the way of peace. Luke 1:68-79

These verses were taken from the Aramaic English New Testament by Andrew Gabriel Roth, who kept the structure of the Semitic poetry, which, as he says, Luke employed. John the Immersers' father,

Zakharyah, appears to be prophesying over his son. However, only verse 76 is about John. Here, he addresses the baby and says, "And you, my child, will be called a prophet of the Most High, for you will go before the face of Master YHWH to prepare his way."

Zakharyah credits Master YHWH for all the Salvation brought to his people, Israel. He then refers us back to David. There is recorded a song of David in 2 Samuel 22 and then is repeated in Psalm 18. 2 Samuel 22:1-3 reads: "And David spoke unto YAHUAH the words of this song in the day that YAHUAH had delivered him out of the hand of all his enemies, and out of the hand of Sha'ul. And he said, YAHUAH is my Rock, and my fortress, and my deliverer; the ELOHAI of my Rock, in him will I trust he is my shield, and the horn of my yeshu'ah, my high tower, and my refuge, my salvation; you save me from violence". As I have covered, it looks like there are two entities here. David credits YAHUAH as being his Rock of Salvation. Who is the ELOHAI of this Rock of Salvation?

I want to point out that David is prophesying a future event. David's people will be scattered. In 2 Samuel 22:17, David says, "He sent from above, he took me; he drew me out of many waters," indicating many nations or peoples. In Psalms 18, it is much the same thing. I have covered concerning YAHUAH thundering from heaven and giving his "Word hailstones and coals of fire" from out of heaven to rain down on Sodom and Gomorrah in Psalm 18:13. It cannot be Sodom and Gomorrah that David is speaking of here in 2 Samual 22:7 where YAHUAH hears David's cry for help and in verse 10 bows the heavens and comes down riding upon a Keruv. In verse 15, after the enemies have been discomfited, it states that the "channels of water were seen, and the foundations of the world were discovered by your rebuke, O YAHUAH, at the blast of the breath of your nostrils." When did this happen? We can see this as a future event being prophesied here because after David is drawn out of many Waters, he is delivered in verse 19 to "a large place." Is this large place from 4 Ezra 7:3? This is the broad place whose entrance was made narrow after the fall of Adam and Eve.

Notice Zakaryah uses the term "set apart" prophets in Luke 1:70. Which could also be translated as a qodeshiym, confirming they are the elect ones as I have covered. All the prophets, including David, prophesied of a redeemer, deliverer, or savior. Remember, YAHUSHA proclaimed himself to be salvation/life in Luke 19:9 when he entered the house of Zakkai and said, "This day is salvation come to this house, for as much as he (Zakkai) also is a son of Abraham. For the son of Adam is come to seek and to save that which was lost". That being the tribes of Israel. Here, salvation is interchangeable with life. We should all recognize by now that life is the life eternal that YAHUSHA promised, and the way to this eternal life is the Torah of Moses as exemplified in the life YAHUSHA the Messiah lived while in the flesh.

YAHUSHA proclaimed this in Matthew 7:12-14 where he said, "Therefore all things whatsoever you would that men should do to you, do you even so to them; for this is the Torah and the prophets. Enter ye in at the narrow gate; for wide is the gate, and broad is the way, that leads to destruction, and many there be which go in there at; because narrow is the gate, and troublesome is the way, which leads to life, and few there be that find it". He also told his disciples in Matthew 19:29, "And everyone that has forsaken houses, or brethren, or sisters, or father, or mother, or woman, or children, or lands, for my names sake, shall receive a hundredfold, and shall inherit everlasting life." This is also quoted in Mark 10:30 and Luke 18:30. Make note here what happens in this life when you follow the way of Truth. Notice things and people you will have to forsake in order to stand on that Rock. YAHUSHA is reminding his listeners of Micah 7:5-7 and Enoch 55:10-11 which reads, "They shall rise up to destroy each other; their right hand shall be strengthened; nor shall a man acknowledge his friend or his brother; nor the son his father and his mother".

Peter describes the way to salvation in his second Epistle, Chapter 1:11. Interestingly, Peter says, starting in verse 10, "Wherefore the rather, brethren, give diligence to make your calling and election sure; for if you do these things, ye shall never fall; For so an entrance shall be ministered unto you abundantly into the Everlasting Kingdom of our ADONAI and Savior YAHUSHA HAMASHIACH." What things? What did Peter say before that we should be doing? In verse one, Peter talks about obtaining belief through the righteousness of YAHUAH and ADADONAI YAHUSHA HAMASHIACH. And we can all agree that Psalm 118 defines righteousness as lawfulness. Then, in 2 Peter 1:3, he says that MASHIACH has given unto us "all things that pertain unto the power of YAHUAH to life and the fear of YAHUAH were through the knowledge of him that has called us to glory and virtue." We now know what leads to life. In verse 4, he tells us that we have exceeding great and precious promises in that, as partakers, we might be partakers of the true nature of YAHUAH. That being the promise of regaining our bright nature and living in the presence of YAHUAH in his kingdom. All of which I have covered.

I have also covered YAHUSHAS divinity statements in the chapter YAHUSHA is YAHUAH in the flesh where he not only raises people from the dead as other prophets had done but also promises eternal life, which is only something YAHUAH can do. So, where did this idea of eternal life come from? And why was it that his disciples believed him? Like YAHUSHA told his fellow travelers on the road to Emmaus, we must begin with Moses (Luke 24:27).

I have made a good enough case that YAHUSHA is the branch, but I have not spoken about trees. I would encourage you to study trees and start with Ezekiel 31, where Ashshur was a cedar in Lebanon. But in verse 8, we are told that "the cedars in the garden of ELOHIYM could not hide him; the fir trees were not like his boughs, and the chestnut trees were not like his branches; nor any tree in the garden of ELOHIYM was like unto him in his beauty." We see here there are many "trees" in the garden. We know YAHUSHA HAMASHIACH is the Tree of Life in the garden in Genesis 3.

At the fall of Adam, YAHUAH Elohim said in verse 22, "Behold, the man is become as one of us, to know good and evil; and now, lest he put forth his hand, and take also of the tree of life, and eat, and live forever: therefore, YAHUAH ELOHIYM sent him forth from the garden of Eden, to till ground from whence he was taken." You see here that to have everlasting life; we must partake of the fruit of the tree of life that is YAHUSHA HAMASHIACH. As I said before, Adam and Eve were banned from partaking of that fruit because they would have remained in their fallen state for eternity. Therefore, YAHUAH had to prepare a way for us to partake of this tree of life that gives eternal life. The way is the living, breathing Torah, our Redeemer, our Father, our groom, our salvation. YAHUSHA stated he was the bread of life twice in John 6. Bread sustains life physically, and YAHUAH gives life eternally. But first, we must partake of it, allowing for it to permeate our being. Remember, YAHUAH is perfect, so we must become perfect.

In Genesis 15, the Word of YAHUAH comes to Abraham and tells him what lies ahead for him and his seed, even in Egypt. In verse 15, the Word tells Abraham, "And you shall go to your fathers in peace; you shall be buried in a good old age." This comes to fruition in Genesis 25:8, where Abraham gave up his spirit "and died in a good old age, an old man, and full of years; and was gathered to his people." This same statement is repeated for Jacob in Genesis 49:33. King David confirms this in 2nd Samuel 12:23, where his infant son had died. He stated, "But now he is dead, wherefore should I fast? Can I bring him back again? I shall go to him, but he shall not return to me".

I will catch some pushback about these passages, but they are not my words. I realize that some believe in purgatory: A place where the dead go, and they are either punished or not depending on the life they lead. They are taught that you can pray for them to be put in a better place in purgatory. There are no scriptures that I have found that agree with that concept. So, paying a priest or paying for masses or whatever you must do to help your loved one move across the chasm to a better place is simply wrong. But you cannot deny that the Messiah did teach what is in the Old Testament scriptures that I just went over concerning Jacob, Abraham, and David. They go to their fathers upon death.

In Luke chapter 16, starting in verse 19, the Messiah gives a parable of a certain rich man who ate sumptuously every day, and outside of his gate was Elazar, who begged for his food. Both men die, and Elazar ends up in the bosom of Abraham, obviously a pleasant place. The rich man goes to a place where he is in flaming torment. The rich man begged Father Abraham to allow Elazar to come to him with a drop of water to quench his thirst. When told that Elazar could not cross the chasm, the rich man then begged Abraham to send messengers to warn his family of this place of torment. The rich man was told, "They have Mosheh and the prophets; let them hear them. If they hear not Mosheh and the prophets, neither will they be persuaded, though one rose from the dead". This is the same instruction Peter gave in Acts 15:21, which reads, "For Mosheh of old times in every city them that preach him, being read in the synagogue every Shabbat. "Sadly, there are those who still refuse to believe even though one has risen from the dead.

All questions are answered in your scriptures. Read your bible. And yes, I realize the Catholics are discouraged from reading scripture, and other denominations discourage reading the books of the Apocrypha, such as the Maccabees, just because in 2 Maccabees 12:41-46 dead soldiers were prayed for because it was discovered they secretly were worshiping idols. They had some sort of charm on their persons as they went into battle, so they prayed for them. The verses do not say that the prayers were helpful to the dead, but they do say that these soldiers who were praying were distraught because of what they had learned about their family and friends in arms secretly living in sin. "They besought him that the sin committed might wholly be put out of remembrance. Besides, Noble Yehudah exhorted the people to guard themselves from sin, for as much as they saw before their eyes the things that came to pass for the sins of those that were slain". Sometimes, prayers are more beneficial to those doing the praying.

Besides Abraham's bosom, YAHUSHA also used the term heart of the earth in Matthew 12:40, where he says, "For as Yonah was three days and three nights in the fish's belly; so shall the Son of Adam be three days and three nights in the heart of the earth." YAHUSHA told the thief on the cross in Luke 23:43 that he would be with him in paradise that day. When you read the book of Nicodemus, you see the thief in paradise, the bosom of Abraham, or the heart of the earth, where YAHUSHA went and preached for three days to the people there.

There was a belief in the first century in the resurrection of the dead, which is the ultimate salvation. The New Testament scriptures, some of which I have covered in YAHUSHA is YAHUAH, and I covered many which would explain why there was such a belief while writing of us regaining our bright nature, but a couple more will not hurt to see. In Luke 11:24, speaking of her brother Lazarus, Martha tells YAHUSHA, "I know that he shall rise again in the resurrection at the last day". Then, there is Revelation 20:4-6 which reads, "And I saw thrones, and they set upon them, and judgment was given unto them; and I saw the souls of them that were beheaded for the witness of YAHUSHA, and for the word of YAHUAH, and which had not worshiped the beast, neither his image, neither had received his mark upon their foreheads, or in their hands; and they lived and reigned with MASHIACH a thousand years." John is directing his reader back to Psalm 122.

YAHUAH tells us through the prophet Ezekiel that they will be judged, or we will be judged according to our ways. Then he says in verse 30, "Repent and turn yourselves from all your transgressions; so, iniquity shall not be your ruin." Then He says in verse 31, "For I have no pleasure in the death of him that dies, says ADONAI YAHUAH: wherefore turn yourselves, and live ye." This is not the death of the flesh but the death of the souls. Remember what sin is. YAH tells Ezekiel in 34:24 that he will be the Elohim of his people and "my servant

David a Prince among them." This was written long after King David's death, making this a prophecy of David sitting on the throne a future event.

Wisdom speaks in Proverbs 8:30-36, "Now therefore hearken unto me, O children: for blessed are they that guard my ways. Hear instruction, and be wise, and refuse it not. Blessed is the man that hears me, watching daily at my gates, waiting at the posts of my doors. For whoso finds me finds life and shall obtain favor of YAHUAH. But he that sins against me wrongs his own soul; all they that hate me love death". Do not be like those in Isaiah 28 who make a covenant with death by denying truth.

The prophecy of death being conquered and the resurrection of the dead in the last days is found in Isaiah 25:8 and 26:19, which states, "He will swallow up death in victory; and ADONAI YAHUAH will wipe away tears from off all faces; and the rebuke of his people shall he take away from off all the earth: for YAHUAH has spoken it. Your dead men shall live, together with my dead body shall they arise. Awake and sing, ye that dwell in dust; for your dew is as the dew of herbs, and the earth shall cast out the Repha'iym". Is death an entity? We are told in Revelation 6:8 that death is the one riding the green horse and She'ol follows after him. And death is given power over a fourth part of the earth to "kill with sword, and with hunger, and with death, and with the beasts of the earth."

Is this Azaz whom I wrote of earlier? Leviticus 16:26 says, "And he that let go the goat for Aza'zel shall wash his clothes and bathe his flesh in water and afterward come into the camp." This name is found in the Cepher and the Targum of Jonathan Ben Uzziel by Lewis Smith. According to Enoch chapter 7, this entity was the leader of the Watchers who fell as told in Genesis 6 or does he pre-date Genesis?

In Enoch chapter 8, we are told that Azaz instructed men "to make swords, knives, shields, breastplates, the fabrication of mirrors, and the workmanship of bracelets and ornaments, the use of paint, the beautifying of the eyebrows, stones of every valuable and select kind, and all sorts of dies so that the world became altered. Impiety increased; fornication multiplied; and they transgressed and corrupted all their ways".

Many of you will be disappointed that I did not name Lucifer. That name did not appear until the late fourth century in the Jerome Vulgate, a Latin translation from the Hebrew. Lucifer is Latin for light bringer and translated from the Hebrew word Halal or Helel, which is found in the Masoretic text where it is used in Isaiah 14:12. From the Targum of Isaiah, this verse is translated, "How art thou cast down from on high, who was shining among the sons of men as the star Venus among the stars; thou art dashed down to the earth, who wast a slaughterer among the nations." From the NETS Septuagint, the same verse reads, "How is fallen from heaven the day star, which used to rise early in the morning! He has been crushed into the earth who used to send light to all the nations!" From the Cepher, that verse reads, "How are you falling from heaven, O Heylel, son of the howling morning! How are you cut down to the ground, which did weaken the Nations!" Then, notice in verse 15 that he will be brought down to She'ol, "to the sides of the pit."

It is important to note that Isaiah 14 starts as a proverb that Isaiah is to say against the king of Babel. So, this Azaz, or this son of the howling morning, is over the territory of Babel. Is this the entity that kept the angel from coming to Daniel's aid? In 10:13, the angel tells Daniel, "But the prince of the kingdom of Persia withstood me one and twenty days; but, lo, Miyka'el, one of the chief princes, came to help me; and I remain there with the kings of Persia." Remember that Babylon is in Persia, and there are many captains or even generals in the host of Azaz. For instance, the Assyrian was in the garden of ELOHIYM, a tall cedar with fair branches from Ezekiel 31.

Enoch listed five angels in the garden before the fall of man. What were they doing there? I wonder if this is what Paul is alluding to in Titus 1:1-3 where he says, "Paul, a servant of YAHUAH, and an apostle of YAHUSHA HAMASHIACH, according to the belief of YAHUAH'S elect, and the acknowledging of the Truth which is in the fear of YAHUAH; our hope of eternal life, which YAHUAH, that cannot lie, promised before the world began; but has in due times manifested his Word through preaching which is committed unto me according to the commandment of YAHUAH our savior." Paul was knowledgeable of the Book of Enoch, just as YAHUSHA was, who called it scripture.

Enoch was shown where this host was destined to go. In The Book of Enoch, chapter 54, we see a deep valley burning with fire during his tour of the universe. He sees monarchs and the mighty being brought there, making fetters of iron of immeasurable weight. Verse 4 states, "Then I inquired of the angel of peace, who proceeded with me, saying, for whom are these fetters and instruments prepared? He replied, these are prepared for the host of Aza'zel, that they may be delivered over and sentenced to the lowest condemnation; and that their angels may be overwhelmed with hurled stones, as YAHUAH has commanded".

Is this the furnace of fire YAHUSHA mentions in Matthew 13:41, where he says, "The son of Adam shall send forth his angels, and they shall gather out of his kingdom all things that offend, and them which do transgress the Torah; and shall cast them into a furnace of fire: there shall be wailing and gnashing of teeth." Then we get the quote concerning our bright nature; "Then shall the righteous shine forth as the sun in the kingdom of their father. Who has ears to hear? Let Him hear". Just something to consider: who is being raptured, the righteous or the unrighteous? I have covered Matthew 25:41, where YAHUSHA on his judgment seat shall say to the people on his left hand, "depart from me, ye cursed, into everlasting fire, prepared for the devil and his angels." In verse 46 of Matthew 25, it says, "And these (the unrighteous, the lawbreakers) shall go away into everlasting punishment: but the righteous into life eternal." The unrighteous will be cast away just as the wedding guest who came to the feast in inappropriate attire (Matthew 22).

YAHUSHA, the Messiah, is our redeemer, the strong arm and wisdom of YAH, our rock, the way, the truth, the life, the door, and the Son who will judge. Everyone knew to be looking for a savior/redeemer who would vanquish death. Job stated in Job 19:25, "For I know that my Redeemer lives and that he shall stand at the latter day upon the earth; and though after my skin worms destroy this body, yet in my flesh shall I see ELOAH whom I shall see for myself, and my eyes shall behold, and not another." Is Daniel speaking of the same event in Daniel 12:2 and 13 when he is told, "And many of them that sleep in the dust of the earth shall awake, some to everlasting life, and some to shame and everlasting contempt? And they that shall be wise shall shine as the brightness of the expanse; and they that turn many to righteousness as the stars forever and ever." Then, in verse 13, Daniel is told to "go you your way till the end. For you shall rest; and stand in your lot at the end of the days".

Luke 2:11 is the most powerful of all New Testament statements concerning YAHUAH as salvation or YAHUAH as the Messiah. Isn't that what the Messiah is? The salvation of us all from eternal separation from our creator? The verse reads, "For unto you is born this day in the city of David, the savior, which is YAHUAH the MASHIACH." Luke points us back to the Prophecies of Messiah found in Isaiah 53:1 and Zachariah 12:10. Luke is trying to explain that the spirit of YAHUAH resided in YAHUSHA because the prophecies foretold that YAH would come in the form of a living man. Isaiah 53:1 reads, "Who has believed our report? And to whom is the arm of YAHUAH revealed? before him as a tender plant, and as a root out of dry ground", referring to the root in Isaiah 11:1.

Zechariah 12:10, 12 is much more interesting when considering Luke's genealogy of YAHUSHA. Luke traces YAHUSHA'S genealogy back to Nathan, son of King David, instead of Nathan's brother, King Solomon, as Mathew does. In Zechariah 12:10, we see the verse which is a prophecy of the Messiah, which states, "And I will pour upon the house of David, and the inhabitants of Jerusalem, the spirit of Grace and supplication; and they shall look upon me whom they have pierced, and they shall mourn for him, As One Mourns for his yachiyd" (beloved son). But further in verse 12, it says, "And the land shall mourn, every family apart; the family of the house of David apart, and their women apart; the family of the house of Nathan apart and their women apart."

Julius Africanus (AD 160–240) clarifies this confusion between the two genealogies in his First Epistle to Aristides. He explains how Matthew, a descendent of Solomon, begat Jacob. Matthew dies, and his wife marries Melchi, a descendant of Nathan, Solomon's brother. Together, Melchi and Matthew's widow have Heli. Heli dies childless, so his uterine brother Jacob (Solomon's descendant) bears him seed: Joseph, the father of Mary, the mother of YAHUSHA the Messiah. Therefore, YAHUSHA can claim heritage to King David by law through Heli, the descendant of Nathan, and by nature, the descendant of Solomon through Jacob, both sons of King David. See Deuteronomy 25:5.

Yes, Joseph was also the name of Mary's father. The word there in Aramaic is gowra, which designates a protector male or a guardian. If you notice, the genealogy ends in verse 17 of Matthew 1, and it begins to tell how the birth of our Messiah came to be. So, we have the past ending in verse 17, and starting in verse 18, we have the present. The two Joseph's are not the same. Joseph, even to this day, is an extremely popular name. I have three sisters and two brothers-in-law named Joseph. I have a friend who married a man named Joseph, and her two daughters married Josephs. But I digress. Paul confirms in Acts 13:23 that this prophecy in Zechariah 12:10-12 has been fulfilled when he states that the promise of salvation made by YAHUAH to all of Israel was completed in the coming of YAHUSHA, the Messiah.

Besides the references to the Messiah prophecies in Isaiah 53 and Zechariah 12:10, Peter repeats the reference of Psalm 110:1. Earlier in Acts 2:33, which I have covered, Peter said about YAHUSHA, "And this is he who is exalted at the right hand of Elohim and received the promise from the Father concerning the Ruach haKodesh" (from the Aramaic). Peter again cites Psalm 110 in Acts 5:31, saying, YAHUSHA, "This one Elohim has established a Prince and a Savior, and he has exalted him by his right hand so that he might give of forgiveness to Israel by repentance of sins." This verse should also bring to mind Isaiah 53. ELOHIYM gives the Messiah to Israel to take away their sins, then sits him at or by his right hand.

Paul is not confused as to who provides our salvation. In 1 Timothy 1:1 and again in 2 Timothy 1:1, Paul tells us that YAHUAH is our life-giver, but that Messiah is our hope. The life promised in Deuteronomy 32 and the promised redemption in Isaiah 50. However, Paul does something extraordinary in 1 Timothy 3:16. I will try to do Andrew Gabriel Roth justice by explaining the wordplay Paul uses in this verse to show just how clever and indeed profound Paul was by offering you the breakdown of that verse in Aramaic and the meaning of the words Paul was using. 1 Timothy 3:16 reads:

"And truly great, is this mystery of righteousness which was revealed in the flesh and righteous in the spirit, and seen by Messengers, and proclaimed among the Gentiles, and believed on in the world, and received up into glory."

The Aramaic reads:

*Sherirayt **rab** (great/high)*

*haw arza hela **d'kanota** (priest)*

***d'atgli b'besra** (revealed in the flesh) **w'atzaddaq** b'rokh (righteous) w'atkhaz **l'malaka** (king)*

w'atkeraz beyt ammah

w'athaymin 'almah

w'astalaq b'shubkha.

Can you see the play on words Paul has employed here? When you see the meanings of the Aramaic, you see Paul is saying, but in reverse, that Malik-Zadok, Melchizedek, has come in the flesh as our high priest who can redeem us. Let us put the whole of what Paul is saying here, starting in verse 14 of 1st Timothy Chapter 3. It reads, "These things I write to you while hoping soon to come to you; but if I should delay that you may know how you should conduct yourself in the house of Elohim, which is the assembly of the living Elohim. The pillar and the foundation of the truth, and truly great, is this mystery of righteousness which was revealed in the flesh and righteous in the spirit, and seen by Messengers, and proclaimed among the Gentiles, and believed on in the world, and received up into Glory ". The truth, the pillar of the foundation of the church, is the fact that the high priest Melchizedek, the king of righteousness, has manifested in the flesh of YAHUSHA, the son of Mary, who contained the spirit of YAHUAH. We know that righteous is another word for the law. So, Paul is saying the king of the law has manifested in the flesh.

Paul addresses this subject again in his letter to Titus, warning against the Gnostic sect of the Sadducees who did not believe in a resurrection of the flesh. They advanced knowledge as being superior to virtue. They also considered scripture in a non-literal sense, and that scripture could only be understood by a select few whose job was to explain the meaning of the scripture to the unclean masses. They also believed that deity could not manifest itself within anything material, such as a body. Paul's wording in Titus 1:3 describes YAHUAH manifesting his word, and at the end of the verse, he calls YAHUAH our savior/Yeshu'ah, which conflates the two. And he repeats this thought in Titus 2:13, where he says, "Looking for that blessed hope, and the glorious appearing of YAHUAH HA'GADOL (the great YAHUAH) and our Savior YAHUSHA HAMASHIACH. " Yes, I see the 'and' there, and no, I do not believe that Paul was telling us to look for two different entities. Paul is equating the two. Great YAHUAH is our savior, just as the scripture at the front of the book states. YAHUAH brought about our salvation/eternal life not by a mere thought but by a fleshly manifestation whose blood atoned for our sins once and for all time.

The Book of John has YAHUSHA preaching eternal life (chapters 3 through 6 and 10, 12 and 17). People will point to John 3:17 and claim that we are not to be judged or that we are not subject to the wrath of ELOHIYM. The verse from the Aramaic reads, "For Elohim did not send his son into the world to condemn the world, but to give life to the world through him." It is true; he was not judging the world at that time. He was showing us the way so that we could repent and sin no more and come into covenant and spend eternity in the presence of the Father. Salvation comes through belief in not just Messiah, but all that Messiah is and represents, which is his Father.

If we believe all this, then as YAHUSHA says in John 3:18-21 (from the Aramaic), "He that believes on him is not condemned, but he that does not believe, is already condemned; because he has not believed in the name of the only begotten Son of Elohim. Now this is the judgment: because the light has come into the world, and men loved the darkness more than the light, for their works are evil. For everyone who does hateful things hates the light and

283

does not come to the light, because his works will be hidden. But he who does truthful things comes to the light that this may be known that they are done in Elohim". Notice the Name comes up here again. Also, notice if you do not believe in the name and you do not come to the light, which is YAHUSHA, then you are already condemned. No judgment is needed.

I have established that eternal life/salvation is given by YAHUAH/ YAHUSHA. Also, Death is an entity, and that entity has a name. Is salvation also an entity? Is salvation a manifestation created by YAHUAH? Is it manifested in YAHUSHA? We know that first-century believers in YAHUAH expected a messiah who would bring them salvation/eternal life. There was also the belief that the Messiah would bring the Kingdom of Israel back into existence as it would have been under King David or Solomon. YAHUSHA fulfilled at least 300 prophesies. It is no wonder why people of his time, as well as ours, come to believe that he was the Messiah.

In Exodus 14:13, Israel is pinned between the Egyptians and the Reed Sea and crying out for salvation. Moses tells them to "fear not, stand still and see the salvation (yeshu'ah) of the Lord which shall be wrought for you this day." Then we are told, as I have covered in the chapter concerning the Angel of the Lord, this angel who was leading the way before Israel went and came behind them, and the column of the cloud "went from before and stood behind them". The Targum tells us that one side of the cloud was darkened for the Egyptians, and the other side shined upon Israel all night before the sea was split and Israel was led across. As a side note, I wonder if this image inspired the yin and yang symbol, the half-white and half-black circle. This salvation of YAH was the angel in the cloud: A manifestation of YAHUAH as the Angel, YAHUSHA the Messiah, the deliverer and redeemer whom Israel saw.

Later in Exodus 15:2, Moses sings a song of praise to YAHUAH and his works of salvation. He sings, "YAH is my strength and song, and he has become my yeshu'ah; he is my EL." Then in Deuteronomy 32:15, Moses sings, "But Yasharun waxed fat, and kicked; you are waxen fat, you are grown thick, you are covered with fatness; then he forsook ELOAH which made him, and lightly esteemed to the Rock of his Yeshu'ah" (salvation). I have covered 2 Samuel 22:2-3 where there is the illusion of two entities, especially in verse 3 where David says, "the ELOHAI of my Rock; in him will I trust: he is my shield and the horn of my Yeshu'ah," whereas before David says in verse 2 that YAHUAH is my Rock. David repeats this in verse 47, saying, "YAHUAH lives; and blessed be my Rock; and exalted be the ELOHAI of the Rock of my yeshu'ah." This makes sense since David says in Psalm 3:8 that yeshu'ah belongs to YAHUAH; your blessing is upon your people".

In Matthew 16:18, YAHUSHA declared himself The Rock on which his Ecclesia would be founded. Peter confirms this in Acts 4:11 and 12, where he declares that YAHUSHA, the Messiah of Natsareth was the "stone, which was set at naught of you builders, which is become the head of the corner.

Neither is there yeshu'ah in any other; for there is no other name under heaven given among men, whereby we must be saved". He is quoting Psalm 118:22. I could go on, but as you read the scriptures, you will begin to see that salvation is The Rock and that salvation is YAHUAH manifested in the flesh of YAHUSHA the Messiah.

In John 8:12, YAHUSHA declared that he was the "Light of the world; he that follows me shall not walk in darkness but shall have the light of life." This statement would hearken his listeners to Psalm 27:1, which states, "YAHUAH is my light and my yeshu'ah, Whom shall I fear? YAHUAH is the strength of my life; of whom shall I be afraid?" Light leads us to salvation, just as the angel who was the guiding light to the Israelites during the exodus. Light is also from Messiah as Enoch tells us in his second parable in chapter 45 where YAHUAH tells Enoch, "In that day I will cause my elect one to dwell in the midst of them; will change heaven; will bless it and illuminate it forever." He further states in chapter 48:3 that the Messiah "shall be the light of nations." See Revelation 21:24.

I have briefly covered Isaiah 49 which is a clear prophecy of the Messiah coming to restore Israel. However, to determine who is speaking in chapter 49 of Isaiah, we need to go to Isaiah 45:11-12 which reads, (from the Targum Isaiah) "Thus sayeth the Lord, the Holy One of Israel, and He that formed him, ye question me about things concerning my people, which shall come to pass; and will ye command me concerning the work of my power? It is I who have made the earth by my Word, and I have created man upon it; it is I who have suspended the heavens by my power, and I have laid the foundation of all the hosts of them." We see here it is YAHUAH who created all things through the Holy One of Israel. From the Cepher, these verses read, "Thus says YAHUAH, the Holy One of Yashar'el, and his Maker, ask me of things to come concerning my sons, and concerning the works of my hands command ye me? I have made the earth and created man upon it; I, even my hands, have stretched out the heavens, and all their hosts have I commanded." Verse 13 continues, "I have raised him up in righteousness, and I will direct all his ways; he shall build my city, and he shall let go my captives, not for price nor reward, says, YAHUAH TSEVA'OTH. "Here, he calls himself Lord of Hosts. In verse 17 of Isaiah 45, YAHUAH admits he is salvation when he says, "But Yashar'el shall be saved by the Word of YAHUAH with an everlasting salvation; ye shall not be ashamed nor confounded world without end." I realize the salvation of Israel, as foretold here, is thought to have been brought by King Cyrus, who is mentioned in verse 1 and earlier in 44:28. King Cyrus the Great (590 - 529 B.C.) did proclaim the Israelites to be free to return and rebuild their temple in Jerusalem. However, it is evident when you get past verse 11 of Isaiah chapter 45 that we are no longer talking about salvation being delivered by an earthly king. King Cyrus did not deliver everlasting salvation. In Isaiah 49:5, we have another instance of YAHUAH speaking of himself in the form of his salvation as though it is in the flesh. The verse reads, "And now, says YAHUAH that formed me from the womb to be his servant, to bring Ya'aqov again to him. Though Yashar'el is not gathered, yet shall I be glorious in the eyes of YAHUAH". From the Targum Isaiah, verse 5 concludes, "And the Word of my God shall be my support." Continuing from the Cepher, verse 6 reads, "And he said, it is a light thing that you should be my servant to raise up the tribes of Ya'aqov and to restore the preserved (H5336) of Yashar'el; I will also give you for a light to the other nations, that you may be my Yeshu'ah unto the end of the earth. Thus says YAHUAH, the Redeemer of Yashar'el and his Holy One, to him whom man despises, to him whom the nation abhors, to a servant of rulers, Kings shall see and arise, princes also shall worship, because of YAHUAH that is faithful, and the Holy One of Yashar'el, and he shall choose you. Thus says YAHUAH in an acceptable time have I heard you, and in a day of yeshu'ah have I helped you; and I will preserve you, and give you for a covenant of the people, to establish the earth, to cause to inherit the desolate heritages; that you may say to the prisoners, go forth; to them that are in darkness, show yourselves. They shall feed in the ways, and their pastures shall be in all high places".

I highlight these verses because it is unclear who is speaking. It is YAHUAH because, at the beginning of chapter 45, it tells us it is YAHUAH speaking. However, the chapter starts, "Listen, O isles, unto me." Instead of 'me,' the Targum Isaiah says, "Listen unto My Word." The Word is speaking these verses, are they not? Isaiah 45:1 from the Cepher continues, "Hearken ye people from far; YAHUAH has called me from the womb; from the belly of my mother has he made mention of my name. He has made my mouth like a sharp sword; in the shadow of his hand has he hid me and made me a polished shaft; in his quiver has he hid me; and he said unto me you are my servant, O Yashar'el, in whom I will be glorified". I know many will say this is talking about the people of Israel, but is it? Is it not talking about the savior of Israel? Is this verse saying YAH will be glorified in the servant or Israel? Israel is not the savior because earlier in Isaiah 43:3,11, YAHUAH is telling Israel that HE is their savior, their Yeshu'ah and that there is no other savior than him. Isaiah 45:17 is very specific about Israel being saved by the Word of YAHUAH. Israel will not be saving itself.

Further, in Isaiah 45: 21,22, which states, "Who has declared this from ancient time? Who has told it from that time? Have not I YAHUAH? And there is no Elohim else beside me; a just EL, and a Savior; there is none beside me. Look unto My Word, and be ye saved, all the ends of the earth; for I am EL, and there is none else". YAHUSHA, the Messiah, taught in the region of Israel and laid down his life in Jerusalem. He was the light that shone upon those who were in darkness. Divorced Israel now has a path back to righteousness, to enter into a covenant with YAHUAH ELOHIYM.

In Hebrews 4:12, the writer tells us that the Word of YAHUAH is quick and powerful, and sharper than a two-edged sword, piercing even to the dividing asunder of soul and ruach, and of the joints and marrow, and is a discerner of the thoughts and intents of the heart". Is this verse recalling Isaiah 49?

Is John in Revelation 1:16 doing the same? John describes the Messiah as having in his "right hand seven stars; and out of his mouth went a sharp two-edged sword; and his countenance was as the sun shines in his strength."

Before I leave these verses, I want to address the phrase 'preserved' of Israel in Isaiah 49:6. Looking at the word preserved (H5336) in the Strong's Concordance, we see it is Nasir from H5341; properly, conservative, but used passively, delivered: —preserved. Fair enough, but the primitive root word H5341 is Nasar to guard, in a good sense (to protect, maintain, obey, etc.) or a bad one (to conceal, etc.): —besieged, hidden thing, keep (-er, - ing), monument, observe, preserve(-r), subtle, watcher (-man). Could Isaiah be referring to a reconciliation of heaven here? Are the Natsariym, the Elect who were with ELOHIYM from the foundation of the world, the same as watchers? The word translated as branch is H5342 Neser. This word is also from the primitive root word H5341 Nasar.

Remember the Prayer of Joseph, where Israel claims to be an angel like Uriel. Now consider Jeremiah 31, where in verse 6 it says from the Cepher, "For there shall be a day, that the Natsariym upon Mount Ephrayim shall cry, arise ye and let us go up to Tsiyon unto YAHUAH ELOHAYNU." These, the Elect from the foundation of the world, causes Jeremiah 31 to be seen more clearly. It reads, "They shall come with weeping, and with supplications will I lead them: I will cause them to walk by the rivers of waters in the straight way, wherein they shall not stumble for I am a Father to Yashar'el, and

Ephrayim is my firstborn." Remember, YAHUSHA is the way, a narrow path beset on both sides with fire and water. I realize this could be considered a stretch because Ephraim is the second-born son of Joseph and his Egyptian wife Acenath, the daughter of Potiy Phera, the priest of On. Israel adopts Joseph's sons and places Ephrayim above his older brother, Menashsheh. If these are the Elect who come to prove their hearts to YAH, then maybe Israel is putting Ephraim in his proper order.

The word Nasar is used again by Jeremiah in chapter 4:16, which tells how these elect or Natsariym will come from a far country and testify against the cities of Yehudah. These will be the followers of the branch of Jesse, YAHUSHA h'anetseriy (the branch). These followers are the remnant from Revelation 12:17 who will guard the Commandments of YAHUAH and have the testimony of YAHUSHA the Messiah as it is written in Isaiah 8:20, "To the Torah and the testimony: if they speak not according to this word, it is because there is no light in them." YAHUSHA and his followers are lights to the nations speaking the words of the Father.

The Arm of YAHUAH brings salvation. Isaiah 59:16-17 says, "And he saw that there was no man, and wondered that there was no intercessor; therefore, his arm brought salvation unto him; and his righteousness, it sustained him. For he put on righteousness as a breastplate, and a helmet of yeshu'ah upon his head". Is this what Paul is referring to in Ephesians 6:17, where he says, to "take the helmet of yeshu'ah, and the sword of the RUACH, which is the Word of YAHUAH "?

It is clear that salvation comes as a person. And that entity is YAHUAH who has and will manifest himself again as Isaiah says in 62:11, "Behold, YAHUAH has proclaimed unto the end of the world, say ye to the daughter of Tsiyon, Behold, your yeshu'ah comes; behold his reward is with him, and his work before him." He is YAHUAH TSEVA'OTH, LORD of the Angelic host, just as Hebrews 2:10 states, "For it became him, for whom are all things, and by whom are all things, in bringing many sons unto glory, to make the captain of their yeshu'ah (salvation) perfect through sufferings." In Aramaic, Hebrews 2:10 states that YAHUSHA is the "prince of our life". The Torah giver, if followed, brings Eternal life, which is salvation.

Hebrews 5:9-10 states, "And being made perfect, he became the author of eternal salvation unto all them that obey him; Called of YAHUAH a high priest after the order of Malkiy-Tsedeq. "The word for 'became' in verse 9 is G1096 ginomai, which means to cause to be. The word author is G159 Aitios, which implies a causer. This word is the same as G154 Aiteo, which means to ask, beg, call for, crave, desire, or require. So, what the writer here in Hebrews is saying is that YAHUAH caused a way or a path to open for us to obtain eternal life. Our husband and high priest died and rose in his glorified state, allowing us to enter into covenant with him.

You will find the rules on divorce and separation in Ezekiel 44:22, where the proclamation is made, that priests are not allowed to marry a widow, or one put away. However, they can marry maidens of Israel or a priest's widow. In Leviticus 21:7, we are told that one cannot marry a whore or a profane woman or one that has been put away from her man, hence the need for our cleansing or purification. In Deuteronomy 24:1-4 we learn that after a man divorces his wife and she remarries and becomes divorced or widowed, her first husband cannot remarry her. Israel received a writ of divorce, see Jeremiah 3:8. And her sister Judah was put away, see 2 Kings 23:27. However, in Isaiah 50, we see a promise of YAHUAH to reconcile himself with his bride. In verse 1, it says, "Thus says YAHUAH, where is the cepher of your mother's divorcement, whom I have put away? Or which of my creditors is it to whom I have sold you? Behold, for your iniquities, have ye sold yourselves, and for your transgressions is your mother put away. Wherefore when I came, was there no man? When I called, was there none to answer? Is my hand shortened at all, that it cannot redeem?"

It is interesting that if you continue to read Isaiah chapter 50, you will see that between verses 5 and 9, you have another occurrence where you must question who is speaking. Is it YAHUAH or the Messiah? Later, you get to Isaiah 53, which is a clear Messianic prophecy where the arm of YAHUAH is revealed and that he will be bruised and wounded for our transgressions and that YAHUAH laid on him the iniquity of us all. Isaiah 53:1 begins, "Who has believed our report?" Who could believe that YAHUAH, the Creator of heaven and earth could reconcile his bride to himself by coming in the flesh and dying allowing her to remarry? We fail to consider the power of our great ELOHIYM, the creator of heaven and earth. We consider his hand shortened in that he would be unable to bring about such a magnificent work of salvation. However, do not forget the bride must also die. Therefore, to enter into covenant, we must die to the flesh.

Salvation, eternal life, is not just something that we gather to ourselves. It can be summarized in the Shema of Deuteronomy 6, which all of Israel learned as children attending synagogue. The Shema reads: "Hear O Yashar'el: YAHUAH ELOHAYNU, YAHUAH is one; and you shall love YAHUAH ELOHAYKA with all your heart, and with all your soul, and with all your might. And these words, which I command you this day, shall be in your heart; and you shall teach them diligently unto your children, and shall talk of them when you sit in your house, and when you walk by the way, and when you lie down, and when you rise up. And you shall bind them for a sign upon your hand, and they shall be as frontlets over your eyes. And you shall write them upon the posts of your house, and on your gates. And it shall be, when YAHUAH ELOHAYKA shall have brought you into the land which he swore unto your father's, to Avraham, to Yitschaq and to Ya'aqov, to give you great and goodly cities, which you built not. And houses full of all good things, which you filled not, and wells dug, which you dug not, vineyards and olive trees, which you planted not; when you shall have eaten and be full; then beware lest you forget YAHUAH, which brought you forth out of the land of Mitsrayim, from the house of bondage. You shall fear YAHUAH ELOHAYKA, and serve him, and shall swear by his name. You shall not go after other elohiym, of the elohiym of the people which are round about you; (for YAHUAH ELOHAYKA is a jealous EL among you) lest the anger of YAHUAH ELOHAYKA be kindled against you and destroy you from off the face of the earth".

The word 'hear' in Deuteronomy 6:4 is Shema H8085 from the Strong's Concordance. It means שמע , shâma', shaw-mah', a primitive root; to hear intelligently (often with implication of attention, obedience, etc.; causatively, to tell, etc.). Therefore, the Commandments are something we hear and then do to obtain life. This is what Paul is talking about when he says in 2 Timothy 1:9-10, "Who has saved us, and called us with a holy calling, not according to our works, but according to his own purpose and grace, which was given us in MASHIACH YAHUSHA before the world began. But is now made manifest by the appearing of our savior YAHUSHA HAMASHIACH, who has abolished death and has brought life and immortality to light through the Besorah". Besorah means gospel or good message. What is the gospel? What was the good message?

By now, you should know that the good news is that our creator, who had covenanted to be our Elohim, whom we forsook and followed our hearts desires, has made way for us to return to that Covenant. We had been put away and divorced. Now, we can accept him, a prospective groom who has made a proposition and stands knocking on our door.

He asks us to put him at the head of our lives: to make him our spiritual ruler, our husband.

In his first epistle to the Corinthians, Paul addresses how we establish our congregations and small gatherings. I say small because your world becomes much smaller once you start walking in the way. My daddy always said it must be wrong if everyone is doing it. Paul is talking about disciplining one another, covering one another, lovingly correcting, sharpening, and encouraging one another. You would do something if you saw a friend running headlong into danger. You would step into the gap and try to avert danger, and that is what the letter to the Corinthians is all about, especially the first ten chapters. So, when Paul is admonished about his stance on women, just remember or keep in mind that that is the subject of the letter: covering each other so that we do not do something foolish that would risk losing our salvation.

You can lose your salvation. This doctrine of once saved, always saved is not established in scripture. Sirach 34:23-26 (Ecclesiastes 34:23-26) states, "When one builds, and another pulls down, what profit have they then but labor? When one prays and another curses, whose voice will YAHUAH hear? He that washes himself after the touching of a dead body, if he touches it again, what avails his washing? So it is with a man that fasts for his sins, goes again, and does the same; who will hear his prayer? Or what does his humbling profit him?" I do not want anyone to think I am dogmatic and forget about Grace. However, I am not sure we know what that is today.

When thinking about what constitutes grace, undeserved favor, I remember an incident at my grandmother's house years ago. Now, we were raised in her house, and we knew the rules. We did not jump on furniture, and we did not sit on the bed. You did not get on the bed during the day unless you were sick. But there was an incident where someone had come with a small child to visit my grandmother, and the mother allowed the child to jump and stand on my grandmother's couch. My grandmother allowed space; she was gracious for this woman to admonish her child and to make her behave because she had told her standing on furniture was not allowed in her house. My grandmother had to admonish the child herself. I would have received a whipping if that had been me, but I cannot say exactly what the correction was. I do not know if she gave the child a spanking or not. I just know the mother was upset. The woman with this child was not kicked out of the house and told never to come again. She was given the rules and provided an example of what you do to bring an unruly child to correction and allowed to complete the visit. It was up to this woman to decide whether she wanted to accept grace by returning to my grandmother's house with a child who had been taught how to behave.

Unlike the man who was caught gathering sticks on the Sabbath and who suffered the death penalty instantaneously due to his law-breaking, this woman was allowed to stay in grandma's house with her corrected child. She was welcomed back if the mother and her child would abide by the rules of the house.

We see an example of grace in Acts 15; James, Peter, and the disciples are contemplating what to do with the gentiles who had not grown up with the rules. These new believers were told not to eat animals that had been strangled, to consume no blood, to stay away from idol worship, and to not fornicate because these new believers would attend synagogue and hear Moses preached thus learning what it is that is expected of them. YAHUSHA said, if you love me, follow my commandments. Our salvation is a heart condition. What is in your heart? Remember the Shema. Love YAHUAH with all your heart, with all your soul, with all your might, and if you do that, you are going to do the right thing because you are going to want to learn and do what he wants from you.

THE BOOK OF LIFE

*I swear to you, righteous, that in heaven the Angels record your goodness before the glory of EL ELOHIYM. Wait with patient hope; for formally you have been disgraced with evil and with affliction; but now shall you shine like the luminaries of heaven. You shall be seen, and the gates of heaven shall be open to you. Your cries have cried for judgment; and it **has** appeared to you; for an account of all your sufferings shall be required from the princes, and from everyone who has assisted your plunderers. Wait with patient hope; nor relinquish your confidence; for great joy shall be yours, like that of the angels of heaven. Conduct yourselves as you may, still you shall not be concealed in the day of the great judgment. You shall not be found like sinners; and eternal condemnations shall be far from you, so long as the world exists. First Book of Enoch 104:1-3*

While intervening for the Israelites in Exodus 32:32, Mosheh said, "Yet now, if you will forgive their sin; and if not, blot me, I pray you, out of your cepher (book) which you have written." There is a book of life, and we can be blotted out of it. The Book of Daniel 12:1-4 states, "And at that time shall Michael stand up, the great Prince which stands for the children of your people; and there shall be a time of trouble, such as never was since there was a nation even to that same time; and at that time your people shall be delivered, every one that shall be written that shall be found written in the cepher. And many of them that sleep in the dust of the earth shall awake, some to everlasting life, and some to shame and everlasting contempt". Notice that not all shall rise.

Enoch is shown the receptacles of the souls, where we go after we die. There were three divisions, and they are explained in chapter 22. In verse 14 it states "a receptacle of this sort has been formed for the souls of unrighteous men, and of sinners; of those who have completed crime, and associated with the impious, whom they resemble. Their souls shall not be annihilated in the day of judgment, neither shall they arise from this place".

In Luke 10:17-20 after the 70 disciples had returned joyfully, reporting they were able to subject devils to their will, YAHUSHA said to them in verse 20, "Notwithstanding, in this rejoice not, that the spirits are subject unto you; but rather rejoice, because your names are written in heaven."

What do we do then to ensure that our names are written in this Book of Life and to make sure that our names are not blotted out? We could begin looking at the differences between the two brothers, Esau, and Jacob, as most of us did as children in Sunday school. In Genesis 25:27, we are told that "the boys grew; and Esau was a cunning hunter, a man of the field; and Jacob was an upright man, dwelling in tents."

In reading the extra-biblical books of Jasher and Jubilees concerning Esau, we learn that he had a total disregard for learning the ways of YAH. We also learn from these extra-biblical books that the patriarch Abraham, as well as Jacob, studied with Noah and his son Shem. The field mentioned in Genesis 25:27 is the world where Esau dwelled, and the tents Jacob dwelt in were the tents of Noah and Shem, where he learned the ways of ELOHIYM. Paul quotes Malachi in 1:3 in Romans 9:13. That YAHUAH hates Esau because he embraced the world and refused to acknowledge his Creator.

In Genesis 17:1, YAHUAH told Abraham to walk before him and be perfect. Deuteronomy 18:13 says we will be perfect with YAHUAH. I have not forgotten about nor am I diminishing the act of grace that we receive from the Most High, which I have covered. We are babes learning how to walk the walk. And do not believe that YASHUAH, the Messiah, did not preach this. In the sermon of the mount, Matthew 5:48, he repeats himself to his listeners and you, the reader, to "be perfect, even as your Father which is in heaven is perfect." It is important to note what YAHUSHA told the rich young man in Matthew 19:17-21, "And he said unto him, why do you call me good? There is none good but one, that is YAHUAH; but if you will enter into life, guard the commandments." The young man then inquired as to which commandment led to eternal life. YAHUSHA listed the commandments, "You shall not murder, you shall not break wedlock, you shall not steal, you shall not bear false witness, honor your father and your mother, and you shall love your neighbor as yourself." The young man said, "I have done all this. "YAHUSHA knew better, notice he had not listed all the commandments, and told the young man, "If you will be perfect, go and sell that you have, and give to the poor, and you shall have treasure in heaven; and come and follow me." In these verses in Matthew chapter 19, YAHUSHA quotes Exodus 20: 12-16 and Deuteronomy 5:16-20 where you will find these commandments.

Remember the parable of the ten virgins who all had lamps. They all had oil, which, as I said, is the name. However, we receive oil as a product of our crushing. Remember the stones from The Shepherd of Hermes. Some of the stones were cast back into the field, i.e., the world because they were not a proper fit. These stones had not been tossed about and made smooth enough to fit into the building, i . e . , The church. five of the virgins needed more oil, so they had to leave their party to gather more.

It is our trials and tribulations James is alluding to when he tells his listeners in James 1:4, "But let patience have her perfect work, that ye may be perfect and entire, wanting nothing." James continues in verse 5, "If any of you lack wisdom, let him ask of YAH, that gives it to all men liberally, and upbraids not; and it shall be given him". Just as YAHUSHA said, ask, and you shall receive. My experience has been that many people do not want to know the truth because once you know the Truth, you must conform. You cannot change the Truth; the Truth must change you. The path then becomes lonely, just like it says in 4 Ezra 7:6. The path becomes so narrow in some places that only one man can walk along at a time. I know this because Christians have become offended by my pointing out that YAHUSHA, the Messiah, as well as his disciples, taught the Torah and its adherence. My Christian friends would ask, 'But what about Paul?" Paul's letters have consistently been used to justify a sinful lifestyle. My answer to this question of Paul is what I have already said. If you think Paul is teaching something other than what his Messiah or the other disciples taught, then you are not understanding Paul. And you need to learn the front of the book just half as well as Paul knew it. Then we become as the householder YAHUSHA spoke of in Matthew 13:52, who "brings forth out of his treasure things new and old."

After Paul declares that YAHUSHA is YAHUAH in Philippians 2:10, he says, "Wherefore, my beloved as you have always obeyed, not as in my presence only, but now much more in my absence, work out your salvation with fear and trembling. For it is YAHUAH which works to you both to will and to do his good pleasure". YAH'S good pleasure is for us to live eternally and not to have our best life now on earth. To obtain eternal life, we must follow the Word of YAHUAH manifested in the flesh.

Read and learn the Song of Moses (Deuteronomy 32). In Revelation 15, we are told of the significance of knowing this song starting in verse 1, which says, "And I saw another sign in heaven, great and marvelous, seven angels having the seven last plagues; for in them is filled up the wrath of YAHUAH. And I saw as it were a sea of glass mingled with fire;

and them that had gotten the victory over the beast, and over his image, and over his mark, and over the number of his name, stand on the sea of glass, having the kithara of YAHUAH. And they sing the song of Mosheh the servant of YAHUAH, and the song of the Lamb, saying, great and marvelous are your works, YAHUAH ELOHIYM TSEVA'OTH; just and true are your ways, King of the qodeshiym".

Notice all the 'ands' in this verse. It is not just the number. It is those people who Wonder or admire this beast whose names will not be written in The Book of Life. The exact verse from Revelation 17:8 reads, "The Beast that you saw was, and is not, and shall ascend out of the bottomless pit, and go into perdition and they that dwell on earth shall wonder, whose names were not written in the cepher of life from the foundation of the world, when they behold the beast that was, and is not, and yet is." Spending time wondering about the beast is nothing but a distraction away from what is truly important.

It is up to us to battle against our flesh. 2nd Samuel 22:24-26 says, "I was also upright before him, and I have guarded myself from my iniquity. With the merciful you will show yourself merciful, and with the upright man you will show yourself upright". This all ties back to the Torah because earlier in verse 22, David says, "For I have guarded the ways of YAHUAH, and have not wickedly departed from my ELOHIYM." Paul speaks to this in Romans 7, where he is talking about people like him being raised in the oral laws and traditions of Judaism and how hard it was in overcoming. Remember, YAHUSHA loosed them from all those little mitzvot that had been made up to keep them from breaking the Torah, which brought immediate death. Paul finishes in verse 22, where he says, "For I delight in the Torah of YAHUAH after the inward man, but I see another Torah in my members, warring against the Torah of my mind, and bringing me into captivity to the Torah of sin which is in my members."

I can only imagine how difficult it would be to overcome a lifetime of traditions, rituals and superstition. I was not raised in a highly ritualized religious environment. However, giving up the pagan holidays was hard enough, in that family and friends do not understand. They recognize YAHUAHs' appointed times as Jewish not knowing that Leviticus 26:2 says, "You shall keep my Sabbaths." They are his Feasts, not ours. We are invited guests to his party. And remember the parable of the wedding feast, we must also come in the proper attire.

James chapter 2:14 says, "What does it profit, my brethren, though a man says he has belief, and have not works? Can belief save him"? The Aramaic says, "can belief resurrect him"? I have covered James chapter 2; however, before verse 14, James quotes the Commandments from Leviticus 19:18, Exodus 20:13,14, and Deuteronomy 5:17, 18. I believe James may be hearkening his listeners back to 2 Baruch 14:12, which reads, "For the righteous justly hope for the end, and without fear depart from this habitation, because they have with you a store of works preserved in treasuries." There is an inventory written in heaven of your treasures and they are your deeds.

We must remember the parable of the tares in Matthew 13:24, which states that the tares in the latter days will be the ones rooted out of the earth, much like what it says in Proverbs 2:21-22 which states for the yashariym (upright) shall dwell in the land, and the perfect shall remain in it. But the wicked shall be cut off from the earth, and the transgressors shall be rooted out of it". This is reiterated in Proverbs 10:29, which states, "The way of YAHUAH is strength to the upright, but destruction shall be to the workers of iniquity. The righteous shall never be removed, but the wicked shall not inhabit the earth". Again, in Proverbs 11:5, we have righteousness, which we know from Psalm 119 is lawfulness, "shall direct the way of the perfect. But the wicked shall fall by his wickedness. The righteousness of the yashariym shall deliver them; but transgressors shall be taken in their own wickedness".

After the writer of Hebrews has made the case that YAHUSHA, the son of Mary, was the Messiah, the Son of ELOHIYM, he states in chapter 10, which I have covered, starting in verse 26, "For if we sin willfully after that we have received the knowledge of the Truth (Commandments), there remains no more sacrifice for sins. But a certain fearful looking for of judgment and fiery indignation, which shall devour the adversaries. He that despises Mosheh's Torah dies without mercy by two or three witnesses; of how much sorer punishment, suppose you, shall he be thought worthy, who has trodden underfoot the Son of ELOHIYM, and has counted the blood of the Covenant, wherewith he is sanctified, an unholy thing, and has done despite unto the spirit of grace? For we know him that has said, Vengeance belongs unto me, I will recompense, says YAHUAH".

The hope spoken of in Enoch in the above-quoted verses is the Messiah who through his mercy is offering a renewed Covenant the one initially given to Adam, Abraham, Isaac, and Jacob and consummated on Mount Sinai. The good news, The Gospel, is that we can enter into this Covenant and receive its promises (Leviticus 26:3-13). If we live in accordance with that Covenant so that at the end of it all, we can be confident when we stand before the Most High Elohim as stated in Revelation 20:12 which reads, "And I saw the dead, small and great, stand before YAHUAH and the books were opened: and another book was opened, which is the book of life: and the dead were judged out of those things which were written in the books, according to their works".

CONCLUSION

Who will inherit land? "Those who endure for the Lord". Perhaps we endure for one who is endurance. For it is written, 'And who now is my endurance? Is it not the Lord?" And just as the Savior is "wisdom," he is "logos" as well; he is "peace"; he is "justice," so he is "endurance." And we become just by participation in him; we become Peaceable by participation in him; we become wise by participation in him; so we also become patient by participation in him. We have participation in the entire saving action of Christ, from whom it is possible to draw and take patience, justice, wisdom, and all things that Christ is said to be in the scriptures. So, it is said, those who endure for the Lord, will inherit the land. — Origen, Homily II on Psalm 36

The Word endurance is defined as the fact or power of <u>enduring</u> an <u>unpleasant</u> or arduous process or situation without giving way. YAHUSHA speaks of our struggle in Mark 13:12,13 when he says, "Now the brother shall betray the brother to death, and the father of the son; and children shall rise up against their parents and shall cause them to be put to death. And ye shall be hated of all men for my namesake; but he that shall endure unto the end, the same shall be saved".

The disciples of YAHUSHA the Messiah underwent many trials and tribulations. In the book of Acts chapter 14, we are told Paul was stoned and presumed dead. However, he did recover, and the verse says he and Barnabas "went on their way confirming the souls of the Talmidiym, and exhorting them to continue in the belief, and that we must through much tribulation enter into the Kingdom of YAHUAH."

James considered the trials and tribulations of life to be a blessing from YAHUAH when he says in chapter 1:2-4, 12: "My brethren count it all joy when you fall into diverse temptations; knowing this; that the trying of your belief works patience. But let patience have her perfect work, that you may be perfect and entire, wanting nothing". Then, in verse 12, he says, "Blessed is the man that endures temptation; for when he is tried, he shall receive the crown of life, which YAHUAH has promised to them that love him."

Peter also spoke of our trials and tribulations in 1 Peter 1:7, where he says, "That the trial of your belief, being much more precious than of gold that perishes, though it be tried with fire, might be found unto praise and honor and glory at the appearing of YAHUSHA

HAMASHIACH." And again, in 4:12,13, Peter says, "Beloved, think it not strange concerning the fiery trial, which is to try you, as though some strange thing happened unto you; but rejoice, and as much as you are partakers of MASHIACH'S sufferings; that, when his glory shall be revealed, ye may be glad also with exceeding joy." Since we are to share in MASHIACH's trials, it would be prudent to ask and then read what YAHUSHA did instead of wondering what he might do given our circumstances. The answers are in your scriptures. Solomon told us there is nothing new under the sun, and he is right.

Since the crucifixion and resurrection of the Messiah YAHUSHA, his followers have suffered tribulations the likes never seen before. Paul tells us of his sufferings. We are told of Peter being crucified upside down by Nero, but Clement of Alexandria also tells us in his Stromata book 7, chapter 11, that before his death, Peter witnessed the torture and death of his wife. We are also told he encouraged her to remain strong in her faith during her trial. According to Clement, the death of Peter's wife is what Paul addresses in 1 Corinthians 7. Paul tells his listeners in verse 29 that "time is short; it remains, that both they that have women be as though they had none." In other words, the enemy will come after your loved ones to get to you, so if you do not think you are strong enough to encourage your loved ones to endure to the end, much like the mother from 4

Maccabees then it is best for you to remain unattached.

Besides crucifixion, we have reports of the followers of Messiah YAHUSHA being dragged behind horses, burned to death, slain with a sword, speared to death, strangled, fed to a fiery furnace, sawn in twain, beheaded, drowned, starved to death, and legs were broken which led to death. The first martyr Stephen, whose last words led to his stoning are recorded in Acts 7. In approximately 62 A.D., the Jews threw James, the brother of YAHUSHA the Messiah, from a pinnacle of the temple while he was preaching in Jerusalem. Then, a fuller of cloth crushed his skull with a club, and then stoned him for good measure. This led to the civil war in Jerusalem, which ended in the destruction of the temple in 70 A.D. The fact that James was thrown off the temple, his head crushed, and then stoned testifies to the anger the Truth stimulates in the sons of darkness.

Our trials and tribulations were foretold in the front of our bibles, so we should not be surprised. YAHUSHA told Paul what he was to suffer, and he followed anyway. Knowing the scriptures, Paul knew what he was being told was Truth. Paul knew the prophecy of Isaiah. In Isaiah 26:20,21, the Targum says, "Come, O my people; produce for thyself good works, which shall protect thee in the time of distress; hide thyself as it were for a little moment until the curse shall have passed away. For, behold, the Lord is revealing himself from the place of his Shekinah to punish the inhabitants of the earth for their sins. The earth shall disclose the innocent blood that was shed in her and shall no more cover her slain". Isaiah 13:9 states, "Behold, the day from before the presence of the Lord cometh, cruel both with wrath and fierce anger, to lay the land desolate and he shall destroy the sinners out of it." Paul knew the prize we would obtain for our endurance of trials and tribulations would be well worth our sufferings. He knew the promise in Isaiah 57:16: "For I will not take vengeance of judgment forever, neither shall my wrath be eternal: for I will revive the spirits of the dead, and the souls I have created."

We are like the believers in the wilderness who were learning the gospel. Paul told Timothy in 2 Timothy 3:15-17, "And from a child you have known the Holy Scriptures, which are able to make you wise unto yeshu'ah (salvation) through belief which is in YAHUSHA HAMASHIACH. All scripture is given by the RUACH YAHUAH, and is profitable for doctrine, for reproof, for correction, for instruction in lawfulness: That the man of YAH may be perfect, thoroughly furnished unto all good works". The scriptures Paul is referring to are in our Old Testament. If it was important then, it is just as important now. In Truth, Paul is referring Timothy back to Proverbs 4:2, which states, "For I give you good doctrine, forsake ye not my Torah."

It was YAHUSHAs' many divinity claims that caused the leadership in Jerusalem to seek his life. The Pharisees recognized YAHUSHAs' claim of being the son of Elohim, the Rock, the True Vine, the light of the world, the Truth, the way and being life itself, all titles which the Most High ELOHIYM proclaimed himself to be in the Old Testament books.

In Revelation 22:13 YAHUSHA said that he was the ALEPH and the Tav, the beginning and the end, the first and the last. He became all things, even last when he went to She'ol and preached to those waiting for him there, possibly even demons. Psalms 88:5 says that he is free among the dead like the slain that lie in the grave. And further in Psalm 88:10 it says; "Will you show wonders to the dead? Shall the Repha'iym arise and praise you?" I understand the word there for Repha'iym can mean dead, but it can also mean the giants from Deuteronomy 2:11, 3:11 and Joshua 12:4, among others. Besides being the first and the last he is also every word in between. My prayer and purpose is to excite you about learning about your Creator so that you will open your scriptures and read them. He is there waiting for you to discover him because the Messiah is written on every page

Many of YAHUSHAs' sayings and works were recorded and foretold in the Old Testament and the prophets. Like I said before, his words on the cross were hearkening listeners back to Psalm 22, and throughout all his preaching, he was calling his listeners back to the Torah with its promises and curses as well. I pray I have piqued your curiosity enough for you to open your scriptures and learn these connections or to prove me wrong. Like YAHUSHA in Luke 24:26, 27, I have tried to show how He was to suffer, then enter into his glory. "And beginning at Mosheh and all the prophets, he expounded unto them in Scriptures the things concerning himself." Of course, I am not the Word, the living, breathing Torah, and I am not as learned as

Paul or any other disciples raised in Torah from their youth. Therefore, there are verses I have not discovered and some I have not included; otherwise, this work would look much like the whole of scripture itself.

With that said, I will leave you with John 18:23, where YAHUSHA tells the high priest, "If I have spoken evil, bear witness of the evil: but if well, why do you smite me"? In other words, do not kill the messenger. If I am wrong, prove it with scripture and not the words of man. I would love to be mistaken concerning our suffering trials, and tribulations. I would love to know that believers will not be here on earth when the great tribulation the Messiah spoke of in Matthew 24:21,29 occurs, that we will be sitting in the mezzanine watching as it happens. However, our Messiah tells us in Matthew 24:21 and 29, "For then shall be great tribulation, such as was not since the beginning of the world to this time, no, nor ever shall be." Notice that it says not until this time. Tribulation began when his people, his chosen people rejected him, and after he had risen, they still rejected him. Then, in verse 29, he says, "Immediately after the tribulation of those days shall the sun be darkened, and the moon shall not give her light, and the stars shall fall from heaven, and the powers of the heavens shall be shaken." Notice that verse 29 says immediately after the tribulation of those days. Most people who believe in the pretribulation rapture think they will not go through tribulation. However, further in verses 30 and 31, YAHUSHA the

Messiah himself says immediately after the tribulation of those days, "Then shall appear the sign of the Son of Adam in heaven and then shall all the tribes of the earth mourn, and they shall see the Son of Adam coming in the clouds of heaven with power and great glory. And he shall send his angels with a great sound of a shofar, and they shall gather his elect from the four winds, from one end of heaven to the other". Then he gives the fig tree parable, which illustrates how we are to know the seasons.

The seasons are the appointed times YAHUAH gave to us in Leviticus 23:2; "Speak unto the children of Yashar'el, and say unto them, concerning the feasts of YAHUAH, which ye shall proclaim to be holy assemblies, even these are my feasts." He does not say they are your Feasts. The first one listed there is the Sabbath, the fourth commandment. Then there are the spring Feasts, the summer Feast of Weeks, and the fall Feasts. We are instructed to meet him at these appointed times. I know the calendar debates, and I have conducted my study and reached my own conclusion as to which one to use. That is another topic for another day but suffice it to say the first commandment is to love YAHUAH with all your heart, mind, and strength. If you do that, you will fervently seek things that please him. I believe the thing that pleases him most is to be sought after. If you do that, he will be found, and that place is in his Word. So, get cracking, read your bible, and pray to be like the believer from Acts 8:27 who insisted on being baptized by Phillip after he had explained the prophet Isaiah was writing about YAHUSHA the Messiah.

And here will I make an end. And if I have done well, and as is fitting the story, it is that which I desired; but if slenderly and meanly, it is that which I could attain unto. For as it is hurtful to drink wine or water alone; and as wine mingled with water is pleasant and delights the taste; even so speech finely framed delights the ears of them that read the story. And here shall be an end. 2 Maccabees 15:38-40

ABOUT THE AUTHOR

Deloris Biocic is retired law enforcement, who 10 years ago went on a journey to discover why or what had happened to cause religion to go so far astray from the truth. Looking for the answer in volumes of scripture and texts, it was while reading the works of Hippolytus (A.D. 170-236) that it was discovered that all the answers to the questions concerning disunity in the ecclesia were contained in the whole of Scripture, including the books of the Apocrypha. In The Refutation of All Heresies, Hippolytus catalogs all the Heresies of his time. These heresies have not changed other than being repackaged for our day. The most important discovery was that It is more important today to read and know the scriptures so as not be led astray from the truth which only the scriptures contain.